Thomas Miller

Turner and Girtin's Picturesque Views of English, Scotch, and Welsh Scenery

A hundred years ago

Thomas Miller

Turner and Girtin's Picturesque Views of English, Scotch, and Welsh Scenery
A hundred years ago

ISBN/EAN: 9783337410667

Printed in Europe, USA, Canada, Australia, Japan

Cover: Foto ©ninafisch / pixelio.de

More available books at **www.hansebooks.com**

TURNER AND GIRTIN'S

PICTURESQUE VIEWS

OF

English, Scotch, & Welsh Scenery,

A HUNDRED YEARS AGO.

EDITED BY

THOMAS MILLER,

AUTHOR OF "HISTORY OF THE ANGLO-SAXONS," "LIVES OF BEATTIE AND COLLINS," "ROYSTON GOWER,"
"PICTURESQUE SKETCHES OF LONDON," &c., &c.

With Thirty Engravings of the Olden Time.

LONDON:
FREDERICK BENTLEY, 62, PATERNOSTER ROW.
1873.

PUBLISHER'S PREFACE.

A SHORT time since, a worthy gentleman rescued the following Plates, engraved with the labours of Turner and his early associate "Poor Tom"* (Girtin), from a cellar, or some equally obscure place, where probably they had been hidden for half a century, forgotten, excepting by the few painstaking collectors, who, at the price of the present volume, had been enabled, on rare occasions, to enrich their stores now and then with solitary soiled and badly-worked specimens. The said worthy gentleman, seeing them beautifully incrusted—to use a collector's phrase—with patna, verdigris, and all kinds of filth (classically called the accumulation of ages), and possessed with the utilitarian spirit of the times, he destined them at once to the refiner's pot, that he might thereby obtain a purer, and to him a more useful metal.

Being myself somewhat of a Fine Art dealer in *Marine* Stores, the old "Temeraire," to wit; the Plates in their "dark and mysterious" state, were

* When Cooke, the engraver, was bringing out his work of the "Rivers of England," Turner heard that he intended to introduce some plates after Girtin's drawing, and the following colloquy took place between them:—Turner: "So you intend to put in some of Girtin's views?" Cooke: "Yes." Turner: "Humph! Who will you get to touch them?" (*i.e.*, the proofs for the engraver to give the proper effect in translating colour into black and white.) Cooke: "You." Turner: "I shan't." Cooke: "Oh! Mr. Turner." Turner: "I tell you, I shan't." Cooke: "But your long acquaintance with Girtin!" Turner: "I tell you, I shan't." And so Cooke left him. A few days after, Cooke saw him again, when Turner began with:—"Well, Cooke, I've thought that matter over, and I'll touch the plates for Poor Tom. Poor Tom!" "Ah!" said Cooke, "I thought you would." "Yes; I'll touch them for Poor Tom. Poor Tom!" and he continued repeating the words, "Poor Tom," as if to himself. Cooke took the proofs to him, and he worked upon them for a long time, bestowing great care, and "making them," as Cooke said, "quite his own;" and, at last, after holding them individually at arm's length, throwing them on the floor, turning them upside down, and flinging them in every direction, he said—"There, poor Tom! that will do. Poor Tom!" and Cooke was about to take the impressions away, when Turner, clapping his arm upon them, exclaimed—"Stop! you must pay me two guineas a piece first."

brought to me, and I saw, as the auctioneers phrase it, that it was a "speculative lot;" and with a love of antiquarian relics—interest I put out of the question—for which the F.R.A.S. ought to create me a member of their learned body, I made an offer, and the plates became mine. Once in my possession, and not having the fear of Morris Moore or a Parliamentary Enquiry before my eyes, I went to work, and, by dint of rubbing and scrubbing with something more than "*hot water*" and "*a ragged towel*"—thanks to her Majesty's ministers for the free use of soap-lees in its pure and unsophisticated state—I found, if I had not hit upon a mine of gold, I had upon a mine of ART, and this, combined with the novelty of the plates exhibiting the works of TURNER and GIRTIN, sixty years since, a generous public would soon convert into a mine of wealth.

The first reward I had for my labours, however, was the intelligence found upon one of the plates, that on "Saturday, October 3, 1801, twenty-five impressions had been worked off, making a *grand* total of two hundred copies"!!!* Two hundred copies, fifty years since, of a popular work, illustrated by the first artists of the day—and one of whom Fame has now placed amongst the first artists of the world—being the entire sale for the United Kingdom! Hear this, ye Longmans and ye Murrays; ye gentlemen that make your fathers' figures to a new book look like the logarithmic numbers in a Hamilton Moore or a John Norie. Only think, if your worthy *forbears* could see and hear your lucubrations over an estimate for an edition of 20,000 copies. What would be their notion of your mental state? Shade of Caxton! Oh, Lackington! and, oh, John Miller, Time works wonders! But, to go on with my "unvarnished tale," I found, when the plates were cleaned and proved, they were in as good condition as they ever had been; and that, as a caterer for public taste, I could present my patrons with the astounding novelty of looking upon their native land, through the medium of a Turner and a Girtin, as their grandfathers saw it.

Here, gentle reader, ends my story; and if the following Engravings

---

* So scarce had impressions of these plates become, that, at Haviland Burke's sale, last year, nine ordinary prints, with the margins cut, sold for five pounds.

afford the same pleasure to the many that they have already done to the few, I shall not regret my dealing in Marine Fine Art stores; and if, by any chance, I am taken, as Turner once was, for " one of our people," I can only hope the mistake may be discovered before it is too late, as was the case with him.*

HAYMARKET, *Dec.* 1, 1853.

---

* When Whittaker was preparing his work of Yorkshire, he applied to a friend in London to send him an artist to make the drawings. His friend engaged Turner, and wrote to Mr. Whittaker, telling him that he would send him the best artist for his purpose, but he must take care of him, for he was a "bit of a Jew." The journey in those days was something different to what it is now, and it was arranged, by Mr. Whittaker's management, that Turner should arrive by the early afternoon coach on Friday, thus giving him, as he said, two clear days to refresh, preparatory to their start on the following Monday. Saturday was spent very pleasantly, and Sunday morning no less so, excepting that Turner had not been invited to join in the family devotions, and the effort made to exclude him was so apparent that he felt annoyed at it. When the time came for Mr. Whittaker to perform Divine Service in his church, he addressed Turner by saying, " he must now leave him for a short time," adding, " and when you are tired of your walk, you will find amusement in the library, for we are going to church." Turner's irritable feeling was aroused, and he said, somewhat gruffly, as was his habit, " I'll go with you!" " You, Mr. Turner!" said the other with evident surprise. " Yes," said Turner, " why shouldn't I go?" " Oh!" exclaimed Mr. Whittaker, somewhat startled; " you!" " Yes," added Turner in the same breath; " why shouldn't I go? What's to prevent me?" " Oh! nothing," replied Mr. Whittaker, hesitating, " but"— " But what?" roared Turner. " Why," said Mr. Whittaker, " I was told you were of the Jewish persuasion."

LIST OF PLATES.

Frontispiece,

PORTRAIT OF J. M. W. TURNER, R.A.

Engraved by C. W. Sharpe, from a Drawing by Count D'Orsay.

TITLE.	ARTIST.
ROCHESTER,	Turner.
CHEPSTOW,	Turner.
BRIDGENORTH,	Turner.
MATLOCK,	Turner.
BIRMINGHAM,	Turner.
CHESTER,	Turner.
MANCHESTER, (*from a Sketch by W. Orme,*)	Girtin.
PETERBOROUGH (Cathedral),	Turner.
ELY (Cathedral),	Turner.
WARKWORTH,	Girtin.
NEWCASTLE-UPON-TYNE,	Girtin.
ELGIN CATHEDRAL, Morayshire, (*from a Sketch by J. Moore,*)	Turner.
FLINT (from Parkgate),	Turner.
WESTMINSTER BRIDGE,	Turner.
BAMBROUGH CASTLE, Northumberland,	Girtin.
HAMPTON COURT, Herefordshire,	Turner.
CARLISLE,	Turner.
GREAT MARLOW,	Girtin.
WOOLWICH,	Girtin.
WINDSOR,	Girtin.
WAKEFIELD,	Turner.
SHEFFIELD,	Turner.
MARINE BARRACKS, Stonehouse,	Girtin.
RICHMOND, Yorkshire,	Girtin.
APPLEBY, Westmoreland,	Girtin.
KING'S WEARE,	Girtin.
CHRIST CHURCH ABBEY, Hampshire,	Girtin.
TARNAWAY CASTLE, Morayshire,	Girtin.
TOTNES,	Girtin.
ROUND TOWER, Abernethy,	Girtin.

Tail-Piece,

THOMAS GIRTIN.

CONTENTS.

		PAGE
LIST OF PLATES,		vii
PUBLISHER'S PREFACE,		iii
BIOGRAPHICAL MEMOIR OF J. M. W. TURNER AND T. GIRTIN,		ix

AUTOGRAPH LETTER from J. M. W. TURNER, to JOHN BRITTON, Esq., on the subject of his remarks upon the picture of Pope's Villa.

AUTOGRAPH LETTER to the same, on the sum to be demanded for a picture he had sold to George IV.

AUTOGRAPH LETTER to Sir THOMAS LAWRENCE, on apologizing for not giving an opinion as to the originality of one of his pictures.

ROCHESTER,	by H. G. Adams, Esq.,	1
CHEPSTOW,	The Rev. J. B. Gabriel, M.A.,	9
BRIDGENORTH,	The Rev. W. Knox Marshall, B.A.,	43
MATLOCK,	William Adams, Esq.,	13
BIRMINGHAM,	Alfred Davidson, Esq.,	18
CHESTER,	Thomas Hughes, Esq.,	23
PETERBOROUGH AND ELY,	Thomas Miller, Esq.,	29
MANCHESTER,	Thomas Miller, Esq.,	45
WARKWORTH,	G. Bouchier Richardson, Esq.,	58
NEWCASTLE,	G. Bouchier Richardson, Esq.,	65
ELGIN CATHEDRAL,	George Anderson, Esq., Inverness,	53
FLINT,	Thomas Miller, Esq.,	73
WESTMINSTER BRIDGE,	Thomas Miller, Esq.,	77
BAMBROUGH CASTLE,	G. Bouchier Richardson, Esq.,	81
HAMPTON COURT,	Thomas Miller, Esq.,	88
CARLISLE,	H. G. Adams, Esq.,	92
GREAT MARLOW,	Thomas Miller, Esq.,	97
WOOLWICH,	H. G. Adams, Esq.,	102
WINDSOR,	Thomas Miller, Esq.,	109
WAKEFIELD,	Thomas Miller, Esq.,	113
SHEFFIELD,	Thomas Miller, Esq.,	116
MARINE BARRACKS,	G. F. Jackson, Esq.,	121
RICHMOND (Yorkshire).	Delta,	127
APPLEBY,	Thomas Miller, Esq.,	133
KING'S WEARE,	Dunsterville Brucks, Esq.,	139
CHRISTCHURCH ABBEY (Hampshire).	Benjamin Ferrey, Esq.,	143
TARNAWAY CASTLE,	George Anderson, Esq., Inverness,	152
TOTNES,	Dunsterville Brucks, Esq.,	156
ROUND TOWER,	Thomas Miller, Esq.,	160

Memoirs

OF

TURNER AND GIRTIN.

WHERE JOSEPH WILLIAM MALLAD TURNER—or, as he afterwards called himself, Joseph William Turner, and which he again altered to Joseph Mallord William Turner (Mallad in the parish register)—was born, it is at present impossible to say, the registry of his baptism in the parochial book of St. Paul's, Covent Garden, bearing the date 14th May, 1775,* being no guide to the date of his birth; and if a certificate of the great painter's birth is ever found, it will either be in the parish registers of Wales, Devonshire, or perhaps Bristol. He was brought up to London from some one of these localities when a little child by his parents, as he himself told Mr. Cyrus Redding when they were in Devonshire; also adding, when Mr. Redding was speaking of the eminent artists Devonshire had produced—" They may put me down amongst the number, for I was born in Devonshire." This statement was made to Mr. John Britton, F.S.A., by Mr. Cyrus Redding. Neither does the marriage

---

* The following is a copy of the certificate of the baptism of Turner from the parish register :—

"Joseph Mallad William, son of William Turner by Mary his wife, May 14, 1775."

certificate* of William Turner and Mary Marshall, found in the parish register of the above-named church, and dated 29th August, 1773, throw any light upon the subject, as there is everything but written proof to support the belief that they were NOT the parents of our artist; for the maiden name of Turner's mother was Mary-Ann Harper, but where she came from has not yet been ascertained.† The Marshalls of Covent Garden were a very old and respectable family; but the William Turner who married into that connexion was not the father of the great painter, nor were the Marshalls ever in any way related to our artist.

Turner, according to his own well-known admission, was born on 23d April, 1769, the year that gave birth to Wellington, Napoleon, and so many other remarkable men; though even this date is doubtful, knowing the vanity of the man, and through his fixing on the birthday of Shakespeare and St. George's Day. He was the same age as Sir Thomas Lawrence, and James Ward, R.A., but the senior of the three.

It is a singular circumstance in the history of the men whose Memoirs we are writing, that it is impossible to reconcile dates, as we shall have occasion to show; and even so late as 1832, the time when Turner raised a tablet to his parents' memory, he is incorrect

---

* The following is a copy of the marriage certificate of the William Turner and Mary Marshall who, it has been stated, were Turner's parents :—

"William Turner, of this parish, a bachelor, and Mary Marshall, of this parish, a spinster, were married in this church by license, the 29th of August, 1773, by me,   EZEKIEL ROUSE, Curate.
"In presence of
    MARTHA PRICE,
    ELLIS PRICE.   Signed { WILLIAM TURNER, MARY MARSHALL."

Copied from the parish register of St. Paul's, Covent Garden.

† Only a few months ago an old lady called on Mr. Spreck, the parish-clerk of St. Paul's, Covent Garden, to inquire about Turner's register, and when it was given to her she at first expressed doubts about its being the same person; but on becoming convinced of the identity, she exclaimed, he must have been christened twice, as she had his register from a church (Mr. Spreck thinks she said) in Devonshire.

as to date, for his father was buried in September 1829, and not in September 1830, as stated on the monument in the church of St. Paul's, Covent Garden.* As a further proof of our artist's age, a drawing of Dover Castle was exhibited in 1787, at the Royal Academy, and entered in the Catalogue of the Exhibition for that year in the name of William Turner; which if it were by him, and the Covent Garden register is to be taken as date for the year of his birth, would only make him twelve years of age when his first drawing was exhibited. Against this we have Turner's own testimony, that neither his own drawings nor Girtin's were anything better than what the generality of boys of that age would produce. It might be argued that Turner had never visited Dover at this time. Even this may be admitted; for in the collection of John Henderson, Esq., of Montague Place, Russell Square, whose father was an early patron of both Turner and Girtin, and to whose collection we shall have occasion again to refer, is a drawing of Dover Castle, made with three or four other views of the same place, from this gentleman's sketches; and they bear a greater resemblance to the works of Malton than any other drawings by Turner that have been met with. It is true, a W. Turner, in the year 1792, exhibited two drawings, one a "View of Paris," and another a

* From the same parish register, the date of the burial of Turner's father is "SEPTEMBER 29, 1829."

In the Vault
Beneath and near this place
Are deposited the remains of
WILLIAM TURNER,
Many years an inhabitant
Of this parish, who died
Sept. 21st, 1830.
To his memory, and of his Wife,
MARY-ANN,
Their son, J. M. W. Turner, R.A.,
Has placed this Tablet.
August 1832.

From the certificate of burial it will be seen that there is an error of a year in the date of this tablet, which is an accurate copy of the inscription.

"View of Chinkford Hall, Essex;" and he gives his address, No. 129 Shoreditch: from which it may be inferred that he is the same artist that exhibited the drawing of "Wansted House;" but against this, and in the same gentleman's collection, are views of Paris by Turner at the same period. Charles Turner, the engraver, tells a story of his sending a drawing to the Royal Academy Exhibition under a fictitious name, and Turner accused him of doing so. The other, not knowing how his fame would stand, denied it; but Turner was not to be so put off, and he said, "I know you have;" and in a half-whisper added, "I've done the same thing myself." The presumption therefore is, that the drawing is by our Turner. Nay, even taking the undisputed dates of the period when he first exhibited his drawings in the Royal Academy, and according to this register of his baptism, it only makes him fifteen; and as he was admitted a student of the Royal Academy in 1789, after working three months upon, and being capable of making, a probationary drawing so correct as to entitle him to admission, it ill accords with his own statement of the bad drawings he then made.

Again, we find him making the drawing of Rochester in the present work in 1793, or when he was eighteen (according to this register); for the engraving, which would take some months to finish after Turner had made the drawing, bears the date of May 1st, 1794: now he must have been well known by his works some time before he would be sent on a mission where he had to compete with masters of repute like Dayes, Hearne, Rooker, Malton, and Paul Sandby.

These facts, which are undeniable, are strong proofs that Turner was six years older than the date given in the baptismal certificate; and that the acknowledgment he made regarding the year of his birth in the presence of Sir Thomas Lawrence and another gentleman well-known to the writer of this Memoir, is a correct statement; and that Joseph Mallad William Turner, the greatest of English painters, was born (perhaps) on the 23d of April, and, there is little doubt, in the year 1769, but at what place is not known. Sir Thomas Lawrence's old servant, Edward Holman, who must be remembered by many still living, and who, as closely as he could, aped the courtly manners of his master, never omitted an opportunity when exhibiting Sir Thomas's pictures of pointing to the portrait of Lawrence, and saying, "Sir Thomas was born in the same year as Wellington, Napoleon, Marshal Soult, Mr. Turner the great artist, and a great many other clever men;" then, with a bow worthy of Sir Thomas himself, he would add, as he gracefully lifted up the corner of his apron, " and — your very humble servant."

THOMAS GIRTIN, whose early history is so closely interwoven with that of Turner, in the commencement of their artistical career, as to render their names inseparable, was born in Southwark, 18th February, 1773. The gravestone erected to his memory states his age to be twenty-seven; but George Dance, R.A., who drew his portrait, has in the most circumstantial manner described the date and place of his birth, Feb. 18, 1773. Chambers, in his "Biographical Dictionary," gives the same date; Edwards, in his "Anecdotes of Painters," states him to be twenty-seven, and Lempriere makes him to have been thirty years old, when he died; in the "Library of the Fine Arts," in the Memoir of Henry Liverseege, it is stated that "Girtin and Liverseege both died at the age of twenty-nine." Of his father nothing is known beyond his being a rope-maker, or roper, as those following that trade are commonly called, and that he died when Girtin was a lad about eight years old. His mother was married again to a Mr. Vaughan, a pattern-draughtsman. Very little, however, is recorded of her; but it appears she carried on business at No. 2 St. Martin's-le-Grand, where Girtin continued to reside up to the year 1796. Girtin had a brother, apprenticed to a writing engraver; and we may suppose it was to the step-father these youths owed their first introduction to the Arts. Still, when a child he is known to have evinced a predilection for drawing, and was seldom without pencil and paper when they could be obtained. In what way Turner and Girtin first became acquainted we have no means of knowing; the chances are, that while Turner was under the tuition of Malton, and Girtin with Dayes (the latter by far the most talented preceptor), they were brought together by

Dr. Monro, who was intimate with both Malton and Dayes: or it might be, that they became acquainted while following the occupation of print-colourers to Mr. John Raphael Smith,* by whom one, if not both, appear to have been employed.

Excepting the boyish sketches he made at home, there is but little doubt that Turner's first essay in the arts commenced in this way, and that for two or three years he was a print-colourer under Smith. Nor was this a bad school in which to commence his career, as it required a great command over the materials to obtain the dexterity necessary to become a print-colourer; for the effect to be got at had to be produced at once, or the print was spoiled. To acquire this facility was, therefore, a work of time, and it is not unreasonable to suppose that Turner was altogether employed in this profession for two or three years, as boys in those days were only promoted step by step; and it may be, that his father's penurious habits preferred the little money he was then earning under Smith to the prospective advantage of a day-school education. It was only when the father came unexpectedly into a legacy, and he was asked by Mr. Tomkinson what he was going to make of William, that he seems to have considered some elementary knowledge necessary, and that he then placed his son under Thomas Malton, the author of the "Treatise on Perspective." What by print-colouring, occasionally selling a drawing,† and putting in skies for one and effects for another, we have pretty clear proof how his time was employed until both he and Girtin, by their talents, obtained invitations to the houses of Dr. Monro and Mr. Henderson, and mingled among brother-artists by several years their seniors, when their artistical career began in earnest.

* John Raphael Smith, who at this time resided in King Street, Covent Garden, was the son of Mr. Smith the landscape-painter of Derby. He was an excellent mezzotint engraver and print-seller, and occasionally painted portraits and other subjects. He was about sixty when he died, in 1811.

† That Turner exhibited drawings for sale in his father's shop there can be no question, and that the elder Turner had some intuitive notion of his son's merits is also a fact, for he has often grumbled to persons still alive about "*Him* making drawings for Dr. Monro for half-a-crown."

Good Dr. Monro, as he was called by Turner, was an eminent collector, residing in the Adelphi,* where he occasionally opened his house for a converzatione; and as old Pine, of "Wine and Walnuts" celebrity, used to say, "what a glorious coterie there was, when Wilson, Marlow, Gainsborough, Paul and Tom Sandby, Rooker, Hearne, and Cozins used to meet; and you, old Jack," turning to Varley, "were a boy in a pinafore, with Turner, Girtin, and Edridge, as big-wigs on whom you used to look as something beyond the usual amount of clay." It was a glorious time, for this truly benevolent patron not only threw his collection open to the young artists, but employed them to make drawings for him, that they might, while having the advantage of study, not lose their moral independence by supposing the benefit was an obligation. Such delicate encouragement has been but seldom given.

The history of artists, in our plain matter-of-fact England, has but little in it that seems to interest the general public. They leave their works behind them, and these seem to be all that the world shows any concern about. They lived and died; but the struggles they encountered, the poverty they endured, and the cold reception they too often met with, are matters about which no record is kept, and for which, until it is often too late, the world shows no sympathy. The vicissitudes that one has battled with and overcome, and which another has combated and perished in encountering, are the history of all;—some have risen to wealth, who are now forgotten; and some have perished in poverty, whose works have realised an hundred times the amount which the artists received while living: and this is almost the whole of their sad, eventful history.

* Mr. Henderson, a gentleman of independent fortune, resided on the Adelphi Terrace, next door to Dr. Monro on one side, and David Garrick on the other. He possessed some fine pictures by Canaletti, which Girtin copied and carefully studied, as he did also the works of Piranesi: but we do not find that Turner attempted the same thing; he seems to have preferred copying the works of the water-colour artists of that day, particularly the drawings of antiquities, &c., by Thomas Hearne, of which Mr. Henderson had a fine collection.

Although Turner's father was stingy to meanness,—so much so, indeed, that when we read the entry of *the* Turner who was married to Mary Marshall with a special license, we are convinced, knowing his penurious habits, that he would have remained single until "the crack of doom," rather than have parted with the necessary sum for such a purpose; still, the son, probably, never had to battle with those severe hardships which so many young artists sink under,—he had always a meal provided, and never wanted bread. But if, like too many, he did not wander homeless "'mid a thousand homes," and was a stranger to the gnawing pangs of hunger, he had for a long period, during the best portion of his career, to endure the chilling neglect, the haughty scorn, the niggard praise, and the averted glances, of those who only measured merit by the notice it attained, and who, from position or connoisseurship—the latter in the hands of the few—either "damned with faint praise," or stood up dreaded Sir Oracles; who, when they spake, bid "no dog bark." What one said, another echoed; they dug a grave for genius with a nod, and buried it with a turn of the heel. The public was a slave to the judgment of the few, and durst not express an opinion of its own.

It is true, excepting at the commencement of his career, Turner always received comparatively high prices for his pictures. Admitting he did, who were his purchasers, and how many did he sell? The large collection he has left to the nation is an answer to that question.

Taste and judgment, with a few honoured exceptions, were at a very low ebb in those days; and although there had been numbers of favourable criticisms on Turner's works, it was not until the eloquent pen of the Oxford Graduate wrote him into fame, and taught Turner to be cared for, if not understood, that his pictures were eagerly sought after.* To this neglect is probably owing his

---

* Turner sold nearly as many pictures during the last six years of his life as were sold altogether before. This does not apply to his drawings, but to the oil-paintings only.

morose manner in after-life; for had he been as uncouth, surly, and churlish, in his early career, as he was in the middle and latter part of it, no one would have tolerated him. By parsimonious habits he grew into independence, and when the time came for his pictures to be sought for, too often as investments, he laughed at the buyers and refused to sell.

They offered him help when he did not need it, paid him homage when he was powerful enough to spurn it, and gave him praise when he turned to it a deaf ear. The gentle blood that flowed through his veins in the days of his youth was turned to gall, and his words were bitter as wormwood. He was no longer the Turner that wandered with "Honest Tom Girtin," as the latter was called by his contemporaries, making sketches in the early morning, and watching the shadows settle down in the grey twilight of evening; but "an adder in the path" of his would-be patrons. And he might exclaim with Jacob of old, "A troop overcame him, but he overcame at the last." Little as there is loveable about the man, he met with rebuffs enough to make him what he was, and when the time came he paid them back with savage interest. His "milk of human kindness" dried up when he lost poor Tom Girtin: he never took another friend to his rough and bear-like bosom. "You must pay me so much," or "I shan't," became ever after his watchword; in this alone did the giant dwarf his mighty proportions: when he knelt, it was on a cushion of gold.

These young artists, whose names will never die while a taste for works of art exist, thus commenced their career; Turner (three or four years the elder) under Malton, and Girtin under Dayes: the world little dreaming that they were destined to shake down an old system, and build up a new,

"Whose dwelling is the light of setting suns."

We have shown, that after acquiring the first rudiments of art they were fortunate in their Adelphi patrons, where they were well schooled by copying the drawings in Dr. Monro's and Mr.

Henderson's collections, which consisted of the choicest works of the period, and many rare prints of an early date.

Turner, from his patient, imitative powers, copied the works of Dayes, Girtin's preceptor, so closely, that it requires careful attention to discover the difference. A close inspection, however, shows the distinction: for Dayes, who had been a miniature-painter, always drew his figures very accurately; while in Turner they are meagre and ill-drawn: the latter, however, even at this early period, exhibit traces of that power in aërial effect that was to raise him hereafter to such high eminence. It must be borne in mind, that the practice they had already acquired as print-colourers gave them great facility. It was then a common custom to colour prints upon an etching, which caused them when finished to have the appearance of drawings,—a task of more difficulty to accomplish than the same work in the present day. About this period, that is, from 1788 to 1790,* during which time Turner had been admitted a student at the Royal Academy, they were also employed by architects to wash in the skies, and, most probably, the flat tints to their drawings; and no doubt they acquired most useful experience from this occupation: for the architectural drawings Turner made some years after this of Cashiobury, for the Earl of Essex, are of the highest quality: one in particular, in the collection of Mr. Windus, where the light falls on the floor of a vaulted apartment through a stained-glass window, stands unequalled. He has introduced a rich

---

* The following quizzical note, which appeared about this period, conveys an idea of the process of washing in skies to water-colour drawings:—
"What a fine, clear morning! I will do my sky. Betty! tell your mistress, if any one calls I can't be seen—I'm skying. Betty! Betty! bring me up a pan of water, and wash that sponge: it really is so hot I cannot lay my colour smooth. Where's the flat brush? Oh, dear! that Prussian-blue is all curdled." "Please, pa, ma says, will you take any refreshment?" "Get away, get away! how ever can your ma think about refreshment, when she knows I am doing my sky? There, you've knocked down my swan's quill, and how am I to soften this colour? it will all be dry before you wash out the dirt. Give me that brush. Oh, it is full of indigo!—there is the horizon spoilt!—Quick, quick! some water! Oh, that's gall! And the sky is flying away! Why did mother send you here? She might have known that I was skying."

Persian table-cover, which for careful finish is as elaborate as anything of the Dutch masters.

They were also employed by amateurs to put in effects to their sketches, some of which were engraved; the drawing of "Elgin Cathedral," in the present work, is one of these by Turner. In the original sketch, made by an amateur, the windows in the nave were closed or built up, but in the drawing Turner made he left them open. On being spoken to about this a few years since, he said, "They ought to have been open; how much better is it to see the light of day in God's house than darkness!"* The "View of Manchester," by Girtin, in this work, is from a sketch by Mr. Orme, and is curious as a joint-production, having received its finishing touches from such an eminent hand. The ardour with which the two friends pursued their studies was most exemplary, and in the next epoch of Turner we find he had taken Cozins for his model, of whom Edwards, speaking in his "Anecdotes of Painters," says, " He produced some drawings of great merit, executed by a process that may be considered tinted chiaroscuro, exhibiting very pleasing effects, and which has served as a foundation to the manner since adopted by Mr. Turner and the late Mr. Girtin, both of whom copied many of his drawings." And here, as we see Turner advance, we find him no longer copying the master's handling, but culling, as it were, the sweets for which he was famed; and his productions now display those aërial effects, the promise of which had been seen in his Dayes' manner, in which the spectator seems to breathe; and whatever his genius in after-life may have done to mature the judgment now forming, the merit must be given to the elegance and brilliancy of Cozins' drawings.

* Turner was always quaint in giving his reasons for what he did. When Mr. J. Pye engraved the plate of Wycliffe for Whittaker's " Yorkshire," Turner, in touching the proof, introduced a burst of light which was not in the drawing. Mr. Pye asked him his reason for so doing. He replied, "That is the place where Wickliffe was born, and there is the light of the glorious Reformation." "Well," said Mr. Pye, satisfied; "but what do you mean by these large geese?" "Oh, they are the old superstitions, which the genius of the Reformation is driving away!"

Girtin never appears to have acquired any style but his own, although the drawings he and Turner made had great similarity; but then it was the similarity to the works of each other when they wrought from their own compositions, or from prints in chiaroscuro, and depended upon their mind's eye for colour and finish.

At this time Girtin was beginning that daring mode of opposition in his drawing which finally overthrew the preconceived notion of the Sandby school, as to the incapability of water-colours to produce more than "tinted drawings." It is recorded that he sketched a picturesque part of Chelsea, drawing the outline at broad day, and had purposed to colour the scene as it then appeared; but in passing near the spot at the going down of the sun, and then seeing the buildings under the influence which twilight had produced, with so unexpected a mass of shadow on the fading light, and that the reflexions in the water still increased the vastness of the mass — moreover, that the bridge opposed its distinct form, dark also, to a bright gleam on the horizon — he was so possessed with the solemn grandeur of the composition, which had thus gained so much in sentiment by the change of light, that he determined to make an attempt at imitation, and by ardent application accomplished the object. This piece was wrought with bold and masterly execution, and led to that daring style of effect which he subsequently practised with so much success. Turner, who was not slow to avail himself of every improvement, gradually began to imbibe Girtin's manner. In a drawing exhibited at the Hampstead converzatione, a few months since, said to be by Cozins, but which was evidently Turner's, is seen a most curious illustration of these two styles in one subject—Cozins's on the trees and sky to the left (as the spectator views it), and Turner's, at this period, on the other portion of the drawing; and it is the first known specimen in which his next, or Girtin manner, becomes visible.

Hitherto the scene of their labours must have been circumscribed—they had become draughtsmen by effective study, and they now sought to become painters by the study of Nature's works.

They threw aside the lessons of the school, and went forth into the out-of-door world to see how Nature herself worked, and to follow her example. Amid ruins, and in hidden nooks, they saw how the touches of Time made even decay look beautiful, by throwing the green moss here, and the yellow lichen there, like a spot of sunshine, and so covering the imperfections of age with loveliness; and into the picture-chambers of their minds they stored up what they saw, and when they again wrought upon their own resources, the inward eye of memory brought back the objects they had visited. And so they made themselves undying names.

By the study from Piranesi's prints Girtin had acquired great vigour, and from Canaletti's drawings and pictures that lineal precision so peculiar to him. If Turner had copied Dayes to advantage, so Girtin seems to have studied Malton; and the drawings Girtin made from the latter's prints are, perhaps, the best examples of his own future originality, for to them, as we have said above, he could only be indebted for outline and chiaroscuro: but as he has coloured them in his own unmistakeable bold style, it shows that the observations on Nature he had stored in his mind were merely waiting opportunity to be developed. The best examples of these drawings are in the collection of Mr. Henderson. But he did not confine himself to landscape and architecture, for the same gentleman has a copy of Morland's "Dogs hesitating about the Pluck" (so called from a sheep's heart, &c. being the object of their probable battle), which, while displaying Morland's subject, has Girtin's manner; so much so that it might pass for an original production.

Their wanderings at this time—probably owing to the limited state of their funds—appear to have been chiefly confined to within a mile or two of the Adelphi, among the picturesque shores of Westminster and Lambeth; for they were picturesque sixty years ago: amongst the old houses occupied by fishermen and their families, and other old buildings, tottering and grey with age, propped and supported by ill-cut posts, pillars, and wide abutments, where overhanging gables frowned defiance at the perpendicular, while here and there a patch of bright vegetation growing in the decaying timber, or some broken bit of wall, tiled roof, or brilliant bit of thatch, newly put up, added to the rich colouring of the picturesque objects, besides sheltering the inhabitants beneath, whose children, in mimicry of their parents' occupation, were amphibiously sporting in all the enjoyment of unsophisticated nature on the muddy shores of the Thames. Or sometimes they were found among the ruins of the Savoy Palace, where the vast fragments of wall and yawning gaps gave to the beholder such glimpses of old London as will never be seen again. A study which Girtin made at this time of the Old Palace Watergate-steps, according to his own testimony, was a lesson of improvement from which he dated all the future knowledge he displayed in depicting monastic and other ruins. Here they studied as friends, each labouring for the other's approbation, free from the slightest touch of jealous rivalry; and the success which attended their labours opened an entirely new field for water-colour painting.

It had always been considered as only capable of representing objects in a thin, washy manner, with a semi-aërial tint, gradually strengthening to the foreground, and then, by warm glazing, to give a little of the hue of Nature; and this was all water-colour was supposed to be capable of, until Turner and Girtin battled with this false theory, and brought such strong proof into the field as overthrew it for ever. Before this, when one of its professors was asked why the beautiful and interesting effects of Nature, as seen at day-break or sunset, were not depicted, the reply was,—"Water-colours have not power sufficient to represent such depth of tone; indeed, the attempt would be vain and fruitless: it is in oil-painting alone that such solemn effects can be obtained." Fortunate was it for the art that these young men were spirited enough to think for themselves, and had energy enough to carry their thoughts into execution.

At this period Girtin's extraordinary talent manifested a decided superiority over Turner, although by careful and laborious study the latter had worked himself into reputation, in spite of the imitative powers, which led him to follow Girtin's style so closely as to cause him to be held in lower estimation.* Hence it is that, while collections exist of Girtin's works of this period, we have none by Turner of the same date; individually, we have proofs of his industry, but none collectively. He, however, could appreciate the excellence he saw, and by diligent and laborious study followed closely in the wake of his volatile fellow-student, who from this period carried all before him.

The broad manner now introduced, led Girtin to seek for a medium to work upon capable of receiving and retaining his labours as rapidly as he could produce the new and startling effects which his genius had struck out. This he at last found in a semi-absorbent stout laid paper, about a royal size, that answered his purpose, which afterwards went by the name of "Girtin's paper," and many a ream was manufactured to be blotted over by the followers of the Girtin manner.† Girtin was not the plodding, painstaking student, that Turner was: by a sort of natural and ready genius he had arrived at a daring but brilliant mode of producing his pictures, and the charm of effect and colour made his productions universally admired. The principle of his mode of work was then novel for water-colour painters, and was the same as that adopted by those who painted in oil; viz. to paint in the local colours as near as possible at once, and shadow each with its own individual tint. By

* Chambers Hall, Esq. has a drawing said to be by Girtin, but which bears evidence of Turner's hand: in it the former—as if by an after-thought—has introduced a boat, with a figure pushing it along by means of a boat-hook; on the hill by the cathedral are some houses. And here also is the same handling and colour, as if, while working upon it, he had seen the drawing weak or defective in that particular part, and retouched it. Mr. Henderson has a copy of the same drawing, but by whom done, unless by his father, it is impossible to say; but it also has the boat and figure above-mentioned.

† Poor Dayes, Girtin's preceptor, destroyed himself about eighteen months after the death of his talented pupil, at his own house in Francis Street, Bedford Square. "Just before Girtin's death," says one of his contemporaries, "he happened to call on a collector of drawings—an old drivelling *dilettante*—who patronised every dashing style, when he saw a smart portfolio, inscribed in gilt letters with the name of one of Girtin's closest imitators. 'What have we here?' said Dayes. 'They are the works of a pupil of your old disciple's,' replied the

this process clearness and transparency were obtained, which added to the grand effects he produced, and fully justified all that his most ardent admirers could say in his praise,—proving him to have been a most attentive observer of Nature in her wildest and most beautiful forms and colours. At one time in the mountain, amidst a war of the elements; at another, when decked with the glorious orb of day, or obscured by mist and rain, one hill opposed to another, until subdued and almost lost in vapour; or standing out in bold relief against a brilliant bit of sky or sunny vale covered with grazing cattle. Moonlight, twilight, the drizzling rain, the pelting storm, the burning heat, or rainbowed skies, all found the pen of a ready writer; and no wonder that he stood alone, the admiration of his little world.

As evidence of the high estimation in which Girtin now stood, Mr. James Moore, an amateur artist, and a Fellow of the Society of Antiquaries, took him to Scotland to make drawings, and put in effects to his sketches: several of which, thus worked upon by Girtin, were afterwards published, bearing only Mr. Moore's name. Mr. Moore's widow lived some time at Croydon, and had in her possession many of these joint productions by her husband and Girtin, together with some of Girtin's original drawings.

But Turner was not neglected: he had also his country com-

---

collector. 'Pray, Mr. Dayes, look at them, and favour me with your opinion.' Dayes untied the portfolio, and on beholding the first subject, a large drawing of a mountainous scene among the lakes in Cumberland, he exclaimed, in his emphatic manner, 'Oh, ye gods! the blue bag! the blue bag!' Dayes was a man of quick discernment, and very pointed in his remarks, and nothing could be more characteristic of the whole collection than his exclamation: and so he kept on, as he turned over every drawing, still making the burthen of his song, 'Oh, the blue bag! the blue bag!' 'So,' said he, 'because Master Tom (Girtin) chooses to wash in dirty water, *ergo*, this puppy—this ass—this driveller—and the rest of the herd, forsooth—must wash in dirty water, too! Yes, by the Lord! and with the very puddle-water, which he has made more dirty!' Then laughing aloud he exclaimed: 'Dietreci begat Cassanova! Cassanova begat De Loutherbourgh! Loutherbourgh begat Frankey Bourgeois (the founder of the Dulwich Gallery): and he, the dirty dog, quarrelled with Nature and bedaubed her works.'"

missions, and made for Mr. Henderson two drawings of Oxford and two of Lincoln, which display talent not inferior to Girtin's.

The time, however, had arrived when the increasing spirit of trade was to place the young aspirants in a new field, and to develope those talents that were to give an impetus to water-colour painting, and enable it to rival its sister art in the pencils of Varley, Havel, Hills, Cotman, Prout, Harding, and others, which, a few short months before, it "was fruitless to attempt." In 1779, Harrison had commenced publishing the " Novelist's Magazine," to which no name added so much lustre as that of Thomas Stothard.* He had been preceded in his publication by several landscape works, such as Hearne and Byrne's " Antiquities," commenced in 1778 ; Paul Sandby's "Views ;" "Virtuosi's Museum;" Watt's "Views of Gentlemen's Seats ;" Milton's "Views in Ireland;" Middiman's "Views," &c. In 1782 Mr. Bell also issued the first part of his celebrated edition of the " British Poets." The taste engendered by these publications caused a growing love for art; and although it was but that dawn of patronage since broken into day, yet, such as it was, the engravers

---

* Thomas Stothard, R.A., was apprenticed to a pattern-drawer in Spitalfields, at that time a very lucrative business for men in the position of mechanics, as its professors were supposed to be; and it will be understood that there was great demand for such artisans, when it is known that it was from the blocks upon which their designs were drawn that our calico-printers used to work, and that this was then done entirely by hand, one colour remaining until the other was dry. Now, seven different colours may be worked upon a piece of cloth thirty yards long in as many minutes. Dod, an artist of that day, had made a drawing for the " Novelist's Magazine," which was so inaccurate that application was made to Stothard to correct it. Instead of doing this, Stothard made another drawing, for which he charged four shillings. This design was so satisfactory to Harrison, that he was employed to make other drawings at half-a-guinea each. One of these, we believe the first, a scene from " Joseph Andrews," engraved by James Heath, was seen by Flaxman; and he was so captivated with it, that he sought out and made Stothard's acquaintance, and from that time they became friends. The new employment being more congenial to Stothard, soon induced him to abandon pattern-drawing. He was, however, not altogether an unknown artist; for the year before, viz. in 1778, he had exhibited a " Holy Family" at the Royal Academy.

d

of the period were almost wholly occupied upon them; and, without disparagement to the beautifully illustrated works that have since appeared, many of them still stand unrivalled. Mr. Walker, an engraver, projected a work which, by employing the united talent of all the other works, should come in for a share of patronage; and, like a man of taste and judgment, cast his eyes on our artists. But Girtin, who was fast rising into fortune as well as fame, for a time refused his services; while Turner was at once engaged; and in the summer of 1793 he took his departure for Kent, to make the drawing of Rochester in this work. It was also at this time he commenced his first oil picture, a "View of Rochester." It was not the first visit he had made to this locality, and on the previous occasion he had received various commissions; but one gentleman, thinking with the Sandbys that water-colour was a secondary material, importuned the artist to work in oil, and actually bought the colours for him to paint with. Whether this picture* was the first finished, is doubtful. Dr. Nixon, the present Bishop of Tasmania, has a picture, painted for his father by Turner, done during this journey, and finished while staying in the parsonage-house at Foot's Cray, which is said to be the first oil picture he painted; but be this as it may, the first oil colours Turner used were those purchased in Rochester. Such a predilection had Turner for the Medway, that he himself encouraged the notion of his being a Kentish man. The result of Turner's separation from Girtin was soon apparent in the works he now produced; and in this print of Rochester we see, amidst his careful touches, those principles of breadth and opposition which attended him through life.

Finding it more profitable to make his journeys at his employer's expense—although, to his credit be it said, he was most moderate in

* The view is Rochester Castle, with fishermen drawing their boats ashore in a gale of wind. The picture is well drawn, and carefully but thinly painted,—in just the manner one might suppose a water-colour artist would paint. He seems to have used semi-opaque colour to scumble with, in so fluid a state that one may distinctly see where it has run down the picture from his brush. It is, nevertheless, a clever production, with a strong resemblance to De Loutherbourg.

his mode of travelling, and as economical with other people's money as he was with his own—he from this time neglected no opportunity of visiting different counties; for we find him busy in Worcestershire and Wales, and for the present work he made the drawings of Bridgenorth, Matlock, and Birmingham; and in the former of these views the characteristics of Turner's style, previous to 1809, are strongly and beautifully marked. His reputation advancing, caused him to be employed upon several works then in progress; and, therefore, we find only two of his plates in this series—Chester and Peterborough—published that year; and in the next, five, viz. Ely, Flint, Westminster, Hampton Court, and Carlisle: but in the two Exhibitions he had nineteen pictures and drawings. In the following year he had six pictures; and for this work he made the drawings of Wakefield and Sheffield; and as if he wished to illustrate his progress, being the last, he has made it one of his best. He had now given practical proofs of his talent as a painter, and the critics were loud in his praise; he also relinquished his engagement with Walker.

The first drawing Girtin made for the present work was the view of Windsor, which contrasts strangely with Warkworth and Bamborough, and with those two beautifully effective drawings of Totnes and Kingsweare. Girtin then made drawings of Pembroke, Marlow, Newcastle, Bamborough Castle, and Warkworth, part of the Marine Barracks at Devonport, Appleby, and Kingsweare, Newcastle-upon-Tyne, Christchurch, Abernethy, and Tarnaway Castle, and last, if not the most artistic, yet one of a very pleasing and interesting character, Woolwich. It was no doubt during his journey into Scotland, as before stated, with Mr. Moore, that, amid the wild solitudes of Nature, Girtin unconsciously gathered materials for producing those startling effects by which he outdistanced all his competitors. Not but what, as we have already shown, he studied Nature in the neighbourhood of London, and long before this period made sketches among the ruins of the old Savoy Palace, amid the vast fragments of which he learnt to copy the mutilated masonry, with an accuracy which did him "yeoman's service" on a future day.

Up to this time, with scarcely an exception, the hues of Nature had only been intimated, not imitated, by weak washes or timid touches; for, as before stated, it was considered impossible to give anything like the effect obtained in oil to water-colour drawings. Girtin, as we have shown, thought differently; and while in Scotland he looked at Nature with his bright, unflinching, eagle-like eye; and saw how, when the sun burst out, the whole landscape was bathed in gold; and how, when it was hidden behind a cloud, the mountains were thrown into gloom and masses; he imitated these changes, making that dark, and sullen, and savage, which had hitherto in landscape-painting been only touched with a little stronger shade than the overhanging sky. He flooded his valleys with a dazzling sunlight, where the golden glory streamed down uninterrupted; and where the clouds hung far away, placed bold dashes of darkness upon the distant mountains, just as he had seen them sleeping under the overhanging shadows. He stamped with sublimity what had hitherto only been timidly touched; he saw how the evening shadows deepened under the trees, and gradually formed the beds on which the descending Darkness first laid down, until her whole length slowly covered the mountain's side, and with a daring hand he drew the mantle over her repose.

Many tried to imitate him, but in vain: for at this period he left his elder competitor, Turner, far behind. He might have become, had he not been what he was universally called, "HONEST TOM GIRTIN," one of the wealthiest artists of the day. Amateurs came rushing daily to him for lessons, exclaiming, "Do but teach us how to draw with this daring and dashing effect, and we shall be content." But Honest Tom saw that the "Divinity stirred not within them," and as one who knew him from his "boyhood, to the day of his death," says, "He was unwilling to minister to their folly, and endeavoured to dissuade them from the attempt." He would neither flatter them, nor waste his time on them, nor take their gold, though he had no secret, but worked openly: no selfishness, but expounded to all his brother-artists the means by which he produced his effects;* he called "a spade, a spade;" and so was voted "low," and the would-be dashing colourists were envious and jealous, because of his unswerving honesty. Tom cared not—he would not pander to their vanity—would not lie to flatter them; but as he looked on their daubs out of his large, flashing black eyes, which could see more than any other artist, excepting Turner, he told them that they had no talent—that they were not "God-gifted"—and so, instead of turning "toad-eater,"

* "It was a great treat to see Girtin at his studies; he was always accessible. (How different from Turner!) When he had accomplished the laying in of his sky, he would proceed with great facility in the general arrangement of his tints on the buildings, trees, water, and other objects. Every colour appeared to be placed with a most judicious perception to effecting a general union, or harmony. His light stone tints were put in with their washes of Roman ochre; the same, mixed with light red, and certain spaces, free from the warm tints, were touched with grey, composed of light red and indigo, or, brighter still, with ultramarine and light red. The brick buildings with Roman ochre, light red, and lake, and a mixture of Roman ochre, lake, and indigo, or Roman ochre, madder brown, and indigo; also with burnt sienna and Roman ochre, and these colours in all their combinations. For finishing the buildings which came the nearest to the foreground, where the local colour and form were intended to be represented with particular force and effect, Vandyke brown and Cologne earth were combined with these tints, which gave depth and richness of tone, that raised the scale of effect without the least diminution of harmony: on the contrary, the richness of effect was increased from their glowing warmth, by neutralising the previous tones, and by throwing them into their respective distances, or into proper keeping. The trees, which he frequently introduced in his views, exhibiting all the varieties of autumnal hues, he coloured with corresponding harmony to the scale of richness exhibited on his buildings. The greens for these operations were composed of gamboge, indigo, and burnt sienna, occasionally heightened with yellow lake, brown pink, and gamboge; these mixed, sometimes, with Prussian blue. The shadows for the trees, indigo, burnt sienna, and a most beautiful shadow-tint, composed of grey and madder brown; which, perhaps, is nearer to the general tone of the shadow of trees than any other combinations that can be formed with water-colours. He so mixed his greys, that, by using them judiciously, they served to represent the basis for every species of subject and effect, as viewed in the middle grounds under the influence of Girtin's atmosphere, when he pictured the autumnal season in our humid climate: which constantly exhibits to the picturesque eye the charms of rich effects, in a greater variety than any country in Europe."

and wallowing in wealth as he might have done, he put on his well-worn hat, and went and smoked his pipe with Jack Harris, the picture-frame maker in Gerrard Street,* and a few other of his homely brother-artists, whom he was accustomed to meet there. He held the golden key in his hand, but refused to "Open, Sesame." What penurious old Turner of Maiden Lane, and his talented son, thought of Girtin, thus throwing away the guineas which they would have hoarded, may be readily imagined; and, perhaps, these thoughts passed through Turner's mind on an after day, when, amid his reveries, they found utterance, as he looked back upon "the days of other years," and exclaimed, "Poor Tom!"

As a proof of Girtin's love of his art, he established a Sketching Society, which was open to talented amateurs as well as brother-artists; and for three years did this little Society of Arts meet on winter evenings to make sketches and improve one another, under the friendly eye of the founder. This alone proves that, however much Girtin might dislike spending his time in the small-talk which formed the staple of amusement at evening parties, when men were willing to meet and spend the evening in intellectual and artistical amusement he at once proposed that they should assemble as a sketching society; and one who was a frequent visitor says, "No little coterie could be more respectable."

The plan that Girtin proposed, and which was carried out, was, that on alternate occasions they should meet at each other's apartments, and at every meeting make a sketch or drawing in colour or chiaroscuro from the same passage, which, before they commenced, was selected from one of the English poets. Each member, at whose house the

---

* Harris, beside making picture-frames, was a dealer in drawings, and through him both Girtin and George Morland often disposed of their works, as they both seemed to dislike dealing with collectors. By this means Jack Harris, as he was familiarly called, made money. Though Girtin was courted by the best society, he seldom mingled in it: perhaps he did not like fulsome praise—perhaps the manners of the upper-classes were unsuited to his old easy habits—and, more probable still, they looked for praise for their daubs; and he was too honest to *lie!* though he occasionally, as will be shown, visited the highest of the nobility.

parties met, supplied in turn the paper, ready mounted on small strainers, together with colours and pencils, and all the designs made during the evening were his property. They had tea or coffee when they first met, at six o'clock; over which they read and talked about the subject selected: after this they worked until ten, when a cold supper was set out, and at twelve they separated. Many of these "impromptu productions" were gems, and were greatly admired. Turner never once joined them: he had no objection to meet Girtin alone, but he seems even then to have thought one of his sketches too great a price to pay for a supper, and not to have cared for the society of talented men. And so these meetings continued until Girtin's health required that he should seek a change of climate.

Girtin was of a kind and friendly disposition, and ready to communicate whatever he had discovered in his practice to those who sought his assistance. He was naturally free, and occasionally associated with persons little qualified to improve his manners; for he had a shyness which made him shun rather than seek the acquaintance of the polite and well-bred world. When travelling to the North, he would take his passage in a collier; and his delight was to live in intercourse with the crew, eating salt beef, smoking, and exchanging jokes. When on shore in search of the picturesque he entered the inn-kitchen for refreshment, as Hogarth had done before him; and from the motley group of wayfarers sketched what struck his fancy, and in the midst of them enjoyed himself for the time, without sacrificing his love of independence; and thus stored up scenes and characters for his works, from the out-door and in-door world. This fidelity to Nature caused one of his contemporaries to say, "He that would sketch like Girtin, must be content to study like Girtin." He also asserts, that "Girtin's admirers tolerated a defect in his drawings, which proves how much allowance the liberal connoisseur will make for the sake of genius. The paper which he most used was only to be had of a stationer at Charing Cross: this was cartridge, with slight wire-marks, and folded like foolscap or post.

It commonly happened, that the part which had been folded, when put on the stretching-frame, would sink into spots in a line entirely across the centre of the sky. This unsightly accident was not only overlooked, but in some instances really admired, insomuch that it was taken for a sign of originality; and in the transfer of his drawings from one collector to another, bore a premium according to that indubitable mark."

Nor must it be forgotten, while speaking of this great artist's homely and social habits, that only a few years before, and even in his day, the first men of the age held their meetings at taverns; —that Johnson, Goldsmith, Burke, Garrick, and Beauclerk, used to assemble in the first-floor room at the Turk's Head Tavern, in Gerrard Street: while on the ground-floor of the same house might be found Hogarth, Reynolds, Wilson, Romney, and others; and amongst them such eminent engravers as Woollett, Strange, Vivares, Brown, and Bazire; and that the upper-room was constantly exchanging visits with the lower, and *vice versâ*.

Even grave family-men, "in these social times, mostly passed their evenings at the tavern, and sometimes prolonged their sittings to the hour indicated on the dial of Hogarth's inimitable picture, 'Modern Midnight Conversation;' for those who had neither imagination nor wit could sit comfortably intrenched behind their pipes, and smoke, and nod, and smile at the lively sallies of their more enlightened friends and neighbours. The pipe, the punch-bowl, and late hours, begat a disposition for mirth; and the morning tale, borne by the lounging amateur from one painter's studio to another, was generally interlarded with the wit and frolic of the over-night." No marvel that Honest Tom Girtin, with his kind, good heart, and easy nature, was often one of the last to say " go," at these merry meetings sixty years since.

Nor must it be forgotten that he lived near that border-land on which, fifty years before, sign-painting, which was not yet out of fashion, had been the first stepping-stone that led to fame, and, what was even of more consideration, to employment, before book-illustrations became so popular. Harp Alley in Shoe Lane, Fleet Street, was the great show and sale-room just before Turner and Girtin's day, and "where," says an eye-witness, "from end to end of that place, the works of the candidates for public favour and employment were to be found—a sort of Noah's ark, in which animals of every hue, kind, and colour, might be seen; from the pencil of Patton, varied by the still-life of Keyse, whose legs of mutton, with every kind of butcher's meat, would not have been less admired for their excellence as works of art in the present, as they were in the past days." The plate-glass fronts of our own time were undreamed of; and it was nothing uncommon for the hosts and tradesmen of those days to expend from fifty to a hundred pounds in the painting and fitting-up of a sign, which, as is well-known, often swung over the centre of the street: as may be seen in Turner's view of Chepstow, in the present work. The style of painting required for this sort of art was a firm pencil and a decided touch, together with an effect which might tell at a distance;—no bad foundation for skilful execution in art. Who can tell, knowing that Girtin's admiration of Morland caused him—as we have shown—to copy one of his pictures at an early period, how often his generous nature may have tempted him to have visited such men as Morland in the taverns, from the owners of which they often obtained employment? Perhaps this feeling of great-heartedness might in his prosperity sometimes induce him too often to frequent taverns, that he might offer his less fortunate brethren a dinner, which they would accept and share with him, though they would have spurned the offered half-crown with as much indignancy as Johnson did the shoes when at school. Through such condescension, springing alone, as it did, from kindness, those who had not a portion in the feeling and manly heart of Honest Tom Girtin might consider him "low." The Sketching Society,* which

* The Society consisted of ten members, viz. :—

Sir Robert Ker Porter,
„ Augustus Callcott,
Mr. T. R. Underwood,
„ G. Samuel,
„ P. S. Murray.

Mr. J. S. Cotman,
„ L. Francia,
„ W. H. Worthington,
„ J. C. Denham,
„ T. Girtin.

Jane Porter, the celebrated authoress, was often present at the meetings, and many of the subjects were from her selection.

he founded and attended during the last three years of his life, shows that, with all his love for sociality, Girtin not only presided over a society of gentlemen, but was beloved by all whom he honoured with his company.

What Girtin's associates might have been, had he chosen to have given the "cold shoulder" to his old homely and warm-hearted friends and companions, will be best shown by stating that Lord Elgin was desirous that he should accompany him to Greece; he was also occasionally a visitor at the houses of the nobility, especially at Lord Hardwicke's, the Earl of Essex, the Hon. Spencer Cowper, who had the largest and finest collection of Girtin's drawings of any gentleman of that day, and Lord Mulgrave's, and that after his death the latter nobleman offered princely aid to Girtin's widow towards placing her son in a position in life, which she declined. The family into which our artist married, and with whom he was a great favourite, as he was with all who were honoured with his acquaintance, was one of some note in the mercantile world of that day; for Mr. Borritt had his house of business, as goldsmith, in Staining Lane, besides his residence at Islington; and it will be remembered that the latter place was the country sixty years ago, and that but few of our old City tradesmen had then their town and country-houses.

Girtin exhibited his first drawing in 1794, at which time he resided with his mother, at No. 2 St. Martin's-le-Grand; it was a view of Ely Cathedral. In the following year he exhibited three drawings; these were views of Warwick Castle, and Peterborough and Lichfield Cathedrals. In 1797 he had removed to No. 35 Drury Lane, and in that year he exhibited ten drawings:—an Interior of St. Alban's Cathedral, two views of Jedburgh, two of St. Cuthbert's Holy Island, four views of York, and one of Ouse Bridge, in the same city. His next residence, in 1798, was at No. 25 Henrietta Street, Covent Garden, in which year he exhibited nine drawings:—Coast of Dorset, Berry Pomeroy Castle, two drawings of Rivaux Abbey, Interiors of Exeter and Chester Cathedrals, Cottage from Nature, a view of a Mill in Derbyshire, and St. Nicholas's

Church, Newcastle. In 1799 he had again removed, and we find him, while residing at No. 6 Long Acre, exhibiting a Mill in Essex, two views of Beth-gellert, Warkworth Hermitage, a Study from Nature, and Tatershall Castle. Girtin next resided with his wife's father, Mr. Phineas Borritt, at No. 11 Scott's Place, Islington, and in 1800 exhibited—Bristol Hot Well, York, and Jedburgh. This year Turner had been elected an A.R.A., and it is possible that Girtin may have aspired to the same honour, which, while he continued to exhibit water-colour drawings only, he could not obtain; we therefore find him, in 1801, sending to Somerset House, for the first time, a picture in oil: this was Bolton Bridge, and the last time he appeared on the walls of the Royal Academy; for in the spring of the following year he went to France, and, as we have already stated, in the autumn of the same year he died.

Amid his numerous works he completed a panorama of London, said to have been one of the finest views of a city ever painted. It was amongst the first of those topographical representations which have, since his day, become so popular, and represented a view of St. Paul's, with the buildings running east and west. It was taken from the lofty roof of the Albion Mills, which were then standing at the foot of the south side of Blackfriars Bridge, and was universally admired, when exhibited at Castle Street, Leicester Square, and in the Great Room, Spring Gardens. For several years after his death it was rolled up in the possession of an architect, named Howitt, in St. Martin's Lane, who, about the year 1825, sold it to a Russian nobleman, and by him it is said to have been taken to St. Petersburgh.

Girtin, never one of the strongest, and fond of society, especially of his brother-artists, who were men of homelier habits than those who stand distinguished in the same profession in the present day, began, young as he was, to feel the effects of the late hours kept at Jack Harris's, and similar places, which, with other constitutional infirmities, brought on a pulmonary disease; and in 1802 his medical adviser recommended a change of climate; and during the patched-up peace of Amiens, he went over to Paris in the spring of that year.

Here he made a beautiful series of drawings, which were purchased by the Earl of Essex, but are now in the collection of the Duke of Bedford, which he etched and published in a style of engraving, then recently introduced but now almost obsolete, called aquatinta.* Not content with these drawings, he executed a great many more—all copied from Nature, in outline—of the principal buildings in Paris, and of one or two of the towns he passed through, which, for boldness, betokened no decay of power. Yet at this very time he was obliged to leave France from the feeling of "solitariness," occasioned by his weak state of health. His return was no way beneficial, for on the 9th of November following he expired at his brother's house in Castle Street, Leicester Square, leaving a widow and an infant son to bemoan a husband and a parent, and his country to deplore the loss of one of the greatest geniuses of the age. He had not even reached the prime of life; but, with all his blushing honours thick upon him, died in the twenty-seventh, as some have asserted, but, as we believe, in the twenty-ninth year of his age. He was, perhaps, the only one who had a place in Turner's memory in after years—one of the few he ever seemed to speak

---

* The first of these etchings he has dated June 10th, 1802, and the last October 4th, of the same year; or but little more than a month before he died. We may almost trace the decline of the master-hand in the appended dates, and by the longer intervals that intervened between the production of each plate: they also prove that he "died in harness," working to the last. The dates are as follow:—

June	July	August	Sept.	Oct.
10	6	4	2	4 !!!
18	12	9	29	
25	16	17		the last.
28	19			

They were published by his brother, John Girtin, a writing engraver, who lived in Castle Street, Leicester Square, until his house and stock were destroyed by fire a few years after his brother's death: his wife, who was ill at the time, died in his arms as he was carrying her out through the surrounding flames. This fire destroyed many of Girtin's best works; and so scarce must we suppose these engravings of the views of Paris to have become, that the British Museum does not possess a copy.

of with regret, and his "Poor Tom!" would sometimes be uttered in such tones as recalled Sterne's "Alas! poor Yorick!"

Turner, who, as an artist, stood unequalled after Girtin died, and who only within what may, by comparison, be called later years, had scarcely a rival competent to contend for the sceptre which he so long and deservedly swayed, had none of those fine social qualities which stood thick as stars on the character of his early and more generous-hearted companion. Nearly all the anecdotes told about Turner—and their name is legion—are illustrative of his selfishness. Once, to the amazement of the whole body of Royal Academicians, he offered to purchase the cloth to re-cover the seats in the room where one of his pictures was hung. Nor was the reason for this apparently generous, and most unaccountable act, at all clear at the time, though, as the end showed, it was only done to serve himself. He was always very particular that everything should aid the effect of his pictures, even to the hanging of those placed around them. To keep up this colour, he would continue painting on his pictures after they were hung, during the varnishing days. On one occasion, however, he was "checkmated," and as he could not produce the effect he wanted by paint, he set about accomplishing it by policy; he studied how it might be done by a foil, and soon found that if he got a mass of bright red in the foreground his object would be accomplished. "The seats are not fit to sit on," said Turner to the hangers; "they are very shabby: they must be re-covered." He was referred to the Council; there was no Council, and so he called upon the President; but some formula was necessary, and delay did not suit Turner's purpose, though he kept his own secret: he muttered something about "It's a disgrace to the Academy!" then said, "I'll do it at my own expense." Lawrence laughed at his liberality, and made no objection. In about an hour he returned, and, going up to the President, said, "Well, I've got the cloth! Suppose I may charge for the men's time and nails?" The President, seeing him so determined, got the necessary permission, and the seats were covered with the cloth Turner had selected, and which he was not allowed to pay for. When the first form was covered he placed the foil in his knowledge of seamanship was picked up during his trips to the North, to which he always went by a Collier. Once he spent a whole summer in drifting about the Thames, for he was fond of the water; and at the time of his death, Mr. "Booth's" boat was moored off Battersea Bridge. Lord Egremont used to assert that Turner had a yacht, but we cannot ascertain this to be the case. In consequence of the prominent part the Téméraire took in the battle of Trafalgar, she was called among the sailors "the Fighting Téméraire," although she had never before or after the battle of Trafalgar a claim to the popular epithet; but Turner had so often heard her called "the Fighting Téméraire," that the name became to him a household word, and as such he entitled his poetical and beautiful picture when it was exhibited. But when the plate was engraved for the Royal Gallery of British Art, and it became necessary to give a brief but authentic history of the ship, and the truth was stated to Turner, he seemed almost in tears when he gave up his pet title, and said, "Call her the Old Téméraire."

With all his selfishness he had a great objection to the "Hail-fellow-well-met" kind of familiarity, and one evening, during a sharp shower, he had taken shelter in a public-house, where he sat in the farthest corner, with his glass before him, when an artist who knew him also came in, who began with "I didn't know you used this house; I shall often drop in, now I've found out where you quarter." Turner listened to him, looked at him, knit his brows, emptied his glass, and as he rose to go out said, "Will you? I don't think you will." While living at Chelsea, a gentleman, who knew him well, chanced to be out on business in the neighbourhood early, and found Turner in the same steam-boat with himself, going towards the City. Seeing Turner clean-shaved, and his shoes blacked, and looking as if he had just left home, he made some remark about his living in the neighbourhood, wondering to see him there so early. "Is that your boy?" said Turner, pointing to the gentleman's son, and evading all questions as to his own "whereabout."

He was not very particular about taking an idea from a brother-artist, and putting him afterwards under an extinguisher, if he had a chance, as was shown when, in 1826, Stanfield had a picture of "A Calm," which he named "Throw us the Painter!" and which he was unable to get finished in time for the Exhibition. Callcott heard of it, and painted "Dutch Fishing-boats missing the Painter;" and the next year out came Turner with his picture, entitled "Now for the Painter!" as if to show that he was the only one competent to handle the *Painter.*

Turner was at first a stern opponent to engraving on steel, and had no notion of supplying plates for "the million." He called upon Sir Thomas Lawrence one day, at a time when he had just received a proof, with which he was very much pleased. He showed it to Turner, and said, "By the way, Turner, I wonder you don't have some of your drawings engraved on steel." "Humph! I hate steel." "But why?" "I don't like it: besides, I don't choose to be a basket-engraver!" "A basket-engraver! a basket-engraver, Turner! what is that?" said the President. Turner looked at Lawrence with that malicious leer, which in his little penetrating eyes, when he meant mischief, conveyed more killing sarcasm than his words, and said, "When I got off the coach t'other day at Hastings, a woman came up with a basketful of your Mrs. Peel, and wanted to sell me one for sixpence." He disliked his works being sold cheap; and no doubt thousands of his engravings were mouldering at the time of his death in his house in Queen Anne Street. Some of the impressions from his plates have realised four times the amount he paid for engraving; and though he made thousands through the aid of the engravers, there is not an instance on record of his ever having rendered assistance to any one of the profession, or, in the whole course of his long life, of having done a generous act. It is, however, stated that he once refused a sum which he lent; but that was after sharing a sumptuous dinner to which he had been invited, and while enjoying the dessert, the host, all at once remembering the transaction, said, "Let me see, Mr. Turner, I owe you a little money."

f

"What for?" said Turner, setting down the wine which he was just raising to his lips. "You paid sixpence for the gate when I drove you down," answered the host. "Oh!" said Turner, with a look of disappointment, as he again had recourse to the glass, "Never mind that *now*."

Although Turner was a close observer of nature, he often committed such errors as placing the new moon with her horns the wrong way—the sun shining from the north—an object throwing two or three shadows from one light, &c.; and when this was detected by his brother-artists it invariably put him into an ill-humour. On one occasion he sent a canvass to Somerset House, with a subject so undefined, that it caused considerable speculation among the Royal Academicians when they assembled on the morning of the first varnishing day, as to what he intended to represent. It was a "Moonlight" with one, and with another a "Storm;" and at last Howard suggested it might be an "Allegory." "Yes," said Fuseli, "the allegoric of blazes at a *déjeûner à la fourchette* wid molten lead!" Turner, who had entered in time to hear the Keeper's remark, said, "No, that's limbo; where they are going to send your 'Sin and Death'" (a celebrated picture). Fuseli threw himself into an attitude of mock terror, saying, "Gentlemen, we are ondone; we all knew *Tourner* to be an imp of de old one transformed into an angel of light by his dooble shadow." "Yes," put in Beechey; "but Turner's shadows are only double when he sees double." "Ah!" added Fuseli, with an affected sigh; "gentlemen, it is what Tourner sees dat concerns us, now he is in his fader's confidence, and he tells him all about de beesiness in his great Fire-ôffice below." The picture was altered, but Turner never again ventured on a joke with Fuseli.

When Turner lectured on Perspective he was often at a loss to find words to express the ideas he wished to communicate. To aid his memory, he would now and then copy out passages, which, when referred to, he could not clearly read. Sometimes he would not make his appearance at all, and the disappointed students were sent away with the excuse that he was either ill, or that he had left his lecture in the coach, or came from home without it. But when the spirit did stir within him, and he could find utterance to his thoughts, he soared as high above the common order of lecturers as he did in the regions of Art. His language was often elegant, his ideas original and most instructive, and it is to be regretted that copies of his graphic diagrams, as sketched on the lecture-boards, were not preserved with his notes. No doubt his illustrative drawings will be found by his executors.

In these brief memoirs we have not space to follow the narrative of events which terminated his long career, and which we only profess to have traced up to Girtin's death. We may, however, remark, that he received the honour of becoming a Member of the Royal Academy in 1802, and more than once aspired to become its President. His life was a strange mixture of shrewd intelligence, independence, liberality in his bequests to the nation and to the decayed painters, and meanness. The materials for his biography are not numerous, as he had a great aversion to writing; still the few letters by him which have come under our notice show that he was shrewd, acute, and occasionally critical in his language. This is verified in the fac-simile letters which are at the end of this Memoir. Whenever he left home his return was uncertain; no one knew whither he wandered, or where he went; and if, by chance, he has been seen, it was only to elicit a " How do you do?" and a " Good-bye ; " he was seen there no more. It was almost useless to write to him on any subject; he would say, " They only want my autograph ;" and his table has been known to contain letters unopened for months.

Turner died at Chelsea, where he had long lived under the assumed name of Booth, on the 19th of December, 1851, in his eighty-second year, and was buried, at his own request, by the side of Sir Joshua Reynolds. Many of the Royal Academicians followed him to his grave.

The dome of St. Paul's, that great landmark of London, which towers a monument above the graves of so many eminent men, marks the spot where the greatest of English landscape-painters, Joseph William Mallad Turner, " sleeps his last sleep."

The remains of Girtin are laid on that side of the burial-ground of St. Paul's, Covent Garden, which leads from Bedford Street to the church on the right.

Just beyond the second tree, a flat stone, which bears neither name nor date, marks his grave. It was not, however, always so, as the portion of the stone here engraved will show, and which

once covered the spot that is still sacred to the memory of "*Honest Tom Girtin.*" These three words ought to have formed the great artist's epitaph, and have been handed down through all time, along with his who won an undying name by his genius in a sister-art, and over whose monument thousands have breathed the words, "O rare Ben Jonson!"

The gravestone was broken by accident some years ago, laid aside, and would, no doubt, have been for ever forgotten, but for the present work. It was originally six feet six inches long, and three feet three inches wide, and was laid *flat* upon his grave. In the appended note * we give the warrant from the "account-book"

---

* " SAINT PAUL, COVENT GARDEN.

"Whereas [*names not known to parish authorities*] hath requested us, the present Churchwardens of the said parish of Saint Paul, Covent Garden, whose names are hereunto subscribed, to permit to have a stone of six feet six inches long, by three feet three inches in breadth, laid FLATT upon the grave of Mr. Girtin deceased, in that part of the churchyard commonly known or distinguished by the of the parish; but by whom it was procured we have not ascertained. Sir William Beechey, Edridge, Hearne, and Turner, followed his remains to the grave. The monument was no doubt erected by his brother-artists, and, perhaps, amongst them the amateurs and members of the Sketching Society which he founded, and a counterpart of which still continues to exist.

After the stone had got broken, it was taken up and reared by chance against the edge of some neighbouring monument, where it remained a considerable time,— so long, indeed, as, nearly a quarter of a century ago, to induce the author of a little sketch, entitled, " Recollections of the late Thomas Girtin " (and who was ignorant of the accident, and knew nothing about the stone having been originally laid flat upon the grave, instead of — as was the custom — placed upright), gravely to state what follows : — " It is a curious circumstance, that the custom of placing the grave stone with its front due east and west was departed from in the instance of this artist. His remains were interred in the burial-ground of St. Paul's, Covent Garden, on the south side, to the left of the paved path (near the west gate of the church) to [towards?] Bedford Street. At the head of this grave, lying east and west, the monumental stone, or *pillar*, is made to front the north ; and from this singular arrangement the passenger who wishes to pay respect to genius may know the site of the grave of Thomas Girtin." Such an error, committed by one who knew Girtin well, would not be credited,

---

name of Henrietta Street Platt, where he now lies interred, in like manner as such grave stones are usually *laid* there : desiring that the sum of twelve guineas may be accepted as a consideration for the same, to be disposed of as shall seem most for the benefit of the said parish.

" Dated 1st day Dec. 1803.

	£	s.	d.
" For a flatt stone over Mr. Girtin - -	12	12	0

" Joseph Muttang,
Richard Ovey, } *Churchwardens.*"
Saml. Skeen,

but for the fact of the warrant here produced for placing the stone *flat* upon his grave; yet many living witnesses, no doubt, might be found who have seen the monument standing as here described, and their testimony would outweigh our assertion, were it not backed by the warrant.

Girtin lived beloved by all who knew him, and died lamented by his friends and admirers. Turner was beloved by no one; and, excepting for his genius, he died unlamented, and without a friend: for his surly habits and suspicious nature were inimical to friendship. Girtin's house, like his heart, was open to all. Turner seldom allowed a human footstep to cross his threshold, nor cared to open his door to a visitor, unless to enjoy the triumph of refusing the object of his mission. Girtin was warm-hearted, liberal, and generous as the sun, that scatters its gold on the good and on the evil. Turner was cold and selfish, and would not have given a brother-artist a shilling to have saved him from starvation; while living, he never gave cause for a human heart, from its full utterance, to exclaim " God bless him!" He had not a loveable atom in his nature—not a redeeming point in him worthy to be placed beside even the faults of Honest Tom Girtin, whose very failings " leaned to virtue's side." But for his genius, Turner would have lived in the world unnoticed, unvisited, and died unpitied. The very men who were instrumental in spreading his fame a millionfold, by whom he made his wealth—the engravers *—he mentions

---

* It has been said that Turner made the engravers, and the experience they have acquired from his works justifies the truth of the remark; but, if he has made them, they have been no less instrumental in making him; and the knowledge he acquired by seeing his works changed into black and white must have given him many a practical lesson in chiaroscuro. To enumerate his prints would lead beyond our limits, for they exceed seven hundred; but we may observe, that no artist of ancient or modern times has been so faithfully translated, or owes so much to the engravers, as Turner. To enumerate their names, when so many are excellent, would be invidious; but we may mention, without hesitation, those of Miller, Pye, Cooke, Goodall, Willmore, Brandard, Wallis, Cosins, &c., which will hereafter stand as high, in connexion with the name and works of Turner, as Marc Antonio's does with Raffaelle, or Bolswert and Edelinck with Rubens. And it is greatly to be feared, that Turner's extraordinary talent will live only not in his will. They, like the water-colour painters, came not under the head of the "Decayed Artists," whom, while living, he neither mingled with, noticed, nor assisted. Peace to his manes! There might be hidden within his heart of hearts, kinder, purer,

to its fullest extent in the productions of the burin; for while these sheets were passing through the press the Vice-Chancellor made the following statement: — " That shortly after the commencement of the long vacation Sir Charles Eastlake, P.R.A., Mr. C. Stanfield, and Mr. P. Hardwick, Royal Academicians, had made their report, which was sent to him, and the result of that report was that, although many of the pictures were damaged by long neglect, it evidently arose from causes existing previously to Mr. Turner's decease, and it would be advisable to keep them free from damp. That the house was abutted upon by two empty houses on one side, and a builder's shop on the other, and, therefore, if they could not be properly attended to where they were, they ought to be removed elsewhere. This (his Honour observed) might have been before predicated, and, in consequence, he had written to them; but, owing to Mr. Stanfield's absence, had not until yesterday received their reply, which was that, considering the difficulty of finding a fit place for them, and in consequence of the serious illness of Mrs. Danby, they should be placed under the care of some respectable man in the house. He (the Vice-Chancellor) HAD SEEN THEM, AND IT WAS EVIDENT THAT MANY OF THEM, FROM NEGLECT PREVIOUS TO Mr. TURNER'S DECEASE, OR FROM EXPERIMENTS, PERHAPS OF HIS OWN, BY VARNISHING OR OTHERWISE, HAD BEEN VIRTUALLY ANNIHILATED; AND SOME, PARTLY DONE IN WATER AND PARTLY IN OIL-COLOURS, HAD BEEN SMEARED SO THAT THE DESIGN COULD SCARCELY BE DETECTED ON THE CANVAS; AND THIS APPLIED TO MANY WELL-KNOWN WORKS. The matter, therefore, had better be considered by counsel." The several parties expressed their willingness to consult on what was best to be done.

It is not often that a judge decides from his own personal observation, and we sincerely trust the exception may, in the above instance, prove erroneous. Turner was in the habit of using oil less boiled than ordinarily, and the consequence is that as the oil dried it exuded its greasy properties, to which the dirt most pertinaciously adhered, and there was no lack of it in his room. The two pictures in the National Gallery are covered with the greasy dirt here spoken of, and, unfortunately, now that it has been varnished over, it has become part of the painting: previously, however, it might have been removed. It was Turner's custom, latterly, to paint much of his pictures with water-colours, using flake white, which turns black through oxidization, without even the addition of gum to bind it; he would then glaze a thin colour over, charged with varnish or magnilp, if he wanted tone; and, if not, he would only scumble over the part some of the before-mentioned oil, and even that diluted with turpentine. The water-colours, not being able to resist the contraction consequent upon the varnish drying, split in every direction, and these evils, it is to be hoped, is the full amount of mischief. They are bad enough, it is true, but not irreparable.

and better motives, than we blinded mortals are permitted to discover. In Christian charity we trust there were, and that for these he has received his reward; and that a measure of happiness is meted out to him a thousand times more bountiful than that which, while living, he meted out to his fellow-men.

In conclusion, and as a testimony of the high estimation in which these great founders of the Water-Colour School of Painting were held, we append the following remarks on their genius. The first, on Thomas Girtin, was written a few years after his death.

An unknown writer says that Girtin closely studied Wilson and Canaletti; and that "much of the knowledge he obtained in the display of contrast of colour in open landscape was derived from the study of Wilson, whose bold and effective pictures in oil Girtin might be said to have translated into water-colour. The vigour and richness of his architectural subjects, which were no less striking, was alike ascribable to his contemplation of the pictures of Canaletti,—indeed, he was alternately designated by his admirers, when he first evinced that power in his works which had never before been seen in drawings, the Wilson and the Canaletti of water-colours, until improving by practice, and increasing in power and judgment, he achieved works that could be likened to nothing in art that had preceded his style." Paul Sandby was the first who produced " pleasing, cheerful, daylight effects on his topographical subjects, slightly coloured: and late in life (he lived to a great age) he improved his style of colouring ; and on a few rural subjects — particularly two—representing ale-houses on the Bayswater road, with wagon-horses at the water-trough, he introduced a very pleasing harmony of tints; but these were executed after Girtin and Turner had displayed, in some of their finest landscape compositions, the superior capabilities of water-colour painting." This is great praise, and a fine compliment paid to genius. For an artist of Paul Sandby's reputation to lay aside a system which he had practised for nearly half a century, and in his old age to become a disciple in the new school of colouring founded by Girtin and Turner, is the greatest honour that could be paid to them.

"Of the subjects which Girtin chose for imitation," says a critic, writing in 1823, "his wild mountain scenery, and topographical views of old towns, were the best adapted for his mode of execution. * * * His masses were bold, broad, and abrupt; his touch large * * * his knowledge of effect exhibited in so captivating a degree, that Nature, and not Art, seemed to prevail throughout the scenes which he represented.

"The variety of light and shadow which he spread over his picturesque buildings, the manner in which he separated the masses, and the brilliancy of certain parts, which received a partial burst of sunshine, diffused a *splendour of effect to these scenes which no artist before had conceived.*

"His fine taste for colour was most evidently conspicuous in his topographical scenes. Every tint of brick, stone, plaster, timber, and tile, was combined, both in broad light, medium tint, and shadow, with such admirable feeling towards general harmony, that no one of the least taste could behold his productions without admiration and delight.

"His skies were generally composed, either of large masses of clouds with partial rays of the sun, which gave variety of light and shadow, or else of a serene character, where the whole piece had a general simplicity of effect. They were rarely composed of many parts. His skies, in general, were extremely luminous."

"It might be supposed," says another writer, "by the bold and broad execution which characterises the works of Girtin, that they were mostly off-hand productions. The contrary, however, is the fact. It is true that he could sketch, and did occasionally dash in his effects with rapidity; but his finely-coloured compositions, though apparently like the pictures by Wilson, the result of little labour, were wrought with much careful study and proportionate manual exertion: in certain of his productions I have frequently watched his progress, which, like Wilson's, was careful, notwithstanding his bold execution, even to fastidiousness. It is true he did not hesitate, nor undo what he once laid down, for he worked upon principle; but he reiterated his tints to produce splendour and richness, and repeated his depths to secure transparency of tone, with a perseverance that would surprise those who were not intimately acquainted with the difficult process of water-colour painting, to produce works that merit the designation of pictures. Indeed it may be truly said, in honour to his memory, that he was, as a painter, unquestionably one of the greatest geniuses of the age."*

An eminent critic, who wrote an article on Girtin and his contemporaries about a quarter of a century ago, after enumerating many eminent names, says, "Greater still, the lamented and ill-fated Girtin, whom his contemporaries placed above Turner, and in whom posterity has seen an anticipator of Bonington, but recognised a higher genius even than Bonington; inasmuch as he was the founder of that school of painting, of which Bonington was only one of the most illustrious disciples."

No sooner had the sun of Girtin set, "darkened at its noon," than Turner began to climb above the horizon, and "flame upon the forehead of the sky."

We give the following as one of the best amongst the earliest criticisms on his works, as it shows that, even more than twenty years ago, there were men of taste and talent enthusiastic in their admiration of his productions:—

"The insight which Turner always possessed of a perfect understanding of his own character and powers, combined with a clear knowledge of the future, taught him in early life the determination of first being able faithfully to portray the commoner scenes of Nature, before attempting a style of art exclusively dependent on a refined and cultivated taste, powerful and vivid fancy

* Library of the Fine Arts, vol. iii. 1832.

and imagination, and the most acute perception of Nature. To such metaphysical and philosophical reasonings the great excellence and superiority of Turner must be attributed—the apparent cause why his latter works* excel those of his more early days in all the qualities of highly-gifted genius. The beauty of his recent works far surpasses his previous performances. By his deep and assiduous study of Nature in his youth, by his fidelity of delineation of the most simple objects, he laid the foundation of that power of execution, grandeur of conception, and knowledge of Nature, which enabled him to portray, with such wonderful facility, the most grand and terrific scenes.

"Landscape, like portrait-painting, will bear a higher style than the mere delineation of outward forms, or of every tree and hillock. The effect of a landscape in Nature, that rivets attention and excites our admiration, is evanescent; and it is left to the landscape-painter of genius for ever to preserve it on canvass. When we recall to memory the many scenes and effects of Nature which Turner has depicted, their variety, beauty, and truth—the almost metaphysical nature of his genius, its comprehensiveness and extraordinary power, further excite our wonder and admiration. Italy,† the gifted country, the chosen land, from whence the light of

---

* The latter works here alluded to are those which he painted above twenty years ago.

† Sir Thomas Lawrence, writing from Italy to Joseph Farington, says:—
"July 2, 1819.
"Turner should come to Rome; his genius would here be supplied with materials, and entirely congenial with it. It is one proof of its influence on my mind, that enchanted as I constantly am, whenever I go out, with the beauty of the hues and forms of the buildings, with the grandeur of some, and variety of the picturesque in the masses of the ordinary buildings of this city, I am perpetually reminded of his pencil, and feel the sincerest regret that his powers should not be excited to their utmost force. He has an elegance, and often a greatness of invention, that wants a scene like this for its free expansion; this blending of earth and heaven can only be rendered, according to my belief, by the beauty of his tones."

Turner, on being made acquainted with Lawrence's opinion, set off to Rome, unknown to any one, and arrived there about the end of October, 1819.

modern civilisation proceeded, never had justice done to her until Turner portrayed her bright sunny skies and 'gorgeous palaces,' her magnificent ruins and relics of departed greatness. Her finest and most poetical scenes and ruins he has painted, and invested them with a grandeur and feeling; 'with an immaculate charm which cannot be defaced,' that never fails when placed before us to recall, in vivid colouring, the past greatness of that fallen nation. To illustrate his genius, we will recall a few of his most popular works. Fuseli, in his third lecture, with considerable minuteness marks the distinction between invention in art and creation in nature; and states that the 'term Invention never ought to be so far misconstrued as to be confounded with that of creation,—incompatible with our notion of limited being, an idea of pure astonishment, and admissible only when we mention Omnipotence.' Still, in spite of this acute reasoning, it is difficult to divest the term 'creation' from the many Italian scenes painted by Turner. 'Palestrina,' 'The Bay of Baiæ,' 'Caligula's Palace,' and 'Italy,' are pictures which, if not of absolute creation, are of the most extraordinary and wonderful invention. When portraying the beauties of an Italian landscape, the imagination of Turner seems unlimited in its invention, exhaustless in variety of forms, and boundless as the universe itself in immensity of space and air.

"Of the many works which he has painted, illustrative either of Italian scenery or her ruins—where all are unquestionably excellent—where there is not one deficient, in the minutest instance, of the full extent of his extraordinary powers, it becomes a hopeless and difficult task to point out any one in particular. The 'Forum Romanum' was little liked, and less understood, yet it is full of grandeur, poetry, and splendid colouring; the careful imitation of every local tint, the exact portraiture of every object, which would have distinguished his early painting of such a scene, have given place to an unlimited indulgence of a vivid fancy, and a poetic and harmonious colouring.

"No picture is more illustrative of Turner's powers than the one which he simply named 'Italy.' It is the portraiture of no particular spot, but a concentration of every varied beauty, of object, and clime of the country,—boundless space, innumerable ruins, a bridge of classic beauty and form, over a river expansive and winding; a group of shepherds dancing in the foreground, and the whole suffused in a blaze of life, clear and warm, combine to form a picture more illustrative of the general beauties of Italy, and the poetic feelings attached to all her scenes, than a hundred written descriptions. The picture of 'Caligula's Palace' is another work of extraordinary merit. Instead of being a mere matter-of-fact delineation of a heap of shapeless ruins, every part of the immense mass assumes a form and character of beauty and grandeur. To enhance the splendour of the effect, to throw additional interest over the scene, the spectator views the towering relics under the poetic aspect of the setting sun. Through the piles of arch upon arches its rays shoot in streams of light, and recall to memory the ages past, when a living multitude peopled the halls, and Rome's most tyrannical despot inhabited the once splendid palace.

"Turner has not confined his powers merely to landscape and marine painting, but adventurously advanced into that style which, while it cannot be designated as the pure historical or heroic, yet is at the same time so identified and so fully imbued with the highest feelings of poetry, that it more than compensated for its digression from the rigid laws of classic composition; particularly such works as the 'Vision of Medea,' 'Polyphemus,' 'Shadrach, Meshach, and Abednego in the fiery furnace,' 'Pilate washing his hands,' and 'Dido superintending the building of Carthage.' The 'Ulysses and Polyphemus' is a picture of the most splendid imagery—fairyland with all its enchantments, its poetry, and unearthliness, seems realised. In its colouring it is intensely beautiful and poetic; and for the display of the most refined taste and vivid imagination it surpasses even all that the painter has ever executed, before or since. When the miscellaneous crowd composing the visitors to the Royal Academy Exhibition first beheld Turner's extraordinary painting of 'Pilate washing his hands,' all experienced the influence of its blaze of light, its gorgeous colouring, and magical chiaroscuro. But its grandeur of conception, its passion, expression, and pathos, few understood, and less appreciated; and the many condemned that which they could not understand, and looked on the noble effort of genius only as a mere mass of unmeaning colour.

"In our opinion the grandeur of idea, the power of invention, and the awfully sublime effect on the mind, cannot receive too much praise. The more than chaotic mass, the infuriated multitude that shouted, 'Let him be crucified!' like an agitated sea undulate before us: we all but hear the Babel-like din of many voices; and by the distance at which is seen the figure of Pilate, with expanded arms, how admirably is given the idea of space! Like Rembrandt, by the mere power of light and shade, and harmonious colouring, Turner can rouse the sublimest feelings of our mind. To accomplish this is the true destiny of Art, and the link by which it connects itself with the regard of posterity. Similar in character to the last-mentioned picture is 'Shadrach, Meshach, and Abednego,' exhibited at the Royal Academy. To say of it that it is an admirable representation of fire and heat is nothing but the truth, and meagre praise after all; when, for justness to the story and awful nature of the effect, it almost defies description. While in the form of the figures, their characters and expressions, there is nothing palpable, nothing accurately defined, yet they float before us with a ghastly and vision-like air.

"The 'Vision of Medea' is another work of extraordinary imagination; the mysterious and shadowy forms composing the funeral train are grandly conceived, and executed with surprising power.

"The marine views to which the English were most accustomed before Turner wrested that department of art from all competitors, consisted of that style which had for its aim a mere portraiture of vessels, without considering the distance at which they might be from the eye; and the vessels were without method in grouping or composition. Turner was the first who gave to this style the expansive breadth, freshness, and brilliancy of nature. Without losing the minutest characteristic of every variety of vessels, he at the same time presents us with pictures full of imagination and poetry. In fact, in his delineation of vessels he is most scrupulously exact in obtaining all their minute peculiarities; and in their trim, according to the quantity of sail they are carrying, he shows how carefully and minutely he has studied them in nature. How brilliant, pure, and aërial Turner's painting always appeared! At whatever distance they were viewed, still the effect was the same,—clear and forcible, with every object distinctly seen, and yet all keeping in their proper places: in fact, the most perfect realisation of the true breadth and air of nature. Scattered objects never offend the eye; fluttering lights and unmeaning masses of shadow are never to be seen. The 'Rotterdam Ferry-boat' is particularly beautiful in the colour and form of the clouds, and extraordinary truth in the delineation of the buildings in the middle distance. In this last quality his power is amazing and wonderful; the tone of the extreme distance, the colour of the vessels, as seen in misty haze in the last-mentioned picture, is wonderfully true. The same effect is seen in the 'Van Tromp returning from the Battle of the Dogger Bank.' To produce effects by harsh oppositions of light and dark has been a very common aim with some painters, but Turner, like the illustrious Reynolds, broke through this incongruity of taste in art, and in the 'Van Tromp' he gives a masterly specimen of the brilliant effect to be produced by the union of light with light, and shade with shade.

"There is no term more generally used and less understood among artists than 'breadth.' With some it signifies light and shade; others, squareness of forms and flatness. There is not one quality for which Turner is more pre-eminently distinguished from among his numerous beauties and excellencies than this knowledge of breadth. Not only does it signify a clear and gradual union of shadows and half tints, but that every picture should present a mass of broken colouring. In his 'Rotterdam Ferry-boat,' and 'Van Goyen looking out for a Subject,' those fine old picturesque men-of-war of the eighteenth century are represented, and finely illustrate his knowledge of breadth; for even in one single vessel the variety of tints and shades are exceedingly numerous, where other men would have painted them all of one tone.

"'The most poetical and imaginative picture of Turner's, since his 'Polyphemus,' is 'The Mouth of the Seine;' perhaps, however, not more so than his 'Fingal's Cave.' 'The Mouth of the Seine' has been vigorously attacked by newspaper critics as a work of extreme extravagance, and inharmonious opposition of warm and cool colour. We think it must be considered a demonstrative proof of the truth of a picture if, on looking at it, the spectator is reminded of a scene in nature.

"This picture, immediately that we saw it, powerfully brought back to our recollection effects of similar beauty we had often observed in nature, and more than ever convinced us of the power of Turner's mind. Unlike Canaletti and Guardi, or Bonington, Turner has not made his Venetian view of the 'Bridge of Sighs' a mere vehicle of splendid handling, and hardly better than a dry transcript of the scene, but thrown over the whole picture of this once city of palaces that death-like stillness and calmness so soothing to the mind, and likewise so characteristic of Venice. Altogether it is a most poetical composition, and brilliant example of the genius of the English artist. 'Watteau's Study,' 'Rembrandt's Daughter,' and 'Jessica,' all prove the splendour, versatility, and giant strength of Turner's genius. The first was a wonderful work, most daring in its attempt and triumphant in the execution. In it were all the great powers of the artist shown with chiaroscuro, colour, and composition. The second was also a splendid delineation of light and shade, colour and management, but is not so elaborate and finished as the 'Watteau.' To scorn tamely following in the beaten tracks of others is a restless curiosity, but an endeavour to discover new combination of objects or refined ideas are powerful characteristics of a great genius, whatever may be his pursuits. Thus the most eminent painters have always been the greatest experimentalists. While other men were content to pursue their art with an apathy to all the deep and intricate beauties of Nature, Turner, after having first well-grounded his talent, emerged as a meteor in colouring. We are aware that on this point he is unceasingly assailed, as sacrificing both Nature and Art to a false taste. It is not for the present age to sit in judgment upon him.

The enemies and contemporaries of the great Reynolds were as actively alive to detract from his genius; he painted not for his time, but for the generations of which we now form a part: and in his works which have descended to us there is no ground on which to accuse him, or call in question his excellency. The same feelings must be our guide to an estimate of Turner; for even in those pictures which are only ten or fifteen years old, time has already subdued the more harsh and glaring properties of colour, and invested them with a warmth, brilliancy, and tone, which could never have been obtained but by a series of experiments in the execution.

" Persons, in judging of the colouring of Turner, look to nothing but the mere body of colour: they have no perception of the combination of the whole. It is unjust, on the part of the public, to dispraise the works of a man whose constant aim is the improvement of Art: instead of censuring, they ought to rejoice in having the opportunity for observing, in his various experiments, the progress and process by which he attempts to embody the more beautiful and difficult effects of Nature.

"Even when he is apparently most outrageous in his oppositions of colour, we can never deny him consummate skill in light and shade, breadth, and splendid chiaroscuro. ' Rembrandt's Daughter' was undoubtedly extravagant, but what other painter could have been so with such propriety? The oft-calumniated ' Jessica,' if too positive in primitive colours, were there not breadth and chiaroscuro? To prove that the principle on which Turner's works are founded is undeviatingly true to Nature, if either ' Rembrandt's Daughter,' or ' Jessica,' were engraved, there would not be a defect to be seen.

" His most beautiful characteristics are, a tasteful combination of forms, vivid imagination, and playful fancy. A refined poetic feeling pervades every part. The theory of Hogarth's line of beauty is substantiated in Turner's works: whether in the form of trees, action, and bearing of vessels, shape and character of clouds, or painting of the agitated sea, the principle of a serpentine line is

h

everywhere perceptible, and marks the acuteness with which he has watched and observed the minutest circumstances in Nature.

"Whenever we stand before a painting by him, the perfect unity of part with part, and the breadth of effect of the whole, form a powerful contrast to the stiffness, crudeness, and scattered appearance of inferior works. We look at Turner's as a condensation of Nature within a limited scale. To contemplate Turner's, is to look on Nature herself:* the same feelings which a real scene would occasion are roused within us. We stand suffused in pleasing melancholy as the eye ranges over the wide expanse of his 'Italy,' or 'Caligula's Palace.' The splendour, magnificence, and imperial glory of Rome, start almost into reality as we calmly contemplate the 'Forum Romanum.' Carthage, with her train of imperial palaces and wide magnificence, over whose ruins Marius mourned, floats visibly almost to our senses. By this great power of imagination his landscapes are imbued with the high feeling of expression.

* "This morning I breakfasted with the Prince (Metternich), his daughter, Comtesse Esterhazy, and their friends, at the early hour of six o'clock, and then set off with them to Tivoli, where I have passed a day of such enjoyment to a painter. Such a union of the highly and varied picturesque, the beautiful, grand, and sublime in scenery and effect, I hardly imagined could exist. Like the Vatican and St. Peter's, it is infinitely beyond any conception I had formed of it, although so many fine pictures by Gaspar and others have been painted from it. The only person who, comparatively, could do it justice would be Turner, who (I write the true impression on my eye and on my mind) approaches in the highest beauties of his noble works nearer to the fine lines of composition, to the effects and exquisite combination of colour in the country through which I have passed, and that is now before me, than even Claude himself. I now speak the clear remembrance of those impressions, when frequently the comparison forced itself upon me. I have pressed your coming to Rome as a measure due to yourself, your requirements, and those circles of literary inquiry and knowledge which have already been so much benefited by your researches; but in Mr. Turner, it is injustice to his fame and to his country to let the finest period of his genius pass away (when, as Lord Orford happily expresses it, it is in flower) without visiting those scenes which, if possible, would suggest still nobler images of grandeur and of beauty than his pencil has yet given us, and excite him to still greater efforts than those which have already proved him the foremost genius of his time."—*Extract of a Letter from Rome to Samuel Lysons, Esq.*, June 1819.

"Of the knowledge and powers of light and shade Turner is admirably gifted. Beyond, or in his point of sight, he never places any objects strikingly attractive. He preserves these generally in the centre of his compositions, where also is to be found the greatest mass of light; and opposed to the point of sight is the darkest and largest quantity of shade.

"But let no man confidently assume, because he paints clouds [*] in whirlwind agitation, or poises his darkest shades against the highest light, that he consequently is then following Turner. No man of true genius can bear imitation; his heart burns for originality. Nature is just the same now as when Turner began his artistical life, and he who would be his equal or superior, must study the same book wherein he discovered the principles which have elevated him to greatness."

The following *fac-similes* of Turner's letters cannot fail to interest all lovers of art and anecdote, not only as illustrative of the language and caligraphy, but also of the extreme rarity of his epistles. The first, to Mr. Britton, shows acuteness of criticism, as well as sound principles; the second alludes to a picture of the battle of Trafalgar, now at Greenwich, painted for George IV., through the recommendation of Sir Thomas Lawrence, and expresses his strong aversion to a custom too common in courts and public offices, of exacting exorbitant fees; and the third confirms his well-known habit and practice of declining to give an opinion on the originality of his own productions. The last two letters have been kindly lent for this work by Archibald Keightley, Esq., the executor of Sir Thomas Lawrence.

[*] To an eminent artist at Rome Sir Thomas Lawrence wrote, in March 1820: — " Try now to get something of more precious character in your skies and distances; don't be content with fair insipid Roman painting (this between ourselves). Clouds, 'tis true, are all softness, but we have been too long accustomed to see them touched with the expression of the pencil to be content with their smooth and spiritless representations; 'tis the same with your distances; they are very accurate, of true and sweet hues, but you do not scumble enough, nor give that finer zest of delicate pencilling that is so exquisite in the finest works of Claude and Turner."

In addition to the letter, we have much pleasure in enriching our pages with the following explanatory note from Mr. John Britton to the Publisher:—

"My dear Sir,

"I enclose for your work, of Turner and Girtin, with both of whom I was acquainted before the present century commenced, a '*fac-simile*' of a letter which the former addressed to me from Farnley Hall, Yorkshire, in 1811, on the proof of an Essay on his justly-admired picture of 'Pope's Villa,' which was then in the gallery of Sir John F. Leicester, in Hill Street, London. I had previously seen the artist, at my house, on the subject, and had read to him part of my proposed comments on that picture; and particularly a passage I had written on certain illiberal and unfair criticisms by Fuseli, in his lectures at the Royal Academy, stigmatising landscape-painters as 'the map-makers, the topographers of art,' &c. Irritated at this sneering sarcasm, I expressed myself strongly, and proposed to test its justness and discretion by reference to Mr. Turner's view of 'Pope's Villa.' Reading the rough proof to a friend, whose judgment I respected, he advised me to omit the passage; and it is evident that Mr. Turner regretted its absence. I had previously printed some comments on the same lecture, in my small volume on 'the Corsham House Collection.' Some years afterwards I met Fuseli at the house of a mutual friend, the scientific dentist, Mr. Cartwright, when the professor complained of remarks which had appeared 'in a trumpery book, by an author of the name of Britton—perhaps your father,' he said, looking at me; 'but the poor fellow knows nothing of art or artists, and, therefore, is below notice.' Though not disposed to wage a wordy war with the learned, but sarcastic professor, I frankly owned the authorship of the comments referred to, by vindicating the integrity and utility of topography, as more worthy of study and praise than romance or fable; and that such landscapes as Claude, Salvator Rosa, Wilson, Gainsborough, Girtin, and Turner, were as admirable and valuable as many pictures which professed to represent poetical or historical subjects.

"Mr. Turner, being on a visit to Mr. Walter Fawkes, of Farnley Hall, Yorkshire, when I wanted to publish the print of 'Pope's Villa,' with my comments on the subject, I addressed a letter, with proof of the letterpress, to him, begging him to make such corrections, additions, or alterations as he wished to see recorded. On a blank page of the same letter he wrote the annexed, and also made three or four pencil remarks on the proofs of the two pages of letterpress. I have often referred to this letter with gratification, not unmixed with surprise, as its critical remarks are at once frank and nicely discriminating; though his usual tone and language in conversation was blunt, abrupt, unaccommodating, and uncourteous.

"Believe me, my dear Sir,

"Yours very truly,

"J. BRITTON."

"*Burton Street, Nov. 30, 1853.*"

TURNER AND GIRTIN'S

PICTURESQUE VIEWS.

ROCHESTER.

PLEASANTLY situated on an angle of land, formed by a bend of the river Medway, which here about is some four hundred and thirty feet wide, is the ancient city of Rochester, called in the old Saxon tongue *Hroffe-ceaster*, that is, Roffe's city or castle, because one Hroffe or Roffe, a great man in his day and generation, built a stronghold here, about which there no doubt grew a little cluster of meaner habitations, belonging to his dependents, or those who, in the dark and troublous times, were glad to live under the protection of his powerful arm. By the Britons the place was called *Dcurbryf*, signifying a swift stream, in allusion to the rapid current of the river, and this name the Romans Latinized into *Durobrovis, brovæ*, or *brovum*, as the case required: so much for the etymology of the place. The Saxon name, we see, has proved the most enduring; nor can we wonder at this, when we consider how largely the Saxon element has entered into the composition of our national character and institutions. Look now at that grim old castle, as depicted by the pencil of Turner, in the view before us; you would never take that for any other than Saxon work. See what a sturdy time-and-element-defying aspect it has! Many centuries have rolled by since those grey walls were built up, and changes—ah! what mighty changes!—have taken place in all things around, yet there they stand, imperturb-

A

able, unimpressible, seemingly as lasting as the hills themselves. Julius Cæsar, they tell us, built a fortress upon this spot, and some antiquaries contend that in the lower portions of the majestic keep they can trace the work of Roman hands. Be it so! What of that? The structure that now looks us grimly in the face, and bids us pull it down if we can—some of us have tried and failed—is Saxon and no other. Built by Norman William? No such thing! Built by Saxon Gundulph. Norman battering-rams and catapults have done their worst against it, and no doubt made some heavy breaches, but could no more destroy it than could the so-called "conqueror" of this realm, destroy the sturdy Saxon independence of the people whom he subdued, as he fondly imagined. He was a stout, stalwart fellow, that Norman William, as he first "loomed large" upon the page of our national history; and it was an iron grasp with which he held our country in subjection; but how like a wax figure in the sun did he melt gradually away! he and his successors, what "little men" did they become —merged in the more expansive and enduring waters of the great wide Saxon sea, which they thought they were born to ride and rule! The laws, manners, and customs which they introduced, the language which they spoke—where are they? Gone, or going fast, as things incompatible with the nation's progress and prosperity, while Alfred and *his* laws and institutions are becoming every day more and more clearly recognized as a part and parcel of ourselves; he the type, and they the natural developments of the Saxon character. Julius Cæsar's fortress, if he had one here, which seems likely, for the position was an important one—being close upon where the great Roman road crossed the Medway—has disappeared. Norman William, with his doings and belongings, has faded like a myth; but there, as we said before, stands the work of the Saxon architect, like an embodiment of the genius of the wonderful people who are spreading over the whole earth, and building up—that is their mission, not destroying—great and glorious monuments of their inventive skill, and energy, and perseverance.

It is near upon eight hundred years since Bishop Gundulph, who also rebuilt a great part of the neighbouring cathedral, erected this massive and enduring memento of his architectural skill, on which, about sixty years ago, Turner looked, as we may well imagine, with delight and admiration, from the opposite side of the river. It is the most prominent feature in the landscape, for the cathedral does not rise sufficiently above the surrounding buildings to be very conspicuous; of this, little more than the main tower can be clearly distinguished in the view, although, from a more elevated spot than that which our artist appears to have occupied, the whole length of the building, upwards of three hundred feet, may be traced, with the two cross aisles, or transepts, one about one hundred and twenty, and the other ninety feet in length; and the two minor towers over the richly carved but sadly mutilated western entrance. Both the castle and the cathedral look from this distance precisely as they did when Turner drew his picture, except that the plain square tower of the latter structure, with its extinguisher-shaped spire, has been replaced by a new tower, also quadrangular in shape, but of a somewhat more elaborate style of architecture, having four enriched pinnacles at the corners. It is, however, much too low to produce a good effect, and it accords but ill with the rest of the building: it was erected about thirty years since.

The print shows little more than one-half of the fine old bridge—that "goodly bridge of stone," built late in the fourteenth century, at the joint expense of the renowned warrior, Sir Robert Knolles, and Lord John de Cobham, who lived at Cowling Castle, some miles away over the hill behind us. At the west—or Rochester end of the bridge—these noblemen also built and endowed a chapel and chantry, where pilgrims and travellers might attend mass, and receive spiritual consolation. It is a noble bridge, and a most picturesque object in the landscape, lying, as it does, close under the castle, one angle of the outer wall of which its parapet nearly touches. It will be seen that the centre opening, as represented in the view, is of a square form: this was originally a drawbridge, but it is not so now, that and one of the side spaces having about thirty years since been made into a single arch. The old wooden bridge, by which the river was crossed, previous to the erection of this more solid and useful structure, was considerably nearer this way, on a line with the high streets of Strood and Rochester, each of which is now connected with the bridge by an abrupt and inconvenient bend of the road. Here it is that the works are in progress for the new bridge of three arches, which is to be mainly of iron. It is about three years since these works were commenced, and the piers are only now beginning to show themselves above the water : the engineering difficulties have, however, been very considerable ; these are nearly overcome, and we may soon expect to see the stately structure spanning the river ; then will be commenced the demolition of the stone bridge ; and by-and-by it will be numbered among the things that were, and we shall be glad to turn to such pictures as the one before us, to recall to mind its old familiar aspect, and the host of historical and individual associations connected with it.

Lovely, indeed, are the green meadows, woods, and corn-fields that slope up on either side above the bridge, where the river goes meandering away towards Maidstone, presenting in its course many a bit of scenery calculated to delight the eye of an artist, and visiting many spots of great historic interest. We would gladly follow it if we might, but our attention must be confined to the objects close about us, on which the eye of Turner dwelt.

Down to the right there, nearly opposite the castle, is the Temple Farm, with but little of the picturesque about it except its situation, but historically interesting as the site and remains of a building once occupied by those warrior priests, or priestly warriors, the Knights Templars. On the left side of the river, close by the castle, is Boley Hill, where stands the house, called by Queen Elizabeth "Satis," to express her high satisfaction at the entertainment which she there received, when she visited Rochester in 1573. Considerable alterations have taken place about this spot within the last half century, the ground having been laid out in pleasant walks, with seats beneath shady trees, and other adjuncts to out-of-door enjoyment. A bathing-house has also been built, and other improvements made.

Nearer to us again, on this side of the river, is Strood, once a mere fishing village, surrounded by marshes—a most amphibious kind of place, we should imagine; it still retains what *Trinculo* would call "a very ancient and fish-like smell"—an eternal odour of stale shrimps, and other marine productions. Turner, however, has excluded it from his picture, so we need not dwell upon its beauties, which are somewhat screened from our view by the very unsightly wooden Railway Station, a blot upon the landscape which our artist was happily spared the pain of seeing, unless he came here much later than 1794, the date affixed to the picture. Near to this ugly station are a couple of rather pretty dwelling-houses of modern construction, and an inn just built; and all about where we stand are scattered luggage-sheds and cattle-pens, and such like necessary accommodations for a considerable railway traffic; there is also an engine-house, once used for pumping water in and out of the Thames and Medway Canal, which commences just about where Turner must have stood to make his sketch, and for which that monster of a tunnel, about three miles long, that stands with open mouth behind us, was bored; the water-way of the arched hollow is now filled up, and the thunder of the iron horse reverberates where once the laden barge glided noiselessly. All this is fresh, and unlike what Turner would have loved to contemplate; so we will leave the spot and ascend the brow of the hill on which stands the pretty picturesque church of Frindsbury. Ah, this is something like a prospect! Up and down goes the river Medway, winding like a silver snake of huge dimensions; on its bosom are vessels of all sizes, from the tiny punt, just big enough for two persons, to the mighty ship of war, that twice in the twenty-four hours swings idly round with the tide, and so will continue to swing until her timbers become rotten, and a contract is taken to break her up, and she will be valued only as so much old timber and metal, although she has never been out of sight of the slip on which she was built. Of such costly monuments of national folly there is no lack in the Medway ; all down the river to Sheerness you may see these great mastless hulls, like sleeping monsters with many eyes. Look now at that busy bustling railway steamer ! She has just left the Sun Pier at Chatham with quite a crowd of passengers, who pay 1d. each, and are conveyed in about ten minutes to Strood, in time for the train. How saucily she dips beneath the bow of the slumbering leviathan, as much as to say, " Well, old useless, here I am again, working for the benefit of man ; while *you*, bah ! you are only an obstruction to traffic. Why don't you go and get cut up for firewood ? You would be of some use then."

That tongue of land which juts out beneath us, and which in the print is nearly bare, has on it now, we see, a number of buildings, among which we distinguish a gasometer ; so there is light for the ancient city of Rochester. And through the iron veins that ramify from thence, flows the subtle fluid up into Strood, down into Chatham, and round that bend of the river there to Brompton and the neighbourhood, miles away. Wonderful ! by the simple turning of a tap, you may quench, as it were, the sun of a social system, and involve a whole district in sudden darkness ! But, to proceed :—Following the line of the river down to Chatham, and round the abrupt turn which it there takes to the north, we notice first the Gun Wharf, or " Old Dock," as it is sometimes called, then St. Mary's Church, and the back of the Marine Barracks, with Melville Hospital higher up to the left, and the elegant spire of Trinity Church, Brompton, peering over it.

Bringing the eye down again, and still bearing to the left, we run along the river front of the Royal Dockyard of Chatham ; "stored," as Camden has it, "for the finest fleet the sun ever beheld, and ready at a moment's warning." Here we see anchor wharf ; building slips and docks ; rope-house ; mast-house ; lead mills ; metal mills ; saw mills ; and all the means and appliances necessary for a great naval arsenal. Frowning above, and enclosing all, are the fortified lines of defence; and from practising ground, and barrack, and citadel, come ever and anon the roll of musketry, the rattle of the drum, and the shrill blast of the trumpet, breaking the peaceful quietude of nature, and making the heart sad for the folly of man. Farther down the river is Gillingham Reach, with its Martillo tower; and on this side, nearly opposite, is Upnor Castle, which was the turning point of the Dutch fleet, when, in 1677, it was sent up the Medway on an errand of destruction. On this side of the castle rise the wooded slopes of Upnor, and out to the left spreads the low marshy ground of the hundred of Hoo, fertile in corn and other life-supporting products of the earth, and also in intermittent fever and ague. And so we complete our survey, and descend the hill again; catching, as we do, a glimpse of the twisted chimneys and gables of the old Quarry House, and thinking that they ought to belong to "a moated grange," with a romantic history; and wondering whether, among the sketches left by Turner, one of this picturesque old house might not be found. Hereabouts the artist must have lingered, watching the lights and shades play upon our beautiful river and the surrounding landscape. He is said to have been partial to the scenery of the Medway, but we cannot learn that the "oldest inhabitant" has ever seen, lingering about those spots that a true artist would be most likely to haunt, one who, as Sir William Allen says, "resembled a Dutch skipper," or who would have answered to the unflattering portrait drawn by the author of 'Turner and his Works'—" He was short, stout, and bandy-legged, with a red pimply face, imperious and covetous eyes, and a tongue which expressed his sentiments with a murmuring reluctance." In his younger days, however, Turner was no doubt a better-looking man; but whether or no, he must be recognized as a great genius, if an eccentric one. Some of the productions of his pencil are truly sublime compositions, and fully entitle him to occupy a foremost position among the great painters of England.

And Turner, too, was a Saxon—a steady, sturdy worker! A man not of words but of deeds, and his works will stand the test of time. The pictures which he has bequeathed to the nation speak loudly, not only of genius, but industry and perseverance—of working on through good and evil report, with fixed attention to the end in view, and attention to little else. Such a man could afford to be laughed and scoffed at! Such a man could bravely *endure* to the end.

D Sir

on your p
same. I
to return
- I am so
Pray info
of sendin
Nov

Sir I rather la
is supposed fa
of Map makin
nature of th
you will find
Two performan
being called Ea
Paper without
difference. - N
one question
is - ought to b
The fourth an
gratefull pos
was in town,
mansion a

P.S. untill
I return en
know what w
as one mon

Sir
to hi
sorry
him T
his Mo
on Plass
be exc
Picture
positively
Wright
Pilkingt.
To his Mo'a

D Sir

Herewith I submit for your inspection, the observations my remarks on your picture of "Pope's Villa" — & if you wish to make any alterations, to the same, I will readily comply with your suggestions — I must beg the favor of you to return this sheet, by the first post — as I must print the account immediately — I am sorry I could not submit it to you previous to your leaving town — Pray inform me if you can make it convenient to oblige me with 2 or 3 drawings of similar forms — they shall be engraved in the very best manner —

Nov 16 - 1811

Yrs truly
J Britton
Tavistock Place

Sir
I rather lament that the remark which you read to me for Mr T — remarks — when I called in Tavistock Place is suppressed for it Espoused the cause of Elevated Landscape against the aspersions of Map making criticism, but no doubt you are better acquainted with the nature of Publication and mine is a mistaken zeal — As to remarks you will find an alteration or two in pencil. Two groups of Sheep Two fishermen are too close. baskets to entrap Eels is not technical being called Eel pots — and making the willow tree the identical Popes willow is rather strained — I cannot give up illusion, and with deference — mellifluous lyre — seems to deny Energy of thought — and let me ask one question "Why say the Poet and Prophet are not often united" — for if they are not they ought to be therefore the solitary instance given of Dodsley acts as a censure. The fourth and fifth lines requires perhaps a note as to the state of the grotto that grateful posterity from age to age may repair what remains — If so I would ask a little more to be added but as it is, use your own discretion and therefore will conclude considering my further with Dodsleys lines.

Your most truly obliged
J M W Turner

PS respecting Landscapes we will have some conversation when I return and you may see the sketches which will not I will and I must if some know what ought all your work before I can positively accept of your proposal as one more I think of being into Liber Studiorum — I have not time to return this by post yesterday — but hope that no delay has been experienced in the printing

Dear

I h
from the Lord
the amount for
demand I tho
asking you of
the 600 £ you
for the service
wishes), the turn
gordaufs to the

In
renew my O,

J, hr Tho' Lawrence

St.
to his
sorry.
him I
hi No
in Rafs
he ever
Picture
positively
bright
Villingt.
J, hr Tho'a

Dear Mr Thomas

I have just now received a letter from the Lord Chamberlains Office stating that the amount for my Picture will be paid upon demand. I therefore feel the necessity of again asking you if you do authorize me in demanding the 600 £ you mentioned, or if in your warmth for the service of the Arts you did exceed (in your wishes) the terms proposed. Do pray have the goodness to tell me?

In regard to the fees I beg to renew my Objections, but do believe me tly

With true regard
yours most faithfully
JMW Turner

To Mr Thos Lawrence

Thursday 2

J M W Turner presents his respects to Sir Thos Lawrence and feels sorry his engagement will prevent him the pleasure of waiting upon Sir Tho.s tomorrow morning. he called in Russell Square to request he might be excused giving any opinion of the Picture in consequence of his having positively declined so doing to Mr.s Knight a particular friend of his Mr. Pilkington on the part of Mr Gray & Sir Tho. Lawrence.

M W Turner presents his respects to
Thos Lawrence and the feels
his engagement who prevent
the pleasure of waiting upon
"tomorrow morning.. he called
in Square to request he might
avoid giving any opinion of the
in consequence of his having
; declined so doing to Mr —
a particular friend of his &c..
to. on the part of Mr Gray
Lawrence.

CHEPSTOW.

Chepstow and its neighbourhood are rich in historical associations and in natural beauties. None can make pretension to an acquaintance with the natural beauties of our island, who have failed to investigate their brightest features in the Tour of the Wye. Chepstow is situated at the mouth of the Wye; and presents in its immediate neighbourhood the commencement of a series of enchanting views, which continue even to its distant source, beside the birthplace of its sister Severn, in the wild heights of Plinlimmon. The accompanying engraving is a copy of an early work of our great artist, Turner, and represents a view of the bridge and castle of Chepstow, as they existed some sixty years since. The original wooden bridge here delineated has given place to a handsome iron structure, erected in the year 1816. One half of it stands in the county of Gloucester, and the other half in the county of Monmouth; the whole spanning the rapid stream at a height above low-water mark far greater than in other similar erections. This is rendered needful by the scarcely paralleled circumstance of the tide rising at times to nearly sixty feet. In the great storm of 1703, the tide flowed over the top of Chepstow bridge, inundating all the low land and devastating whole farm-yards. The inn represented in the engraving is still standing, though a little changed from its original self. It is now known as the Bridge Inn. The other buildings are much changed in their appearance.

The old bridge was a favourite promenade for the inhabitants. It was, like its iron successor, of great height—built on piles—and its length is thus described by William of Worcester :—" Longitudo pontis de Chepstow 126 virgæ." A sad calamity, connected with this bridge, drew from the pen of the poet Campbell an epitaph on a lady and her two daughters, his personal friends, who perished by the upsetting of their boat, which struck against the wooden pier in the centre arch. The tide was running strong at the time. Their lifeless remains were afterwards recovered, and buried in the churchyard of Monkton Combe, Somerset, beneath a tomb which bears the poet's inscription :*—

> " In deep submission to the will above,
> Yet with no common cause for human tears,
> This stone to the lost partner of his love,
> And for his children lost, a mourner rears.
> One fatal, one o'erwhelming doom,
> Tore, threefold, from his heart the ties of earth ;—
> His Mary, Margaret, in their early bloom,
> And HER who gave them life and taught them worth.
> Farewell, ye broken pillars of my fate!
> My life's companion, and my two first-born;
> Yet while this silent stone I consecrate
> To conjugal, parental love forlorn,
> Oh, may each passer-by the lesson learn,
> Which can alone the bleeding heart sustain,
> Where Friendship weeps at Virtue's funeral urn—
> That to the pure in heart, *To die is gain.*" †

The castle, also here represented, is one of the many relics of feudalism possessed by the Duke of Beaufort. It was originally founded by William Fitzosborne, Earl of Hereford, for the protection of the many possessions in Monmouthshire and the neighbouring counties, bestowed upon him by his kinsman, William the Conqueror. It passed in the time of Henry I. into the hands of the renowned " Strongbow, Earl of Striguil, Chepstow, and Pembroke." In the reign of Edward IV. it was held by Herbert, Earl of Pembroke, who was beheaded in 1469. It afterwards descended to Sir Charles Somerset, who was afterwards created Earl of Worcester.

* Life and Letters of T. Campbell, vol. ii., p. 278.

† It is remarkable, that they had attended the church on that day, and heard a sermon from Philippians, chap. i. ver. 21 :—" For to me to live is Christ, and *to die* is gain."—Note by T. C.

The history of the castle, during the civil wars of the Commonwealth, is full of the liveliest interest. In 1645, it was garrisoned by the king's troops, under Robert Fitzmaurice, but was taken, after a few days' siege, by Colonel Morgan, the Governor of Gloucester, under Cromwell. It was afterwards surprised by a body of Royalists, under Sir Nicholas Kemeys, and retaken. Cromwell then directed his whole strength against it—and succeeded in regaining possession of it, after the garrison had been reduced to the verge of starvation. This closing scene of its warlike history took place in May, 1648; and from that date to the present time, the castle has remained " a picturesque and dismantled ruin."

In the Parish Register there are found many records connected with that disturbed and eventful period. Several " souldiers" of the castle, many of whose names are stated to have been " unknowen," were buried in the years 1644 and 1645. One is described as a "souldier of Colonel Russell's regiment, a Suffolk man," who, " being killed, was buried." Another "died in the (castle) ditch." Another was "killed with the fall of a wall." Three of the inhabitants of the town are recorded in succession as having been " killed with the fall of an house"—probably during the siege. " A souldier dying at Pearsfield (now Piercefield), was buried." Another " dying at the George," (an hotel now existing,) " was buried;" and several others, who were either drowned, or fell on the field, at Longcaute (now Llancaut) " in the battell fought there"—give a painful interest to the record of those days, when every man's hand was against his fellow.

The present appearance of the castle has slightly changed since the period here represented in the accompanying engraving. The roof of the circular tower, or keep, has long since fallen in; and the noble chestnuts in front of the entrance have disappeared. But the fine old door, concealed by those trees, still exists, and turns as at first on its massive hinges. It is covered with iron bolts and clasps—a genuine relic of the feudal stronghold. The knocker now in use is an old four-pound shot, suspended by a few links of heavy chain. A striking contrast to the original occupation of this fortress is now twice in the year presented within its area, by an exhibition of flowers and fruit, which is unrivalled by any provincial display of horticulture.

The circular tower, or keep, was the place of confinement occupied for twenty years by Henry Marten, whose vote, with those of his fellow-regicides, at the trial of Charles the First, consigned that unfortunate monarch to his untimely end. Marten died of apoplexy in September, 1680, and was buried in the parish church of Chepstow. He retained his republican principles to the last—having asserted to Mr. Lewis, the owner of St. Pierre, near Chepstow, that if the times were to come again in which he had lived his life, he would act the same part he had done. His epitaph, written by himself—an acrostic—is engraved on the stone which covers his remains. His remains lay interred at first in the church, but were removed by a later vicar, named Chest, who, in the staunchness of his loyalty, considered that they ought rather to lie at the entrance to the sacred precincts. They now repose in the vestry at the entrance of the church.

Such are the main features of the objects of interest here represented. It would be easy to enlarge, but such additions as could be made are already to be found in the modern guidebooks.

One record of the reverend vicar, above referred to, may be mentioned, not so much for the credit of himself as for the ingenuity of the writer. It is the production of a person named Downton, who married a daughter of Mr. Chest, and who, whatever might have been his affection for the lady, held the father in unmitigated ridicule and contempt. He satirized him thus :—

> " Here lies at rest, I do protest,
> One chest within another;
> The chest of wood was very good,
> But who'll say so of t'other ?"

MATLOCK.

MATLOCK, the name attached to our view, properly belongs to the village, about one quarter of a mile distant. The term "Matlock-bridge" is the name usually applied to the bridge and the cluster of houses which occur on each side of it. To the bridge, which probably was built in the twelfth century, is attached some interest, from the fact of its being built for the use of *pack-horses*, then the only means of transport across the country; hence, when the traffic increased with the improvement of the people, then all such bridges had to be widened or doubled. This is the case also with the neighbouring bridges, Cromford and Darley, spanning the same stream (the Derwent). The view is taken from the upper side, showing the *new* addition to it; and some curious mistakes and disputes have arisen from this fact, by the architecture of the older and newer parts differing; for instance, the old part, or first-built narrow bridge, has pointed arches, seen on the lower side, while that seen in the view consists of plain round arches.* Our ancestors were not always particularly nice in matching the additions to their buildings.

There is another peculiarity, too, and that is, the bridges named are all built at *shallows*, or ancient *fords*; hence the term, "Cromford," "Nets-ford," and "Mettes-ford." The site of the last named has long been lost sight of. The name appears in Dooms-

---

* Two London artists had a dispute on this head, and had to send a competent person down to settle it, about Cromford Bridge, when it turned out *both were right*—for the one had carefully copied the upper, and the other the nether side of the bridge.

day Book, showing that *Matlock* belonged to this Mettesford. A clew has lately been given to the exact site of this ford, by cutting the railway close to the bridge, in one of which a "cist" was discovered in the cutting—that is, two rough slaps of limestone set on edge, and then covered by a similar one, within which was found a *sun-dried* round jar, containing burnt bones in the bottom; and a very small jar within it, placed on the bones, just large enough to contain the heart—which was the usual custom of the ancient Britons and Romans, at least with regard to their chiefs.

Other indications appeared to justify the supposition, that a British mining village once existed here, which we will call the long-lost Methsford.

These fords were once the great highways of communication in a past age, when all the traffic went to and fro, from east to west—that is, from the eastern *corn-growing* counties to the mining districts of the High Peak, and into Staffordshire; and especially to the celebrated salt mines of Nantwich in Cheshire. Hence Salterslane on one side of our bridge, and the old road, leading to Alfreton, Mansfield, Nottingham, and Lincoln, on the other side; and such also, as stated, was the *slow* and imperfect mode of transfer in those days. And it is only since the year 1822 that we had our present excellent road down our valleys to Bakewall, Buxton, and Manchester. Within one mile of the bridge, to the north, is a rather lofty insular hill, called "Oker," which occurs about the middle of Darleydale. Here was a Roman encampment, probably formed to overlook and overawe the inhabitants and miners in this rich mining district; for it is well known that immense quantities of lead were found in this neighbourhood during the Roman rule. Pigs of lead, of *their smelting*, as well as the tools employed in working, have been found here, together with silver coins and warlike instruments—all testifying to the proximity of an ancient village, and a military station close by. Gisborne, in his reflections—a Poem—has some good lines in his remarks on this hill:—

> "So insular thy form,
> So steep, irregular iu daring height—
> From whence no movement of insidious foe,
> Ambushed in Cowley's thickets, could escape
> Rome's piercing eye. But now, what forms remain
> Of all thy warlike sternness? Tearing down
> Each bulwark of antiquity, the plough
> Feels no remorse; and peasants smile to view
> Greensward, that once so gracefully adorned
> Thine opening brakes, of ever-blooming gorse,
> All withered—all upturned."

But how many changes have taken place since our great artist looked upon the scene, and made the sketch! The new road has been made and levelled; some of the dwellings on the right, and the old houses on the left, have given way to newer and more comfortable dwellings; and the "rail," that extraordinary innovator of the past, has done still more to alter the features of the neighbourhood. But the rocks and hills beyond wear somewhat of the same stern character they did then. For below, in close proximity to the bridge, we have the bold and curved limestone rocks, mantled with the loveliest foliage, on a part of which the fine old church stands, which has sent out (in winter) its peal of the "curfew-bell" over the beautiful dales, ramifying in all directions, for centuries—perhaps ever since the Conquest. The bridge is the commencement, from the *north*, of some of the finest rocky scenery in the world. In a few minutes from hence, walking southward, we find ourselves in the midst of the crags and rocks of the High Tor and Masson Low, heaped one upon another, like "Pelion upon Ossa." The mighty Tor, with its bold and splendid adjuncts, is a fine sight; and when viewed before human habitations were built in the dale, and the foot of man, except the miner, seldom trod this once rough and difficult defile, it could not fail to be highly impressive.* The Tor towers from the bed of the river, almost *perpendicularly*, for about four hundred feet; and the massive ribs of rock which seem to support Masson Low, form, what is called by the celebrated Dr. Darwin, the "marble jaws of Matlock."

* There was no road through it of any kind eighty years ago.

Just about a mile beyond this narrow pass, turning a sharp angle beyond the Tor, we come upon Matlock Bath, nestled amongst the rocks and hills, beautifully situated in what we may call a *sheltered nook*. It is well called "far-famed Matlock" Bath,* for it would be difficult to find so sweet a spot. The combinations of the beautiful, and even the more sublime, in natural scenery, is here all compressed into one lovely picture. The lofty rocks, forming a barrier to the eastward—the still loftier Masson and the "Heights of Abraham" to the west—the fine river flowing between—all covered with the richest foliage, and seen especially in the "*changing leaf*"—exhibit a grouping of objects "of the first order of things," covered with beauty which perhaps cannot be seen elsewhere.

It is not our object to speak of the "Bath," as it is called—now become the post town of the district, and containing within itself every accommodation the traveller may wish, and which had no existence two centuries ago—but with the old village, which dates farther back into time, with its embattled old church, and its fine old pinnacled and embattled square tower, which is a very striking object in our print. The present church, dedicated to St. Giles, was rebuilt and enlarged in the 12th century, in which there has been no external alteration since that time. Within, the heavy stone columns, however, have been removed from the centre, and iron columns substituted in their stead, and galleries erected to give greater accommodation. The roof of the nave exhibits a striking specimen of village painting. It is covered with emblematical representations of the four Evangelists trampling upon various forms of error; and one, "Death," pointing to the open tomb, and old Time opposite, is an effective piece of its kind. On the right, as we enter the church, a dozen or two of strange-looking things, in the shape of wreaths and crowns, meet the eye, suspended from a beam of the gallery. These are the

* The latter term, "Bath," is seldom appended to it; but it should be so, to distinguish it from the village of Matlock itself. The hot springs being discovered, and baths erected, gave to it the appellation of Bath.

relics of a bygone age, when it was the custom to carry one before the bier of every virgin buried here. Two young maidens, dressed in white, carried it suspended on rods, painted also white, and, after the ceremony, it was hung up in the church as a memento of the departed—a custom now long obsolete. A monument of the old family of Wolley is in one of the side aisles, and it is recorded of one of them, born in 1558, that he lived with his wife the extraordinary period of 76 years, and died at the age of 100. His wife lived to the age of 110, and died in 1669. This family had considerable property in the neighbourhood, and once lived at Riber Hall, now converted into a farm-house, not far from the " Hirst Stones," or cromlech, on the top of Riber Hill, seen in the background of our view. The last relict of this family, Adam Wolley, an attorney, died in 1827, and bequeathed his valuable manuscripts to the British Museum.

The cromlech on Riber Hill top, already alluded to, is one mile above the village. Mr. Bray mentions, that part of it much resembled the Cornish logon-stone ; others that it was a mere signal-post, or beacon, commanding the valley to the north ; and others a Druidical altar ; but of this there is no doubt, it is a relic of the religion of our ancestors, but now unfortunately broken up to build the fence walls with ; and the plough, as on " Oker " top, has done its business, and almost erased it.

One more spot we have to notice in this delightful neighbourhood. To the north-east of Riber is a secluded glen, rich in wood and water. Here a beautiful mountain stream is seen leaping from ledge to ledge of the gritstone rocks, and dashing over the broken fragments, forming a beautiful cascade. The scenery of this spot has been said to be " fit for the pencil of Salvator Rosa."

With these remarks, we bid adieu to Matlock.

c

BIRMINGHAM.

The town of Birmingham presents one of the most striking instances of industrial progress on record in modern times. Without distinction, as having been the theatre of any of those important events which, in a bygone age, have exercised an influence over the destinies of a nation, she has no historic past to which she may appeal. Her annals are those of the onward progress of the human mind—her triumphs those of industry and skill—her victories the extension of every art calculated to benefit mankind. Her name is familiar wherever the foot of civilized man has trod, and her fame co-extensive with the bounds of the habitable globe itself; while her productions are to be found both in the palace of the monarch and the cottage of the peasant.

Long prior to the Reformation, the inhabitants were extensively engaged in manufacturing pursuits, the situation of the town, within a short distance of the coal and ironstone mines of Staffordshire, affording peculiarly favourable facilities for their occupation. Leland, writing in the time of Henry VIII., speaks of "many smithes that use to make knives and all manner of cutting tooles, and many lorimers that make bittes, and a great many naylors, so that a great part of the towne is maintained by smithes, whoe have their iron and sea cole out of Staffordshire;" while Camden, half a century later, described it as "swarming with inhabitants, and echoing with the noise of anvils." The town contained but one parish church until the reign of George I.; and the registers, which commence in 1554, show that the population, at the period

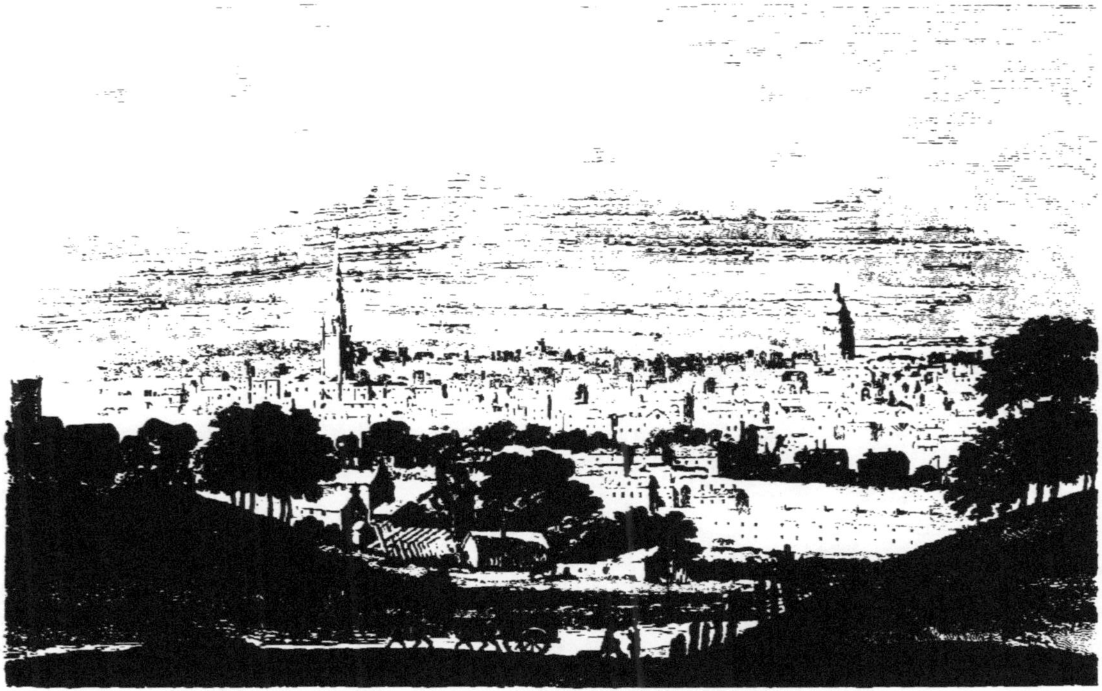

just named, must have been limited, as a month frequently intervened without any entry being made. In the time of Charles I., the inhabitants had increased to nearly 6,000, and so warmly espoused the Parliamentary cause, as to oppose Prince Rupert's entrance into the town: they were, however, defeated with great loss.

In 1801, the census was taken for the first time, the number of inhabitants being 73,000; and so rapid has been the increase since that period, that the population at the present time amounts to a quarter of a million. The houses have also progressed in the same ratio, from 15,600 in 1801, to 50,000. This extraordinary advance is mainly to be ascribed to the complete development of the industrial resources of the population, stimulated to the highest point by the keenest rivalry; and also to the superiority of the articles manufactured being now so generally appreciated as to procure a ready market.

Within the incredibly short space of time that has elapsed since the discovery of the wondrous process of electro-plating, that beautiful art has been cultivated with extraordinary success; and specimens of manufacture of the highest excellence in gold, silver, and bronze, are now produced in great abundance, many hundreds of persons being employed in this branch of manufacture. Elegant articles in papier maché, the details of which are exquisitely elaborated, are produced to a large extent, and many of the houses engaged in this branch of art have acquired a European reputation by the perfection to which they have carried it. In the article of ornamental glass, so exalted is the fame of some of the Birmingham artists, that numerous specimens of their skill are to be found in the palaces of the crowned heads of Europe; while even the Sultan of Turkey and the Pasha of Egypt have shown their appreciation, by becoming liberal purchasers of superb specimens of this manufacture. The production of stained glass and church furniture is also carried to a high degree of perfection, specimens, in every style, being widely scattered throughout the kingdom. Jewellery and plate, in every variety of elegant form, and adapted to every conceivable purpose, here dazzle the eye and bewilder the imagination of the beholder; while table and other lamps, both in glass and metal, display such exquisite beauty, both in design and execution, as almost to approach absolute perfection itself. Steel pens form an important item in the trade of the town, not fewer than 750,000,000 being annually manufactured; and the gun trade—first stimulated by Government patronage in the time of William III.—still maintains its reputation. Metal buttons, though in diminished numbers, are still made; but shoe-buckles, once a leading article of fashion, are now entirely discarded. The general brassfoundry trade is carried on to an immense extent, and the manufacture of metallic bedsteads, gas pendants, &c., affords great scope for the taste of the designer and the skill of the artisan.

In the vicinity of the town are the gigantic establishments of the contractors for the erection of the Crystal Palace, and the works where the whole of the glass required for that wondrous edifice was produced in so short a period of time; while the manufacture of steam-engines is carried on in the neighbourhood of the world-renowned Soho, though that establishment itself has been closed for a considerable period. The general condition of the numerous artisans, by whose assistance the various branches of trade are carried on, is that of comfort and even prosperity; and their habitations far superior to those occupied by persons in the same class of life in most other large towns.

The charitable institutions are numerous, embracing two hospitals and a dispensary for general diseases; institutions for the relief of deafness and diseases of the eye; a lying-in hospital; self-supporting dispensaries; schools for the instruction of deaf and dumb, and blind; a Magdalene asylum; numerous alms-houses; and an asylum for decayed licensed victuallers. Many of the buildings connected with these institutions have been erected of late years, and display considerable architectural taste.

The Free Grammar School of Edward VI. is one of the greatest ornaments of which the town can boast. It was erected (on the site of a former edifice) from the designs of Mr. Barry, and is in the perpendicular Gothic style. This magnificent structure contains two stories, divided into compartments by buttresses, terminating, above an embattled parapet, in pinnacles, enriched with elaborate crockets and finials. This royal foundation, in its principal and branch schools, provides education for 2,000 boys and girls, and the annual income amounts to £16,000.

In the Queen's College, established 1843, a collegiate education is imparted, and this important institution is rapidly rising in public estimation. The Blue Coat School provides instruction and maintenance for nearly 300 children of both sexes; and numerous schools, conducted on almost every system, are carried on for the benefit of the young. In addition, there is a college for the training of students for the ministry in connection with the Congregational body.

The churches of the town are twenty-six in number, eighteen having been erected within the last thirty years. The dissenting chapels are numerous; and the Roman Catholics possess a cathedral and episcopal residence. There are also three cemeteries, the grounds attached to them being laid out in good taste.

The town first sent members to Parliament in 1832, and in 1839 was constituted, by royal charter, a municipality; the corporation is the only governing body, having recently obtained a transfer of the powers vested in the several local boards. Within the last few years, a gaol, lunatic asylum, and public baths, have been erected by the town council; and a workhouse, of handsome elevation, has also been recently built. A spacious market hall, opened about 1833, and ornamented with a beautiful fountain, affords accommodation to the numerous country persons and others who frequent the town. Near to this building is a statue to the memory of Lord Nelson.

The town hall, the noblest building of which Birmingham can boast, is in the Corinthian style. Its distinguishing ornaments are a series of fluted columns, resting on rustic bases, and supporting a bold entablature on the sides and at the back, while the front is relieved by a magnificent pediment. The external length of the structure is 195 feet. Near to the hall is the Society of Arts and School of Design, the principal feature of this building consisting of a tetrastyle Corinthian portico.

An important agent in the extension of Birmingham, of late years, has been the development of the railway system, lines from all the large towns in the kingdom here uniting in one common centre. To accommodate the constantly augmenting traffic, an immense central station is now in course of erection, composed entirely of iron and glass, and of so ample dimensions as to afford space for ten lines of railway, four platforms, and a carriage-way beneath its roof.

That portion of the town shown in the view is seated on a gentle declivity; and the point from which the artist has selected his subject of illustration is an elevated spot on the eastern side. The only public edifices shown are the churches of St. Martin and St. Philip, the former being recognized by its tapering spire, now in course of re-erection. The small tower midway between the churches surmounted the Free School, a building possessing no architectural beauties, having been erected in 1707, when taste was at a very low ebb; and the same remark is applicable to the edifice to the extreme right, the chapel of St. John, Deirtend. The water displayed in the foreground is the Oxford Canal, constructed but a few years prior to the sketch being taken. Its banks are now thickly studded with manufactories, the greater number of which have sprung up within the last quarter of a century; and not a vestige of the sylvan scenery of "sixty years since" remains at the present day. Even the canal itself is now hidden from view, by the accumulations of buildings called into existence by the increasing demands of commercial enterprise. So rapid, too, have been the changes of the scene, that it is impossible to identify the ranges of buildings to the left of the view with any edifices at present in existence. The entire absence of large chimneys will not fail to be noted, especially as, at the present time, they form one of the most prominent features in the landscape; and "Birmingham smoke" has even passed into a proverb.

Within the last half century a marked improvement has taken place in every part of the town. Public buildings have arisen, rendering Birmingham an attraction and a pleasure. The evidence of her growing wealth and taste are visible on every hand —in her banking and mercantile establishments, in the shops of her retail tradesmen, in the suburban residences of her manufacturers, in her places of worship, and in her numerous charitable institutions. And precisely in the same ratio as the ability of her sons shall cultivate those

"Arts that make fire, flood, and field,
The vassals of her will,"

will be the measure of her future progress.

CHESTER.

The genius of the painter is here employed on a luxuriant scene. Before us in the picture lies the rare old city of Chester—the identical creation of the legions of Agricola—and the city which, of all others, retains within itself the most incontestable proofs of its Roman origin. The vagaries of time have played but little havoc with its ancient character—the same old Walls which, 1600 years ago, rose in stately majesty before the genius of the Roman masons, still surround the city. The veritable altars, and other pagan relics of their religious worship—the baths, the pottery, the statues, the pavements of this refined people—abound at every turn. The covered Rows, too, which intersect the principal streets, to the wonder and admiration of the visitor, owe their first existence to the same remote source. In fine, if any there be who desire to see a city of the past enshrined in, and coexistent with, a city of the present day, let them journey to Chester, and every aspiration of their soul will be incontinently gratified. It was here that King Edgar was rowed in his barge on the Dee by eight tributary sovereigns, while himself sat at the helm; and Ethelwolf and two other British princes were crowned at this place. It is also noticed, among other curious facts, that Henry IV., Emperor of Germany, died and was buried here, after living a hermit in the neighbourhood ten years unknown.

In the sketch before us, our artist has presented to us a panorama of considerable extent, and of no ordinary interest. We see beneath us—for we are on the eminence between Overleigh and Handbridge—the placid waters of the Dee, the sacred river of

the Ancient Britons; to the extreme right we catch a partial glimpse at the Old Bridge, which here connects the city with Handbridge, and was, at the date of Turner's visit, the principal avenue of communication between Chester and North Wales. Further to the left, and somewhat obscuring our view of the bridge, stand the City Mills, founded in the 11th century by Earl Hugh Lupus, nephew of the Conqueror. On the failure of the line of Norman Earls, these Mills were seized by the Crown, and were bestowed by Edward the Black Prince on Sir Howel-y-Fwyall, who won his spurs on the field of Poictiers, where he took the French King prisoner.

Still further to the left, and crowning the tops of the intervening houses, the venerable tower of St. John's "lends enchantment to the view," and reminds us that 1000 years have passed away since the foundations of the church were laid by Earl Ethelred—incited, we are told, by a curious vision, to "build it upon the spot where he should find a white hind." This church is, in architectural grandeur, without its equal in the county. Beautiful in its ruins—for but half the building is now occupied for Divine worship—the other half stands forth in all its shattered splendour, a warning to "the powers that be" of their awful responsibility for the preservation of the remainder. Assuredly its present state, both interior and exterior, is such as to excite the anxious fears of every lover of antiquity. But to proceed with our survey.

Advancing towards the centre of the plate, the Norman towers and bastions of the ancient Castle—the camp and court of Hugh Lupus and his successors—meet our gaze. 'Twas in this fortress that the punishment of "pressing to death" was first administered to those criminals who refused to plead—'twas here the Cambrian chieftains assembled to do homage to their first English Prince, Edward of Carnarvon—'twas here that King Richard II. rested, on returning from Wales as the prisoner of Henry Bolingbroke—'twas here, again, the luckless Queen Margaret, before the battle of Bloreheath, cemented to her cause the loyal hearts of the men

D

of Cheshire—and 'twas here that King Henry VII. lodged, with his Queen and retinue, on their way into Wales, " when Richmond was the cry!" The Castle has, since the date of our sketch, been almost entirely swept away, and, "like the baseless fabric of a vision," has "left scarce a wreck behind;" the only part now remaining of this once redoubtable stronghold being a portion of the higher ward, with the smaller of the two towers depicted in the engraving. In a small chapel in this tower, King James II., a while before his abdication, caused mass to be celebrated before him, during his temporary residence in Chester.

Again we proceed on our course, until the eye rests on the twin church towers of St. Michael and St. Bridget, which, at this time, stood opposite to each other in Bridge Street. The latter edifice was demolished in 1827, to form a better approach to the Castle of the present day, and to that stupendous triumph of masonic skill, the Grosvenor Bridge, which, almost at the very point chosen by Turner for his sketch, now spans, with its noble arch of 200 feet, the rippling waters of the languid Dee.

And now, kind reader—for kind you have indeed been to follow us thus far—we would lead you still farther northward, until our progress is arrested by the vast proportions of the mother church of the diocese—the Abbey, and now Cathedral, Church of St. Werburgh.

> " Lo! where triumphant o'er the wreck of years
> The time-worn fabric lifts its awful form;
> Scathed with the blast its sculptured form appears,
> Yet frowns defiance on the impetuous storm.
>
> " What powers—to more than giant bulk allied—
> Thy firm-compacted mass conspired to raise!
> Then bade thee stand secure to latest days,
> Wonder of after-times—of Cestria's sires the pride!"

Ever the most prominent object in the landscape, towering majestically above its suffragan neighbours, the sacred fane of St. Werburgh commands universal respect and veneration. Upon the very spot which had been previously occupied by the Roman

PONT-Y-POOL.

Temple of Apollo, it is recorded that St. Werburgh, the virgin daughter of Wulpherus, King of Mercia, founded, in 666, a more seemly temple, dedicated to the Most High. This remained until towards the end of the 11th century, when the famous Earl Hugh, seeking, after the fashion of that day, to salve his troubled conscience by some outward act of piety, commenced the foundation of the present massive structure. Oh! then, in that day,

> "It must have been a cheering sight to see
> Each arch and aisle, in fair proportion, rise
> Before the Norman craftsmen;"—

and now, even now, when time has stripped the splendour of its once gorgeous exterior, the ancient fabric, full of years and honour, is still the "admired of all admirers"—the pride and glory of the citizens, and the magnet of every stranger that comes within their gates.

To the extreme left, and courting, as it were, the protection of its aged parent, the modest steeple of St. Peter's raises its diminished head. This church is situated at the apex of the four original Roman streets of the city, and stands, in all probability, on the site of the ancient Prætorium. It was formerly surmounted by a spire of goodly dimensions, on the summit of which, in 1489, the city records assure us, the parson and wardens of the parish ate a goose and its accompaniments, to the satisfaction of themselves and of the beholders, casting the well-picked bones into the four principal streets below!

Lower down in the view, we see the ancient Walls twining their devious course through the entire panorama before us, skirting in their progress that spacious and verdant mead, the Roodeye, or Island of the Cross—so called, it may be, from an old cross, the remains of which, until lately, stood within it, and marked the boundary of a neighbouring parish. Here, on this grassy plain, the races have been annually held for nearly 250 years; and certainly no amphitheatre of ancient times was ever more adapted for the requirements of the competitors, or the contentment of the spectators. Momentarily hidden from our view by the large clump of trees in the immediate foreground, again we see the walls stretch menacingly onwards, laved by fair Deva's tide, towards the Mills and Bridge. Thence they continue eastward, and, as with a girdle of stone, complete the circuit of this unique old city.

Thus have we endeavoured, imperfectly, it is true, to describe to our readers this "ancient of days;" and if we have succeeded, however slightly, in imbuing them with a desire to explore it for themselves, our end will be attained—our mission accomplished.

PETERBOROUGH AND ELY CATHEDRALS.

Rich as England is in ancient records, which date as far back as the Roman Invasion—while the Welsh Triads are believed to be even older than this remote period—there are no documents that enter so fully into minute detail as those describing the destruction of the churches in the fens, by the Danes, about a thousand years ago. There are few things connected with the past so easily to be accounted for as the preservation of these minute and lifelike descriptions. The monks were generally the historians of the period; and many of them witnessed the destruction of these ancient monasteries, and re-collected, with their own hands, the relics of the saints, which were scattered and kicked about, and half-burnt, by the misbelieving Danes. Their heathen creed taught them to believe that they could render no greater service to the god, Odin, than by slaying the Christian Saxons, whom they considered renegades for having forsaken their idols, and by destroying the Christian churches; for the Saxons and the Danes were originally of the same race, and both alike worshippers of the war-god, Odin. It was in the spring of the year, when the Danes quitted their head-quarters in Northumberland, crossed the Humber, and destroyed the Abbeys of Croyland, Peterborough, and Ely. They were led by two sea-kings, named Hubba and Ingwar, the sons of Rognar Lodbrog, who had come over to revenge their father's death; for Rognar had been taken prisoner by a Saxon chief named Ella, and, with his wounds still bleeding, was thrust into a dungeon, where he died. His death-song is one of the finest specimens that has been preserved of the old

Scandinavian poetry. It is in a broken and irregular measure, but the following is nearly word for word a literal translation of a portion of it :—

> " We struck with our swords!
> When I went out, in the flower of my youth,
> To prepare the banquet of blood for the wolves,
> From that great combat I sent crowds to the halls of Odin!
>
> We struck with our swords!
> Hundreds lay around the horses of the island rocks—
> The great sea promontories of England.
> With the uprising sun we chanted the mass of spears!
> The blood dropped from our swords!
> The arrows whistled in the air as they went in quest of the helmets.
> Oh! it was a pleasure to me equal to what
> I felt when I first held my beautiful bride,
> Aslanga, in my arms!"

And so it runs on for some forty or fifty lines. Every sea-king swore on his bracelet of gold to revenge the death of Rognar Lodbrog, and not to leave a priest alive or a Christian church standing in England.

Why they were so embittered against the priests on this particular occasion is not clearly shown, nor is it necessary to explain more than their general hatred of Christianity. It was about the spring of 850, when the Danes desolated Lincolnshire, ravaged Northamptonshire, and destroyed Ely—sweeping onward like a destroying tempest from north to south, trampling the young corn beneath their feet, and leaving behind death and desolation wherever they trod. Where, in the morning sunshine, the pleasant village and the busy borough stood on the cliff, or from their green mounds looked over the wild wold, watery mere, or reedy marsh, the twilight dropped down on smoking ruins and blackened ashes, while such of the inhabitants as escaped the fire and slaughter, either sheltered in the gloomy forest, where the grey wolf had its lair, or in the sedgy swamp, where the tall water-flags waved, and the wild swan swam, and built, and led forth her cygnets. Wherever a church stood above the landscape, thitherward they hastened; for, to slay the priest at the foot of the altar, make the

choir ring with their war-cry, and, instead of holy hymns, chant what they called "the mass of spears," was their greatest delight, for they called savage and cold-blooded murder victory. But sack, slay, burn, and destroy, are words that fall with almost an unmeaning sound upon the ear, unless we can depict to the "inward eye" of the reader the very actions of these savage sea-kings, through the green spring, flowery summer, and yellow autumn of that terrible year.

It was evening when the tide of battle turned against the brave Saxons, who had thrown themselves between the Danes and their own hallowed monasteries; for but a few miles divided the Abbey of Croyland from that of Peterborough, and before the former they made a noble stand. Even the Saxon serfs fought in defence of their altars, and the humble swineherd blew his horn to summon his fellow-slaves to the combat.

The battle had lasted all day, and the assembled Danes had obtained no advantage. Over the wide fens and the watery marshes a dim mist began to gather, and on the eastern ridge, where the wild forest spread, the shadows of evening were slowly settling down, when the Danes, wearied and enraged at having been so long repulsed by a force which consisted chiefly of the neighbouring peasants, feigned a defeat, and retreated before the Saxons, who blindly followed in pursuit, in spite of the warning voice of Algar, their leader. The Danes suddenly turned upon their pursuers—Hubba made a circle to the right with his cavalry—to the left the centre rolled back like an overwhelming wave. The Saxons were surrounded. All was lost. But few escaped. Those who did, availed themselves of the approaching darkness, and, plunging into the adjoining forest, hastened to the Abbey of Croyland, to which the scene now changes, on a morning in autumn, one thousand and ten years ago.

It was the hour of matins, when pale, weary, and breathless, two or three of the Saxon youths who had escaped from the scene of slaughter, rushed into the choir of the monastery, with the tidings that all excepting themselves had perished. The abbot uplifted his hand to command silence when he saw them enter, and the solemn anthem in a moment ceased. He then bade the monks, who were young and strong, to take a boat, and carry off the relics of the saints, the sacred vessels, jewels, books, and charters, and all the moveable articles of value, and either to bury them in the marshes, or sink them beneath the waters of the lake, until the storm had passed over. " As for myself," added the abbot, " I will remain here with the old men and children, and peradventure, by the mercy of God, they may take pity on our weakness." The children were such as at that period were frequently brought up, by the consent of their parents, in the habits of a monastic life, and who, in their early years, sung in the choir. Amongst the old monks were two whose years outnumbered a hundred. Alas! the venerable abbot might as well have looked for mercy from a herd of ravenous and howling wolves, that came gaunt, grey, and hungry, from the snow-covered wintry forest, as from the misbelieving Danes, who were then fast approaching. All was done as he commanded; the most valuable treasures were rowed across the lake to the Island of Thorns; and in the wood of Ancarig, those who were not brave enough to abide the storm, found shelter. One rich table plated with gold, that formed a portion of the great altar, rose to the surface; and as they could not sink it, it was taken back, and again restored to its place in the monastery.

Meantime the flames, which shone redly between the forest trees, told that the last village had been fired. Every moment brought nearer the clamour of the assailants, until at last the tramp of horses could be distinctly heard. Then the ominous banner, on which the dusky raven was depicted, hove in sight, and the whole mass came up with a deep threatening murmur, which drowned the voice of the abbot, and silenced the chant in the monastery. At the foot of the altar, in his sacerdotal robes, was the abbot hewn down; the grey hairs of the venerable priests protected them not; those who rushed out of the choir were pursued and slaughtered; there was scarcely a slab on the floor of the sacred edifice that was not slippery with blood. Some were tortured, to make them confess where their treasures were concealed, and afterwards beheaded, for the Danes acted more like fiends let loose to do the work of destruction, than like men. There was an exception on that dreadful day—one human life was saved by the intervention of a Dane, and but for him every soul would have perished. The prior had been struck down early in the massacre by the battle-axe of Hubba; as he lay dead upon the pavement, a little boy, about ten years of age, clung to him and wept bitterly, for he had been greatly attached to the prior. The slaughter was still going on, when Sidroc, one of the sea-kings, paused, with the uplifted sword in his hand, to gaze on the boy, who knelt weeping beside the dead body of the prior. Struck by his beautiful and innocent countenance, the Danish chief took off his cassock, and throwing it around the little chorister, said, "Quit not my side for a moment." He alone was saved, excepting those who had previously fled with the boat and the treasures. Disappointed at finding neither gold nor jewels, the pagans broke open the tombs, and scattered around the bones of the dead, and as there was no longer any one at hand to slay, they set fire to the monastery. Laden with cattle and plunder, they next proceeded to Peterborough, burning and slaying, and destroying whatever they met with on their march.

The Abbey of Peterborough was considered at this time as one of the finest ecclesiastical edifices in England. It was built in the solid Saxon style, with strong stunted pillars, crypts, vaulted passages, oratories, and galleries, while the thick, massy walls were pierced with circular windows. It also contained the finest library which had ever been collected in Britain, and which had accumulated through the gifts of many a pilgrim who had visited the still proud capital of Italy. The doors of this famous building were so strong, that for some time they resisted the attacks of the Danes; and as the monks and their retainers had resolved to defend themselves as long as they could, neither the besieged nor the besiegers remained idle. From the circular windows, and the lofty roof of the abbey, the monks and their allies threw down heavy stones, and hurled their sharp javelins at the enemy, who had hitherto endeavoured in vain to break open the ponderous doors. At last, the brother of Hubba was struck to the earth by a stone, and carried wounded into his tent.

This act seemed to redouble the fierce energy of the Danes, and in a few minutes after they drove in the massy gates. In revenge for the wound his brother had received, the brutal Hubba, with his own hand, put eighty-four monks to death; he demanded to be the chief butcher on the occasion, and the request was freely granted him. The child whom Sidroc had rescued from death at Croyland, stood by and witnessed that savage slaughter, and the friend who had saved him stooped down, and, whispering in his ear, bade him not approach too near Hubba. The boy, as we shall see, needed not a second warning. All who had aided in defending the monastery, excepting the few who escaped at the commencement of the attack, were put to death. The library was burnt, the sepulchres broken open, and the abbey fired; and for nearly fifteen days was that noble edifice burning, before it was totally consumed. Many a deed, and charter, and valuable manuscript, which would have thrown a light on the manners and customs of that period, were consumed in the flames.

Laden with spoil, the merciless pagans next marched towards Huntingdon. Sidroc had charge of the rear-guard, which brought up the plunder. Two of the cars, containing the spoil of the monastery, were overturned in a deep pool while passing a river; and as the sea-king lingered behind, and was busily engaged in superintending his soldiers, and aiding them to save all they could from the wreck, the child, who had witnessed such scenes of bloodshed, took advantage of the confusion and escaped. Having concealed himself in a wood until the faint and far-off sounds of the Danish army had died away, he set off across the wild marshes alone, and, in the course of a day and a night, found his way back again to Croyland. Poor little fellow! the smoking ruins and the weeping monks, who had returned from their hiding-place in the Island of Thorns, and who were then wailing over their murdered brethren, were the melancholy sights and sounds that greeted his return home. A stern school was that for a child of ten years old to be nursed in! He told them all he had witnessed at Peterborough; they gathered around him to listen; they ceased to throw water on the burning ruins until his tale was ended; they left the headless body of their venerable abbot beneath the mighty beam which had fallen across it, nor attempted to extricate it until he had finished "his sad eventful history." Then it was that they again wept aloud, throwing themselves on the ground in great anguish, until grief had no longer any tears, and the sobbing of sorrow had settled down into hopeless silence. That over, they again commenced their sad duty: the huge grave was deepened, the dead and mutilated bodies were dragged from under the burning ruins; and placing the abbot on the top of the funeral pile, they left them in one grave, covered beneath the same common earth, to sleep that sleep which no startling dream can ever disturb. That child afterwards became an Earl of Mercia, and distinguished himself in many a battle against the heathen Danes.

Scarcely was this melancholy duty completed, before the few monks who had escaped from the massacre of Peterborough made their appearance. They had come all that way for assistance; for, excepting themselves, there were none left alive to help to bury their murdered brethren, on whose bodies the wolves from the woods, they said, were already feeding.

With heads bent, and weeping eyes, and breaking hearts, those poor monks had moved mournfully along, leaving the wolves to feed upon their butchered brothers, beside the blackened ruins of their monastery, until they could find friends who would help them to drag the half-consumed remains from beneath the burning rafters, place them side by side, and, without distinction, bury them in one common and peaceful grave. How clearly we can picture that grave group on their journey! their subdued conversation by the way of the dead, whose good deeds they discussed, or whose vices they left untouched, as they recalled their terrible ending; the country through which they passed, desolate; the inhabitants, who were wont to come on holy days to worship, fled; here a hamlet reduced to ashes; there a well-known form half consumed, and stretching across the charred threshold. We can picture the wolf stealing away until they had passed; the raven, with his iron beak and ominous note, making a circle round their heads, then returning to the mother or the infant, half hidden in the sedge beside the mere, with her long hair floating amid the tall water-flags, where she was stabbed, as she hurried away from the unbelieving Danes, shrieking, with her child in her arms. Wherever they turned their eyes, there they would behold ruin, death, and desolation—see the remains of once happy homes, which the fire had consumed; or, where the children had escaped, they would witness them weeping, fatherless and motherless, beside the blackened walls. Let us, however, hope that there were a few like Sidroc amongst them, and that the raven and the wolf were not their only attendants; but that the Angel of Mercy, though concealed in a pillar of cloud by day, and in a pillar of fire by night, was still there, and often stretched out his unseen hand to save. The same scenes were enacted when the Danes reached the Abbey of Ely. One description serves for all—murder, fire, and the destruction of the churches, marked their course; they left nothing standing of the Abbey of Ely, says the monkish historian, but the foundation. It makes us shudder to think what they who once lived and moved as we now do, must have endured; while, after the lapse of nearly a thousand years, we cannot portray their sufferings without sympathising with their sorrows, and experiencing a low, heart-aching sensation. The grave that covers up and buries the past, inters not all pain and sorrow for the dead, but leaves a portion behind, that the living may feel what they once suffered; the agonizing shriek, and the heart-rending cry, ring for ages upon our ears, though such sounds disturb not the silent chambers of the dead. But enough of these gloomy pictures; who will now glance at what time has left us?

All that remained of the old Abbey of Peterborough, after the ravages of the Danes, and the further inroads of time, was destroyed by an accidental fire, which also burnt down a great part of the town, in 1118. There might probably be a portion of the ancient Saxon foundations left, on which John of Salisbury, the abbot, began to rebuild the present Cathedral; but he died in 1125, and left the building unfinished. In 1125, Martin de Vecti brought the relics into the new church, on its dedication, at which the Bishops of Lincoln, Thorney, Croyland, Romney, and others, were present, and to whom the arm of St. Oswold was exhibited. King Stephen, while at war in this ancient neighbourhood, was blessed with a sight of this relic of St. Oswold, and to which he made an offering of his ring.

The present building consists of a nave with side aisles, a transept, a choir terminating at the east end semicircularly, and surrounded with a continuation of the side aisles of the nave, and the whole terminated at the east end by what is called the new building. In the centre is a tower rising from the four arches, by which the several parts of the structure are connected together. The west front is formed by a portico, or porch, of three lofty arches, in the centre of which is a small chapel. Many years elapsed before the whole of the building was completed. The choir, with its aisles, from the circular extremity at the east, to the commencement of the transept on the west, and which is the oldest portion of the building, was finished in 1143, the year before the dedication. The transept was erected between 1155 and 1177; and between the latter period and the year 1193, the nave with its aisles were completed, to the termination of the pillars which divide the nave and side aisles on the west. In 1288, the space between the extreme pillars and the west entrance was finished, and which form a projection on each side of the western extremity, terminated by the two towers. What is called the new building at the eastern extremity of the choir, was erected by Richard Ashton, in the middle of the fifteenth century, and completed by Abbot Kirton in 1518. This was the last addition made to the building before the dissolution of the monasteries by Henry the Eighth.

The length of the Cathedral, externally, is 471 feet; of the nave, from the west door to the entrance of the choir, 267 feet; of the choir, 117 feet; and from the altar of the choir to the east window, 38 feet; making altogether 422 feet. The transept, from north to south, measures 180 feet; height of nave from floor to ceiling, 81 feet; and of the central tower from bottom to top, 135 feet. The breadth of the nave, from the north to the south wall, is 78 feet, and the breadth of the west front 156 feet. These are the measurements given in Gunton's History of Peterborough Cathedral.

It is stated in the 'Beauties of England and Wales,' page 232, Vol. XI., that Queen Katherine, the first wife of Henry the Eighth, was buried here, between two pillars on the north side of the choir, near the altar; and that her hearse was covered with a black velvet pall, crossed with a white cloth of silver, which was exchanged for an inferior one, and the latter taken away during the Civil Wars. In the same work we also find mentioned, that the funeral of Mary Queen of Scotland was here solemnized, and which is described as follows:—"The body of the queen was brought from Fotheringhay Castle, where she was beheaded on the night of Sunday, the 30th of July, 1587, and at two o'clock, on Monday morning, was committed to the vault prepared for it on the south side of the choir, close to the bishop's throne, which was immediately closed, without the performance of any religious service. A rich hearse was erected near the grave, and the choir and church were hung with black. The performance of the funeral service took place on Tuesday afternoon, and was attended by thousands of spectators, and many of the nobility, the heralds, and other officers of the Crown. Those of the kingdom of Scotland, who had thus far beheld the fate of their queen, here stopped, and bade an adieu to her remains for the last time. They indignantly refused either to enter the church, or to be present at the last ceremonies."

The following is a curious specimen of the "trimming" practised in these stormy times, and there is no doubt that cautious Dean Fletcher had the fear of Elizabeth in his eye, and a perfect knowledge that every word uttered over the headless trunk of the unfortunate and martyred Mary, would be carried back to the ears of the royal vixen. There are, however, two or three sparks of independence in it, and "more meant than meets the ear," in the last sentence attributed to "Father Luther." It is as follows:—

"Let us give thanks for the happy dissolution of the high and mighty Princess Mary, late Queen of Scotland, and Dowager of France, of whose life and death at this time *I have not much to say, because I was not acquainted with the one, neither was I present at the other.* I will not enter into judgment further, but because it hath been signified unto me, that she trusted to be saved by the blood of Jesus Christ, we must hope well of her salvation; for as Father Luther was wont to say, 'Many an one that liveth a papist, dieth a protestant.'"

Twenty-five years after the period of the interment, King James had the body of his mother removed from Peterborough Cathedral to Westminster Abbey; and it is said, that the epitaph which recorded the death of the ill-starred queen, was, after her removal, taken from the wall, over the vault where her remains had reposed, and cast out of the church. About thirty years after, the monument of the Queen of Scotland had been cast out like "an unclean thing." Cromwell's Roundheads entered Peterborough, and almost made as much havoc of the Cathedral as the Danes of old had made of the first monastery. They broke the stalls and richly-painted windows, tore up the books, and tore down the organ; destroyed much of the beautiful carved work, and defaced many of the monuments, and seem to have only left undemolished what it was impossible, without much labour, to destroy. And in this state of ruin it remained for eight long years, until after Charles I. was beheaded, when sufficient repairs were made to allow of its being again opened for Divine service. This sacrilege broke poor old Bishop Towers' heart, and he died at Peterborough, in 1648, in "great poverty and distress;" and so, from this period to the Restoration, a gloom settled down upon all the churches in England, and the Roundheads had everything their own way.

Ely Cathedral is a magnificent structure, though erected at various periods, and contains fine specimens of what is called the mixed style of architecture. The north and south transepts, which are the oldest parts, were erected in the reigns of the Red King and Henry the First, and here are found circular arches, as also in the nave. About 1189, Bishop Rydel erected the great west tower, which was formerly flanked on the north side by a similar building to that on the south, but which seems either to have fallen, or else to have been taken down, though at what period is not known, and another building erected in its place, but never carried beyond twelve or fourteen feet in height. The interior of the great tower, which is decorated with small columns, and has several stories of arches running round it, is very splendid, and its beauty is greatly enhanced by the light from so many windows. But here modern innovation has crept in with its belfry floors and unsightly beams, which have been put up to guide the bell-ropes, and assist in producing "triple-bob-majors." The choir was commenced by Hugh Northwold, the eighth bishop, in 1234, and finished sixteen years after that period. But, in 1322, the three western arches were destroyed by the falling of the stone tower, which stood on four arches in the centre of the building, and which was caused by the arches giving way. This tower was never rebuilt, but in place of it the present magnificent octagon was erected by the sub-prior, Alan de Walsingham, who was no novice as an architect. It is supported on eight pillars, the capitals of which are ornamented with historical carvings, illustrative of the principal events in the life of Etheldreda, and covered with a dome, terminated by an elegant lantern. This octagon, which was completed in 1342, is almost unequalled, and may rank beside the finest that remains in any of the stately cathedrals in England. The three arches eastward of the octagon were rebuilt by Bishop Hotham. They are very beautiful, and divided into regular compartments by various ribs, which spring from the capitals of the pillars, and shoot into the vaulting. The capitals are ornamented with flowers and foliage of exquisite workmanship. The arches of the second arcade, with the windows that surmount them, are decorated with the most elegant tracery found in any building erected at this period; and the good people of Ely may well be proud of their splendid and ancient Cathedral.

At the east end of the north aisle there is a beautiful chapel, which was erected by Bishop Alcock, who died in 1509. His tomb, much defaced, is under a stone arch on the north side. In the south aisle is another chapel, erected by Bishop West in 1530, which is very elegant and richly ornamented. Both these chapels were defaced by the ornament-hating Puritans during the civil wars, and we almost wish that there had been another stone tower to have fallen on them while committing such wanton sacrilege.

Nor were the Roundheads the only parties that disfigured this beautiful Cathedral. Many of the monuments which stand in the aisle, and which are of excellent workmanship, are covered over with coatings of whitewash, which fill up all the interstices of the beautiful carving. In conclusion, it is only necessary to add, that the length of the Cathedral from east to west is 535 feet; that of the transept, 190 feet; the height of the lantern over the dome, from the floor, 170 feet; and that of the western tower, 270 feet. The two towers on the south wing are 120 feet high; the nave, 203 feet long; and the roof over it, 104 feet high; the height of the eastern front to the top of the cross is 112 feet. What remains of the old monastery which the Danes ravaged and burnt, it is difficult to ascertain, though there is no doubt but that Simeon, the Abbot of Ely, made use of some portion of the ancient foundation when he first commenced erecting the oldest portion of the present structure, in the year of our Lord 1081. This good old abbot saw a great portion of the building finished before he departed this life, for he lived to the patriarchal age of one hundred years, and at a period when many of the misbelieving and murderous Danes still resided in England, and followed their heathen creed.

BRIDGENORTH.

BRIDGENORTH is beautifully situated on the river Severn, on the west side of the ancient forest of Morfe. Camden erroneously traces its name to Burgh-*Morfe*. In the most ancient records, it is called Brugia, and Brugge. In a charter granted by King John, it is called Bruges. In more recent times, Brugge North— all having evident reference to the stately bridge of seven arches which spanned the Severn, and connected the high and the low towns. In the year 986, the Danes marched to Quatbridge, now Quatford, a village about a mile south of Bridgenorth: there they fortified themselves and wintered; and doubtless this place was called Bridgenorth, because its bridge lay northward of the bridge at Quatford. It was built in the time of the Saxon Heptarchy, by Ethelfleda, oldest daughter of Alfred the Great, and Queen of the Mercians. She was widow of King Ethelred, who died in 912. It was walled about by Robert de Belesme, son of Roger de Montgomery, Earl of Arundel and Shrewsbury, who added a castle for the further strength of the town. It is divided into two unequal parts by the river Severn, but united by a fair stone bridge of seven arches, the east of which is represented in the print, which had formerly a gate and gate-house, and other houses on it for defence or ornament. During the last century the gate-house was used as the borough prison, and the prisoners let down a basket through the floor to beg alms or provisions from the passengers. The building on the pier to the south of the gate, was occupied as a barber's shop. The bridge was much injured by the high flood in 1794; finally, it was repaired and reconstructed in the present century, under the direction of John Simpson and John Smalman, Esqrs.; the gate-house was removed, and the present handsome bridge produced. The chapel of St. Osyth stood near the ancient bridge gateway. The situation of the town is one of the most picturesque and beautiful in England; its noble walk round the castle-hill, commanding a view of the river and valley, was the favourite promenade of King Charles II. and Prince Rupert, when they were detained here in the time of the Rebellion.

MANCHESTER.

Manchester is the great mart of commerce—the mighty metropolis of trade; nowhere in the world beside can a town be pointed out that, in a few years, has risen to such opulence and political importance, as the thriving and densely-populated town of Manchester. We look back upon it at the time when the present sketch was made—when the giant steam, like the Titon of old, lay buried in the bowels of the earth, as if sleeping in the coal formation and fossil forests, till touched by the finger of science, when he sprang up, and with him Manchester, rubbing its eyes, and looking round on the old houses and the old streets, and shaking them at once out of centuries of slumber, with the building of princely warehouses, and the clatter of wonder-working machinery, that filled the world with marvel and admiration. Ships went freighted with her commerce to the remotest corners of the globe; and in distant climes, far away over the sea, cotton-fields were planted, to feed her ever-gaping looms. She gave a new impetus to trade—sent her sons to legislate, and make laws for the neighbouring cities, and stood " second to none" in her proud pre-eminence; and all this she did within the brief space of half a century.

To Manchester we are indebted for Mechanics' Institutes, which were first suggested by Dr. Thomas Barnes, as far back as 1785. In Manchester the first steam-engine for spinning cotton was erected; and it may be said to be the cradle of the mighty locomotive power, which now bids defiance to time and space. It established its own Tract and Missionary Societies, and, while it increased in wealth, dispersed religion and knowledge amongst the benighted heathens in remote lands. No measure was ever proposed for bettering the condition of the human race without Manchester stepping forward, with purse in hand and shoulder to the wheel, ready to pay to, and labour in, the promotion of the good work. From a population under fourteen thousand, in 1773, her inhabitants, in fifty years from that date, numbered above a quarter of a million of souls.* To write the history of Manchester, would require more quarto volumes than we can devote pages to the subject. We shall therefore confine our remarks to the locality of the accompanying view, and glance at the changes which have taken place in the neighbourhood, here pictured, since our sketch of the old College and Bridge was made; for the history of Manchester is the history of England, from the commencement of the present century.

How those "grey forefathers" would gaze round in amazement, who lived at the time the present drawing was made, could they but arise and look on the gigantic Manchester of to-day —on the Town-Hall, erected by Goodwin at an expense of £40,000 —on the Royal Institution, built by Barry at a cost of £30,000; with its Theatre (where the British Association held its annual meeting in 1842; and its literary unions have been presided over by some of the most eminent men of the present age); and its Rooms for Exhibitions, Lectures, Museum, &c.—on the Manchester Athenæum, immediately in the rear of the Royal Institution—on that princely-looking establishment, the Royal Infirmary, more fitting as a palace for monarchs—and, lastly, on our Exchange, erected at a cost of £22,000. These are sights that would startle the spirits of the old cotton-spinners, such as we see pictured in conversation at the foot of the bridge, as if conversing

* The census of 1851 gives the Municipal Borough of Manchester, . . 303,358
Parliamentary Borough, ... 316,190
Municipal Borough of Salford, ... 63,851
Parliamentary Borough, ... 85,099

about the riots, caused by the high price of corn, that took place in the same year the present sketch was made. Even the volunteer, in his grenadier's cap, stands like a landmark, pointing out the events of the period; for, in the same year, the Manchester and Salford volunteers were first drawn out; and to show that the order-loving inhabitants had no sympathy with the rioters, they raised about £16,000 for the support of Government. We have not space to dwell upon its Chamber of Commerce, Customhouse, Banks, Albion and Union Club-houses; its Theatre-Royal, capable of holding above 2,000 people; its Cemeteries, Zoological Gardens, and Public Parks; Victoria Park, with its picturesque villas; and Peel's Park and Cornfield Hall, with their Museums,—all proclaim the opulence and intelligence of magnificent Manchester.* We gaze with amazement on its tall chimneys, which point out the hundred and twenty factories that are worked by steam power, and in which five million pounds of cotton, chiefly supplied from America, are worked up every year. And our marvel increases, when we find that this wonder-working machinery can take one single pound of cotton and spin it into four hundred and sixty hanks, each hank of which measures eight hundred and forty yards. As a spider folds up a fly in the winding-sheet that it spins, so could the factories of Manchester, in a single year, with their hundreds of thousands spindles, bury a large town within the white cocoon that they could weave. The piles of princely buildings, now erecting on every spare space of ground, while the old and unsightly piles of brick are as rapidly disappearing, are proofs of the prosperity of the Manchester merchants; and could the old traders draw up with their traves of pack-horses, on which they carried their goods through England, from market to fair, in the reign of George III., they would flee in affright from the mountains of bales that are now sent out, and doubt whether England contained horses

---

* We would refer our readers to a more detailed account of the numerous magnificent institutions, both charitable and useful (and point out Manchester second to no other city), in a work by Mr. Duffield, entitled " The Stranger's Guide to Manchester."

enough to remove such monstrous loads. The old pack-horse in the engraving belongs to the Manchester of the past.

We have here a view of the oldest and most interesting portion of Manchester, as it appeared sixty years ago, and of which but little more than the College, and what is now the Cathedral (the tower of which is seen in the distance), are remaining. The old bridge is gone, and is replaced by a handsome stone bridge of one arch, and named Victoria Bridge; and the house to the right—which then stood in a pleasant garden, though marked by a leafless tree—is now the site of the Lancashire and Yorkshire Railway Station. The picturesque little cottage at the foot of the bridge, and its tall neighbour, then a famous public-house—with the lock-up, or jail, adjoining it, as if in readiness for the tavern brawls, which were so common amongst our ale-drinking forefathers—are all swept away, even down to the old grammar-school, which has been rebuilt. The present view is from Hunt's Bank; and on the old bridge there formerly stood a chapel, no doubt similar to the one engraved in the view of Wakefield. It was, in those times, called Salford Bridge, and appears to have been the only one which spanned the river Irwell at that period. In the will of Thomas-de-la-Boothe, who appears to have built the Chapel on the Bridge about 1365, is the following clause:—
"I also give to the Bridge of Salford £30, payable in the three years next following (my death), in equal portions," for prayers to be said in the chapel for the benefit of his soul. At that remote period, the banks of the Irwell were fringed with deep woods, and the river was so celebrated for its eels, that the warden of the college rented the right of fishing to supply the tables of the clergy during Lent. The first stone of the Collegiate Church was laid by Thomas West, on the 28th of July, 1422, in the reign of Henry V., and on the following year the present College, which forms the principal object in our engraving, and which was then called the Old Baron's Hall, was the residence of the clergy, and so remained, no doubt, until the Collegiate Church was completed.

Thomas West, called Lord de la Warre, who founded this church at a cost of £50,000, was lord of the manor and rector of Manchester—not a poor rector, like too many of the present day, but one possessing baronial rights, and of importance enough to take his seat in Parliament. In 1540, the Collegiate Church of Manchester obtained the privilege of sanctuary " to all offenders and malefactors, of whatsoever quality, kind, or nature their offence might be." There were, however, certain exceptions; and any one committing murder or highway robbery, or wilfully setting fire to house or barn, was not sheltered in the sanctuary. The old church had its "ups and downs" in the stormy reign of Queen Mary; and George Collier, who was deprived of his wardenship for refusing to acknowledge the supremacy of the boy-king, Edward VI., was restored by her, while John Bradford, a Protestant, suffered martyrdom. In 1578, Queen Elizabeth gave the College a new charter, took the electorship of the warden into her own hands, fixed his salary at four shillings a day, that of each fellow at sixteenpence; chaplain, sixpence three farthings; each chorister, fourpence halfpenny; each singing-boy, twopence halfpenny; and inflicted a fine of twentypence on the warden for every day he was absent, and eightpence for the same from every fellow of the Collegiate Church. But the old church was appropriated to other purposes than those of Divine service; and on the 28th of April, 1584, the heads of Bell and Finch were exposed on the College, by command of Elizabeth, and the offence for which they suffered death was that of being Catholic recreants.

The old Free Grammar School, which has been rebuilt, was founded by Hugh Oldham, Bishop of Exeter, who died in 1519. The copy of the foundation is dated April 1, 1524, in the sixth year of Henry VIII. There is something very pleasing and very quaint in the wording of the will, expressing the motives which induced the good bishop to undertake and accomplish so worthy a work. He says—" Considering the bringing up of children in their adolescence, and to occupy them in good learning therein, when they should come to age and virility, whereby they may better know, love, honour, and dread God and his laws; and that the liberal science or art of grammar is the ground and foundation of all other liberal arts and sciences; and for the good mind which he did bear to the county of Lancaster, where the children had pregnant wits, but had been mostly brought up rudely and idly, and not in virtue, cunning, education, literature, and in good manners." Good old Bishop Oldham was, says his biographer, "a foe to monkish superstition;" still he was a follower of the ancient faith, as the following curious clause in his will proves, and the fulfilment of which has no doubt long since been abandoned. It says, "The master and usher which first cometh in the morning shall openly with the scholars say this psalm, 'Deus misoratur nostri,' with a collect, as they use in the churches on dominical days; and every night, on such like manner, the master and usher to sing an anthem of our Blessed Lady, and say 'De profundis' for the souls of the late Bishop of Exeter, Hugh Oldham, founder of this school, his father and mother, and for the souls of Sir Richard Arderne, Henry Trafford, and Thomas, his wife deceased, and for the souls of George Trafford of the Garret, and Margaret, his wife; then next immediately ensuing, when or at what time it shall please God of his mercy and grace to call for the said George and Margaret, or either of them, and for all the souls of the feoffes and benefactors of the same, then departed, and all Christian souls, and to say with an audible voice in the school, before the beginning of 'De profundis,' in this manner, for the soul of Hugh Oldham, late Bishop of Exeter, founder of our school, and his father and mother's souls, and for the soul of George Trafford, and Margaret, and for all the souls they are bound to pray for, and for all the benefactors' souls, and all Christian souls."

The Old College, the most prominent object in the present engraving, and which, beyond a little renovation, has scarcely undergone any change since it first became the residence of the clergy in 1423, was purchased by the feoffes of Humphrey Chetham's charity, in 1654, and is now called Chetham's Hospital. The author of the "Annals of Manchester" says, "Humphrey Chetham, Esq., founder of the hospital and library which bear his name, died October 12, 1653, in his 74th year, and was buried in the chapel of the Chethams, at the east end, and behind the altar of the Collegiate Church, but there is no monument erected. He was descended of an ancient family, which derived its name from the existing township. He was born at Crumpsail, and baptised at the Collegiate Church, July 10, 1580 (the very year that the new jail was built at Hunt's Bank), and, it is said, received his education at Bishop Oldham's Free Grammar School. His wealth was chiefly derived by supplying the London market with fustians, a material of dress then in almost general use throughout the nation. By this commerce, which was probably conducted on an extensive scale, he acquired wealth, whilst his strict integrity, piety, and charity, secured him the respect and esteem of those around him. 'He was,' says Fuller, 'a diligent reader of the Scriptures, and of the works of sound divines, a respecter of such ministers as he accounted truly godly, upright, sober, discreet, and sincere. He was High Sheriff of the county of Lancaster in 1635, discharging that office with great honour, insomuch that very good gentlemen of birth and estate did wear his cloth at the assize, to testify their unfeigned affection for him.' During his life he had maintained fourteen boys of the town of Manchester, six of the town of Salford, and two of the town of Droylsden; and by his will, dated December 16, 1651, he directed that the number of boys should be increased to forty, bequeathing the sum of seven thousand pounds for the purchase of an estate, the profits of which are to be applied to the support of the establishment." He then wishes that the old College may be purchased; and thus describes it as it then stood above two hundred years ago:—" And my desire is, that the great house, with the buildings, outhouses, courts, yards, gardens, and appurtenances, in Manchester aforesaid, called the College, or the College House (no doubt from the clergy of the Collegiate Church having resided in it for above 120 years), may be purchased and bought for the same purpose (if it may be had and obtained upon good terms, and for a good estate)."

It was had, though the purchase was not completed until after the Restoration, when the feoffees were a body corporate, under the charter granted by Charles the Second. Such is a brief summary of the principal buildings represented in the accompanying engraving. It will be remembered that, in Manchester, Free Trade had its birth—that there the infant Hercules was cradled who strangled Monopoly with one hand, and crushed Protection with the other ; struck the fetters from Commerce, and then threw to the million its bread untaxed. Cotton Lords, without any heraldic device, or any other war-cry than that of " Free Trade," entered the lists, and shouldered their way through the old chivalry, using neither lance nor shield, but making all yield before them, only because they " willed it"—often threatening, but never striking, though compelled to exclaim, " If thee keeps on aggravating I, I'll hitten thee, I 'ool."

ELGIN CATHEDRAL.

If St. Mungo's, at Glasgow, is the grandest, that of the Holy Trinity, at Elgin, was undoubtedly the most beautiful and most symmetrical of our Scottish cathedrals. With some slight traces of an older fane in one or two round-headed windows, with short rude columns on the south side, indicative of the Norman period, as a whole it stands forth a stately and elegantly proportioned example of the *early English* style of Gothic architecture, in its purest pointed, and also in its more advanced or decorated, form. In our drawing, the building is exhibited in its *desolation*, as it stood at the close of the last century, before it was taken under the protection of the Crown, and before John Shanks, its native and self-constituted preserver, thought of arresting its farther decay and ruin. He, with the plodding and persevering use of his shovel and wheelbarrow, removed the rubbish which ages of neglect had accumulated round the foundations and bases of the columns; while Mr. Isaac Forsyth, a bookseller in Elgin, a man whose unsullied integrity, great and useful activity in business, and excellent literary taste, will cause his name to be long spoken of with respect, was mainly instrumental in awakening public interest to the beautiful gem which lay hidden in the north, and in securing it from farther destruction. He also published, about thirty years ago, a series of beautiful engravings of the cathedral, with minute measurements and letterpress descriptions.

Elgin is one of the few ecclesiastical-looking towns to be seen in Scotland. The streets abound with picturesque and fantastic-like houses, some of them of considerable antiquity, which, besides every variety of shape, often display projecting wooden balconies and piazzas, overhanging and partly encroaching on the public way, and one or two of them have still the mark of the old Templars' property on them—a high iron cross on the topmost chimney.

But the glory of Elgin is its venerable cathedral, now in ruins, long and justly styled "The Lanthorn of the North." (*Speculum patriæ et decus regni.*) Of this edifice there are standing only the two large square western towers (84 feet high), but without their spires, though, fortunately, the intermediate large doorway, and part of the window above, are entire; as also, at the eastern end, the choir and its cloister, the grand altar, and double-rowed and orieled windows above it, with the two eastern terminal turrets and adjoining chapter-house. The length of the cathedral measured 282 by 86 feet over the walls, and the transept was 115 feet in length, while, in the centre of the whole, a magnificent tower, supported on massive pillars, rose to the height of 198 feet. A flight of spacious steps received the visitor on his approach, and landed him at the great western entrance, the floor of which represents the general basement level of the whole structure. Traces of this pavement have lately been discovered, and the ascent of steps may yet be restored. The chapter-house is of an octagonal form, with windows of variously-patterned tracery; and its flat stone roof is supported by a clustered pillar, nine feet in circumference, rising from the centre of the chamber beneath, and from the top of which, beautiful light-groined arches proceed round the building, and unite with those composing the windows. While the general dimensions of the whole cathedral (which, as we have said, is in the style of the early English and decorated Gothic) attract admiration for their symmetry, the workmanship of the chapter-house (erected, it is supposed, about 1480) is peculiarly deserving of notice for its lightness, richness of ornament, and great delicacy in the execution of the minuter tracery, and the flowered fillets and capitals of its columns. The cathedral stands at the east end of the town of Elgin, and was surrounded by a high wall 1,000 yards in circuit, having four gates. The officials had each a manse and garden within the precinct, in a street still called the College, and a glebe in a large adjoining field. But little is known of the original building of this noble minster, which alone, of the Scottish cathedrals of the thirteenth century, had two western towers.

The diocese of Moray was constituted by Alexander I., in the year 1115, and the foundation-stone of the cathedral was laid, on 19th July, 1224, by Bishop Andrew, of the ancient native family De Moravia, nephew of that St. Gilbert who, on the opposite shore of the Firth, at the same time, raised the humbler walls of Dornoch. The work was afterwards completed through the exertions of the Popes, who caused collections in aid of the undertaking to be made in different parts of Europe, and sent artisans and architects from Rome to forward and superintend its execution. Along with the towns of Elgin and Forres, this magnificent pile was, in 1390, burned by the ferocious " Wolf of Badenoch," Alexander Stewart, son of Robert II., who also, to avenge himself on Bishop Bar, for refusing to recognise him as his liege lord, set fire, at the same time, to the College, the Maison Dieu (an hospital, it is believed, for lepers), and the Town Church of St. Giles, which, with their whole writs and documents, were all reduced to a heap of ruins. Well might the old Church Chronicler style those as days in which there "was no law in Scotland, but the great man oppressed the poor man, and the whole kingdom was one den of thieves. Slaughters, robberies, fire-raising, and other crimes, went unpunished; and justice was sent into banishment beyond the kingdom's bounds." The bishop, making his lamentation to the king of the damage done on this occasion, describes the cathedral "as the pride of the land, the glory of the realm, the delight of wayfarers and strangers, a praise and a boast among foreign nations—lofty in its towers without, splendid in its appointments within—its countless jewels and rich vestments, and the multitude of its priests." It had seven dignitaries, fifteen canons, twenty-two vicars-choral, and about as many chaplains.

A second plundering and burning of the town and cathedral was perpetrated in 1402, by Alexander, third son of the Lord of the Isles, a worthy rival of the ferocious Wolf, who, like him, was previously sworn, bound by writ, "not to allow his men, nor any other *Kethranes*, to beg or strole through the country of Moray, nor to annoy or destroy the inhabitants!" Both incendiaries had speedily to propitiate the Church, and obtain absolution by costly presents. The rebuilding of the cathedral was commenced by Bishop John Innes, a son of the family of Innes, in 1407, but was not completed till 1420. In 1506, the great tower fell, and its re-erection was not finished till 1538. On the 14th of February, 1568, the Regent Murray and his Council issued an order to strip the roofs of the Cathedrals of Elgin and Aberdeen of their lead; but the vessel freighted with it, is said to have sunk in the Bay of Aberdeen. Since that period, the building has been, till of late, totally neglected, and suffered to fall into its present state of decay. A small sum was latterly given, by the Barons of Exchequer, to the self-constituted guardian, John Shanks, above mentioned, (who displayed great taste and industry in clearing away the rubbish, and restoring the ground-plan of elevation,) and is still continued. It is difficult for us, who lavish so much on our own "coiled houses," to appreciate the sentiments of the age that decorated so profusely the house of God; but even after visiting Melrose Abbey, the stranger will be obliged to confess, on beholding Elgin, that "enough yet remains of it to entitle it to rank as at once the grandest and the most beautiful of our cathedrals, if not the most superb edifice of Scotland."—(*Reg. Morav. Preface.*) Elgin, as remarked by the learned author whose words we have just quoted—(Cosmo Innes, Esq.)—"long retained a strong impress of its ecclesiastical origin. Within the memory of some yet alive, it presented the appearance of a little cathedral city, very unusual among the burghs of Presbyterian Scotland. There was an antique fashion of building, and withal a certain solemn, drowsy air about the town and its inhabitants, that almost prepared a stranger to meet some church procession, or some imposing ceremonial of the picturesque old religion. The town is changed of late. The dwellings of the citizens have put on a modern trim look, which does not satisfy the eye so well as the sober gray walls of their fathers. Numerous hospitals, the fruits of mixed charity and vanity, surround the town, and, with their gaudy white domes and porticos, contrast offensively with the mellow colouring and chaste proportions of the ancient structures. If the present taste continues, there will soon be nothing remaining of the reverend antique town but the ruins of its magnificent cathedral."—(See Registrum Moraviense; article on the Scottish Cathedrals in 'The Quarterly Review' for June, 1849, and G. & P. Anderson's 'Guide to the Highlands,' last edition. A. & C. Black, Edinburgh.)

WARKWORTH.

DESPITE the corroding tooth of time, and the systematic dilapidations of man, Warkworth Castle still presents one of the finest examples of the feudal residences of which England has so many to boast; and though, in its general arrangements, its appearance does not excite the idea of one of those rugged fortresses destined solely for war, yet it possesses all the defensible qualities to be found in the most advanced stage of Edwardian castremotation. Seated on the very summit of a lofty peninsula, formed by the meanderings of the Coquet, about a mile from its mouth, it commands not only the town which clothes the steep beneath its northern walls, but has an outlook over the adjoining country of the most extensive and varied character. On the south side, where the castle-yard is on a level with the country between it and the sea, the entrance has been defended by a deep ditch, crossed by a drawbridge. The great gateway tower, which has been provided with a portcullis, machicollations, and arrow-loops calculated to scour every part of the south ditch, has been of greater height than at present. It formerly contained a prison, the porter's lodging, and the constable's apartments over all. Passing through the archway, the visitor enters the court-yard, an enclosure about eighty-five yards long from north to south, by sixty-six from east to west, and containing rather better than a square acre. Against the west wall have been built the common hall and kitchen, which, like that within the keep, has had two large fireplaces and ovens. Between these and the keep is a postern, opening to the steep banks which here impend over the Coquet. To the north, placed

on an artificial mount, is the *keep-tower*, which is of a square figure, with semi-octagonal projections on each of its sides, and the whole surmounted by a lofty exploratory turret. A flight of steps leads to the principal entrance, which is in the southern tower. The lower apartments, of which there are eight, have arched stone roofs, and are each dimly lighted by a narrow loop-hole. These were probably receptacles for cattle during Scottish invasion. In the floor of one of them is the opening to a gloomy bottle-shaped dungeon, fifteen feet square at the base, to which the only access is by a ladder or rope; as well might the wretched captive be buried in the bowels of the earth, as in this darksome cavern. From this tier of apartments, one large and two smaller staircases lead to the next story, the former terminating in a spacious landing, round which stone seats are fixed, and which has been a sort of vestibule or waiting-room to the great hall. The hall itself is thirty-nine feet long, and twenty-four feet wide, and has been about twenty feet high, extending to the roof, which has been wholly removed. Two capacious open arches in its west side have led to a dais, adjoining which are retiring closets for the noble owner. On the same floor are various other apartments, and the presence of fireplaces and corbelling, with walls above them, indicate still another tier before the roof was reached. On the same floor as the hall, and closely adjoining it, is the kitchen, with its stone floor, capacious fireplaces, and enormous chimneys, where, doubtless, many a glorious feast has been prepared for the favoured guests of the Earl's own table. It is worthy of remark, that the *sinks* and *latrinæ* have all been constructed upon principles which would put to shame many buildings of pretension of the present day. The latter are so situated as to be immediately accessible from the principal sleeping chambers. From this flat, smaller staircases lead to the roof and exploratory tower. The masonry of the whole is in excellent order, and only requires roofing and flooring, and the filling of the windows with glass, to put it into habitable condition.

It is a source of satisfaction that the good taste of the present

Duke of Northumberland has done much for Warkworth Castle, and that he is at present putting two or more of the apartments of the south tower of the keep, with the adjoining principal staircase and entrance, into habitable repair, to be used by him when business requires his presence in the neighbourhood.

Within the court-yard, immediately south of the keep, and stretching across from east to west, have been exhumed the foundations of the massive piers and ground-plan of an ecclesiastical structure, being the vestiges of a collegiate church intended to have been there founded in the reign of Edward VI., and of which all trace had been lost till the recent excavations instituted by his Grace. The remains display a nave, chancel, central tower, and transepts, and have beneath them an extensive series of strongly-vaulted chambers. South of this, the enclosure would seem to have been unoccupied with buildings. The buildings erected against the inner face of the walls are generally much ruined, but exteriorly the masonry is so perfect as to convey an impression that the castle is in a state of almost thorough repair.

But for the barbarous demolition of 1672, the keep would, in all probability, have yet been in good repair, and formed a rare example of a medieval structure descending to us in all its integrity. In 1672 (observes Chatto in his *Oliver's Rambles in Northumberland*), one of the auditors or stewards of the family, named Joseph Clarke, obtained of the Countess of Northumberland a gift of the materials of Warkworth Castle, in order that he might build himself a house at Chirton, near North Shields; and he accordingly unroofed the keep for the sake of the timber and lead. What other injury the building might sustain through the cupidity of this *honest* steward—who had obtained from the youthful countess permission to dismantle the castle of her ancestors, in order to build himself a sty—does not appear: the walls were probably spared, because he had found it would be more expensive to pull them down, and separate the stones from the hardened lime, than to purchase new stones from the quarry! In order to carry out his intention, this unblushing fellow, in virtue of his office, pressed into his service all her ladyship's tenants in the neighbourhood, with their wains; and, in the plenitude of his considerateness and liberality, engages to "allowe every waine half-a-crowne, in regard they are like to be out three days ere they gett home." He also provides for the punishment of those who refuse his behests, in terms which, it is well for the sake of Mr. Clarke's reputation, are now wholly illegible from the decayed state of the document.

There is no direct historical evidence to show when this desirable site was first crowned with a fortress; though, from a return made to an assessment in 1166, it appears that the castle and manor of Warkworth were then held by Roger Fitz-Richard by the tenure of one knight's service. In this family the place remained till the reign of Edward III., when, becoming the property of the crown, the king granted the castle and manor to Sir Henry Percy, governor of Berwick, in lieu of a yearly allowance of five hundred marks, payable out of the customs of that town. From the date of this grant, in 1334, to the present time—with the exception of periods of forfeiture, when Warkworth became the temporary property of the Nevilles, the Umfrevilles, and the Ogles—the castle and manor of Warkworth have continued in the possession of the Percy family.

The picturesque old bridge and bridge-tower, which occupy so prominent a position in the view, are in much the same state as when Girtin saw them; in the same state, in fact, as they were three hundred years before. A survey, made at the instance of the Percy family, in 1567, states that the "sayd towre ys without roof and cover; and without amendment will in a short tyme utterlye decay: it shall be therefore very requisete that the towre be with all speed repaired, and the gates hanged upe; which shall be a great surety and comoditye for the towne." The recommendation to repair the tower was not attended to, as there was little reason at that time to apprehend danger from the hostile incursions of the Scots. The importance of such a defence must often have been found in warding off, at least for a time, the sudden attack of a marauding party. The town of Warkworth did not escape the evils generally experienced by the inhabitants of a frontier country. After William the Lion, of Scotland, made his disgraceful retreat from the castle of Prudhoe, in 1174, he beset the castle of Alnwick with his whole army of 80,000 men. Being repulsed for some time, he formed a blockade, and drew off many of his forces in marauding parties to pillage the country; one of which, as Benedict of Peterborough says, commanded by Earl Duncan, entered the town of Warkworth, burnt it, and put all the inhabitants to the sword, without distinction of age or sex; the soldiers broke open the church of St. Lawrence, in which, and in the house of the minister, they slew above one hundred men, besides women and children. In more recent times, the Earl of Northumberland, in a letter to the king and his council, says, that he dressed himself at midnight, by the light of the surrounding villages, which were set on fire by the Scotch marauders. The agricultural riches of the inhabitants of this district often excited the cupidity of the borderers, and they were much exposed to their daring inroads.

The church, of which mention has been made, is a spacious and interesting structure, with a fine stone spire upwards of a hundred feet in height. Its south wall and the greater part of the tower are Transition Norman in their architecture, while the whole of the rest of the building is Perpendicular. The chancel has a groined roof, and the east end of the north aisle is cut off by a pierced oaken screen of the latter style. This was formerly used by the Percys when at church. At the opposite extremity is the recumbent funeral monument of a mailed warrior, with a more modern inscription to this effect—" The Effigies of Sir Hugh de Morwick, who gave the Common to this town of Warkworth." The erection of the original church here is attributed to Ceolwulf, King of Northumberland, about the year 738.

The *Hermitage* of Warkworth, which has been correctly designated "the best preserved example now existing of those numerous oratories in secluded spots, formerly viewed with great veneration," has gained additional celebrity from the pleasing ballad, 'The Hermit of Warkworth,' which appeared from the pen of Percy, Bishop of Dromore, in 1771. The most convenient mode of approach is by taking a boat from a little above the castle, and rowing a short distance between high banks, most beautifully clothed with wood, the visitor lands at the foot of a pleasant walk, which leads directly to the Hermitage. This secluded retreat consists of three small apartments, excavated in the face of a lofty freestone cliff, embowered in trees, and from whose summit spring and impend, from the clefts and fissures of the rock, others of scarcely less magnitude. An ascent of seventeen steps leads to the outer apartment, which is about eighteen feet long, seven and a half wide, and about the same in height. Above the doorway are the remains of an inscription, which is understood to have expressed, from the Latin version of the Psalms, the words, "*Fuerunt mihi lacrymæ meæ panes die ac nocte:*" "My tears have been my meat day and night." The roof is chiselled in imitation of groining. At the east end is an altar occupying the whole width of the apartment. Near to the altar, on the south side, is carved on the wall the monumental effigies of a lady, much defaced. There is not within the Hermitage the slightest vestige of armorial bearings or inscription, to inform us as to whom this represents. In a niche at the foot of the monument is the figure of a man kneeling, supposed to indicate the first hermit. From this apartment a doorway opens to an inner one, in which there is also an altar, and a seat cut in the partition wall, and an opening, cut slantwise, to admit of one seated or reclining there to see into the chapel, and view the effigy of the lady. In the same wall is an elegantly-formed window, which lights the inner apartment. To the north of this is another excavation much smaller, which leads to a gallery having a view of the river. A flight of steps cut in the rock leads to the hermit's garden on the top—a little patch of ground, planted with a few shrubs and flowers. Beneath, on the ground level, are the remains of a stone building, which has seemingly contained the later hermit's kitchen and sleeping apartments. From the style of architecture prevailing in the Hermitage, it would seem to date about the commencement of the fourteenth century; and Chatto thinks that the site may originally have been a place of concealment, and afterwards, that the first hermit, finding a great part of these excavations already made, had been induced to make choice of them as a place of retirement, enlarging them and ornamenting them in after years. The Percys certainly continued a priest in the Hermitage, for the benefit of their own and their ancestors' souls; but there is no good evidence to show that they regarded the memory of the former hermit, as is stated by the accomplished writer of the ballad. The universal tradition is, that the first hermit was one of the great Northumbrian family of Bertram, and that he imposed this penance on himself to expiate the murder of his brother.

This curious memorial of devotion, so venerable for its antiquity, and so interesting from the delightful solitude in which it is placed, is a source of continual attraction to visitors throughout favourable weather; and it is gratifying that it has never suffered damage of any material character by the hand of man, though the falling of part of the rock has broken down and obliterated some portion of a projecting gallery, which, it is stated, was originally supported by a pillar cloisterwise.

NEWCASTLE-UPON-TYNE.

MORE than half a century has elapsed since the capital of the North of England presented the appearance which Girtin makes it to have had. When we consider, that since this period Newcastle has trebled her size and population, it is difficult to realize the idea that she could have been so inconsiderable at so comparatively late a period.

The first object that attracts the notice of the visitor to the "Coaly Tyne," is the immense activity which pervades every inch of ground which borders upon the river, from Shields up to and beyond Newcastle. The shores are clothed to the very water's edge with quays, coal-staiths, waggon-ways, iron-foundries, brick and cinder ovens, and ship-building yards. The steep hills, between which flows a river laden with a forest of masts from every quarter of the globe, are clad to their very summits with chemical works, and their chimneys of dizzy height vomiting forth their fumes; refineries for extracting silver from lead, with vast conduits and apparatus for condensing their noxious exhalations; the clanking pumps and engines of coal works; and at the very apex on either side, long trains of waggons filled with coals, goods, or passengers, as the case may be, hurried along by hissing locomotives. At night, the voyager may, without putting his imagination to any very violent stretch, conceive himself sailing up the pitchy river of hell, and making his *entree* to the infernal regions. In whatever direction he may turn his gaze, he is met with hideous sights—a score of huge cones belch forth fierce tongues of flame, furnace-doors suddenly burst open and disclose what seem vast caverns of liquid fire, great sheets of flame licking the blackened walls, which hardly confine them within bounds, or shooting forth aloft into the darkness, rendered doubly dark by contrast. The ear is afflicted by the thunder of the forge, the continual clanging of hammers, and the hideous ringing of huge plates of metal, as they are incessantly smitten; the panting of mighty bellows, the fierce roaring of the furnaces howling and shrieking as they are chafed into whiter heat; the clanking and hissing of machinery, ever and anon varied by the stentorian cries of the workmen—all contending for mastery in this chorus of horrible discords. In the midst are seen dusky forms, hurrying to and fro, with unearthly-looking instruments, stirring up the fires into fiercer flame, and suddenly casting athwart the murky waves huge streaks of light, as if to reveal the astonished voyager to the fiends, who seem not ill-prepared to give him a *warm* reception.

Sixty years ago, and there was comparatively none of this—the town was mainly confined within her walls, her manufactures were few, though her trade was always considerable, and she had then received but little of the impulse which drives our modern towns into the great commercial activity which is their principal characteristic. Like other ancient boroughs, before the Reform Bill, its progress was impeded by commercial restrictions, which not only discouraged competition, but put an inseparable bar in the way of manufactures, or enterprise of any description. Capital, which is the soul of modern business, had no field for action, as its exercise would have aroused the jealousy of all who were less fortunately situated. The people lived on in a quiet dreamy state, all moderately well off, many enriching themselves, and some there were who were enjoying the fruit of their ancestors' toil. The defensive wall, which had shielded their predecessors, still afforded them its now needless protection. The old streets and thoroughfares remained all but intact from the days of Elizabeth or James, and the very heart of the town, which for centuries had contained the gardens and pleasure-grounds of two conventual institutions, remained devoted to similar purposes, though the bodies who had originally owned them had long been extinct. Appropriately enough, it is in the very heart of the place that the most radical changes have been made, not within sixty, but within twenty years. Grainger, like a modern Aladdin, has, by the mere force of his own genius, called into existence, where before there was nought but an open, useless waste, streets of palaces, sumptuous tiers of architecture, and magnificent public buildings, which, both from their design and material, may safely be asserted as unsurpassed in any city of the empire. But it is not only centrally that Newcastle has advanced within the same period. Urged by the impetus that unrestricted industry and untrammelled commerce have given, she has thrown down her ancient barriers, uprooted her towers, levelled her gates and ditches, gone a-field with her streets, and enlarged her boundaries in all available directions. She has planted herself and her dense population on what but yesterday were quiet fields and stack-garths, and her extremities are now three times as far asunder as they were at the date of our picture.

Newcastle, like all our old garrison towns, was surrounded with a defensive wall, which in her instance was upwards of two miles in circuit, and of such effective construction and architectural grandeur, as to have elicited from old Leland (Henry the Eighth's antiquary) expressions of the highest admiration. What with wall and ditch, the almost insuperable barrier which forty feet would constitute, was presented to the enemy, and this flanked and strengthened with seventeen circular bastions, seven great gates, and fifty watch-towers, served for some five or six hundred years to secure, to the opulent burgesses of Newcastle, uninterrupted possession and enjoyment of their wealth and privileges.

So placed as to be the great frontier town, and the principal check upon the southward progress of the Scots in their repeated and ruinous invasions, Newcastle has ever held the highest position as a fortress; and as a place of trade, its antiquity and importance may be estimated from the fact, that the charter of its Company of Merchant Adventurers dates anterior to that of London, while it is one of the three towns in England possessing a Trinity-house.

But if Newcastle was shielded from one enemy by her fortifications, they had their part in breeding another within, and that of a much more deadly character; for, besides the fact that the wall-begirt town was a stranger to the free admission of pure air, the presence of the stagnant waters of the moat must have largely aided the numerous other factors of malaria in the town itself. Much as we may pity the condition of the poor of our modern towns in this respect, they suffer in an immensely diminished degree from their ancestors, with their crowded streets, narrow thoroughfares, ill-constructed unwholesome dwellings, total want of scavenging, and systematic disregard of sewerage. In the middle ages, Newcastle presented—ay, less than sixty years since—the features of an ancient walled town, in what were at once their picturesque and repulsive forms. Huge tiers of what Dr. Dibdin calls "the overhanging glories of the Elizabethan era," set side by side, packed, as it were, in close order, the roads between them mere horse-tracks, and story after story bulging out, till at last those at the summit so closely approximated, that if the occupants could not absolutely shake hands, they could converse with ease and comfort. Beneath, the roads were miry and ill-kept, and what with the smallness of the windows, and the little light which could penetrate from above, the dwellings were rendered so darksome as to interfere very materially with health. One of the most remarkable portions of ancient Newcastle, and one which remains to all practical intents unaltered, is the Quayside, and the block of buildings extending northward to the base of one of the numerous hills upon which the town is built. This quarter, which is some hundreds of yards in length and of proportionate width, is traversed from north to south by twenty narrow lanes or alleys, which, in the dialect, are called *chares*, and are so narrow that all but one (by way of distinction called the

Broad-chare, though it will only admit a cart) may be reached by the outstretched arms; one is even so narrow at its outlet, that the body must be turned sideways to gain egress. This block of buildings is computed to be more densely populated than any equal portion of her Majesty's dominions, and though now occupied (with the exception of the merchants' offices in the front) mainly by the lowest order of the inhabitants, was anciently tenanted by the commercial magnates of the place; and the dirty narrow lanes, which we now think so noisome and disagreeable, gave egress and ingress to the dainty dames and daughters of Newcastle's best merchants, so late even as the beginning of the eighteenth century.

The Quayside, with the Sandhill, Close, and all the low-lying portions of the town, are built on ground gained from the river, which at high tide washed the bases of the higher grounds. The ballast, which for ages has been brought from the bed of the Thames in the holds of colliers, coming hither for cargoes of the invaluable fuel for which Newcastle has a world-wide celebrity, and which *ornament* the banks of the Tyne on both sides of its course, in the shape of mountains of gravel and chalk, has been used to heighten the slimy shore, so as to fit it for the erection of the localities in question.

The *Sandhill*, with its sufficiently significant name, yet presents some of the finest extant examples of the domestic architecture of the era of Elizabeth and James, as also the street winding around the flank of the Castle-hill, and thence termed *The Side*. These have all numerous projecting stories, long rows of casemented windows, and the other characteristics of the style. Their occupants, in former days, viewed the many pageants, and other public spectacles, of which, in times past, there was literally no end. Then, the office of a king was really no sinecure; and he who would worthily fill it, must move about at the head of his armed men, and, if necessary, wage war with the invading Scot. Here it was that the unfortunate Charles repeatedly availed himself of the hospitality and aid of the loyalists of Newcastle, dined and slept, created knights and kept court—where he was imprisoned, and eventually handed over to the Parliament; here has the redoubted Oliver Cromwell supped, and been regaled with music from the town's minstrels; here has the sapient James been received by the mayor and aldermen, presented with addresses, and with, what was infinitely more acceptable to him, money. Close by, was the Princess Margaret, daughter of Henry the Seventh, sumptuously entertained by the Earl of Northumberland, on her way to marriage with James the Fourth of Scotland —and at earlier periods was Newcastle the frequent residence of the martial Edwards, Henrys, and John.

The main part of Newcastle is seated on three hills, which rise swiftly from the Tyne to a considerable elevation, between which flow four ancient streams, which pour their waters into the Tyne, and form the main sewerage of the place. Though these are for the most part covered over, and in some places, by engineering contrivances, now some forty or fifty feet below the level of the roadways of the streets which are built over them, they yet run as they have for centuries past, laden with the manifold impurities of a populous town. Upon the summit of the most western of the eminences referred to, stands the august *keep-tower* of the Norman castle, in full command of both the bridges; the one occupying the site of that erected by Hadrian, and the other spanning the river at a dizzy height, the product of the genius of Stephenson. The castle itself is an object of double interest, for not only is it one of the finest extant specimens of Norman military architecture, but it has been made the *locus* of the Society of Antiquaries of Newcastle, and their valuable museum of northern archæology deposited within its time-honoured walls. Close by, and springing proudly to the height of about two hundred feet, is the elegant spire of St. Nicholas, unique both in point of architectural construction and majesty of effect. The adjoining eminence is crowned by the church of All Saints, rebuilt in the latter part of the last century.

The great *barrier-wall*, drawn by Hadrian across the island, from the Tyne to the Solway, passed through the midst of the site of Newcastle, where was seated one of the stations on the line, Pons Ælii; but so completely have the mutations of centuries obliterated every remnant, that the precise site of the structure is an unsettled question, and the course of the wall itself, so far as the town is concerned, a matter of as great uncertainty. Numerous Roman remains, however, have from time to time been turned up near the castle, indicating clearly that a portion of its area has been hit upon; but, in all probability, the real grave of Pons Ælii is at a depth far beneath that to which most modern excavations need be carried. The *military road*, which accompanied the wall all the way, may still be traced through the town by means of a series of ancient streets, following one another in the line assumed as that of the wall, while their uniform width and character tend to confirm the opinion. Further attention to the subject will end in placing it beyond a doubt, that this Roman road was originally the only street of Newcastle—the road from east to west—the West*gate*—along the sides of which were erected not less than nine or ten churches, convents, and hospitals, for the spiritual and bodily comfort of the wayfarer. Between these, along each side of the road, would be built dwelling-houses, after the manner of the street—like villages of the present day. Subsequently, other streets would be made to branch thence in all directions, of which the principal was Pilgrim Street, so named from its being used by the devotees to the shrine of the Virgin, at Jesmond, near Newcastle. The conventual institutions within the town were very numerous, and richly endowed.

Until a few years ago, there existed, close to the magnificent railway station, an unpretending little ecclesiastical building—the chapel of one of these conventual institutions—which had been appropriated to the purposes of the Grammar School, refounded by Queen Elizabeth, and from which has emanated a goodly roll of names, whose fame has extended far beyond the place which gave them birth. It was here that were nurtured the early minds of the illustrious Collingwood, and the brothers Stowell and

Eldon, two of the most accomplished judges which England has produced. Ridley, the Marian martyr, learned his grammar at Newcastle; and Dr. Bryan Walton, the learned polyglottist, is understood to have had his rudimentary tuition here. Newcastle produced her Bewick, the reviver of engraving on wood, the revered re-originator of an art which now delights thousands upon thousands of our countrymen, and which is hardly second in importance to printing itself, as a means of educating and ameliorating the condition of the people. To Newcastle belongs Harvey, Jackson, Landells, the Dalziels, and many others whose works are in every one's hands. Newcastle also produced Bulmer, whose praise it is to have been the reviver of first-class printing. Nor in painting is she behindhand. If she be not a great patron of art herself, she sends forth her artists—the accomplished but ill-fated Clennell, the gifted Ewbank, the imaginative Martin, the Richardsons, and Carmichael, are not unknown, and she saw and fostered the early days of Lough the sculptor. George Stephenson, the first to perfect the railway system, and his son, Robert Stephenson, whose engineering triumphs are world-known, may fitly close a list of worthies, of whom Newcastle possesses at least her proportion. So, for the present, adieu to "this fine English town on the Tyne—the centre of the coal-trade—of intelligence of every kind—and of engineering knowledge."*

* *Times*, 4th November, 1853.

FLINT.

FLINT, at the time this view was taken, contained about three hundred houses, and but little more than eleven hundred inhabitants, half of whom were occupied in trade and agriculture. It was, however, at that time frequented as a bathing-place, and during the summer months visited by what were considered fashionable people; but Parkgate, from whence the view is taken, and which stands on the opposite side of the estuary of the Dee, was then slowly increasing in importance and respectability, though the marshy beach was a great inconvenience to the bathers. Flint is described, in a work of the period when Turner made his sketch,* as "the ancient deserted capital of the county, and was probably once a Roman-British town, being formed on the plan of a Roman encampment, rectangular, and surrounded with regular entrenchments and ramparts, with four portal or fortified gates." Mention is made of several Roman remains, coins, &c., that have been discovered in the old washes, and the place is described as having the appearance of a deserted village—the lines of the streets being broken and dilapidated—that mooring rings were still visible in some of the remaining walls, which showed that when the Dee wound round the foot of the castle, Flint was a maritime place, although then—sixty years ago—it could only admit small vessels, "capable of taking the ground at the ebb of the tide." So low had it sunk at this period, that the sessions had been removed to Mold, and the market discontinued. The point of view is so distant in the

* 'The Cambrian Guide.' Stourport.

engraving, that it presents no traces of the old castle, which stands upon a rock, on a marsh by the banks of the Dee, which river formerly ran by its walls, though now they are only reached by high tides which flow up the estuary. The age of this castle is doubtful. Camden says it was built in the time of Henry II.; Leland in the reign of Edward I. During the insurrection, when Prince David seceded from the English party, the fortress was captured. Edward III. granted it to the Black Prince; and in 1385, Richard II. granted it to the Earl of Oxford; and after his attainder it came into the possession of Percy, Earl of Northumberland, who, by some means, allured the generous monarch into the fortress, and then handed him over to Bolingbroke. That beautiful scene in the third act of Shakspere's Richard II. takes place at this castle, in which, when Percy tells the ill-starred king, that Bolingbroke attends in "the base (lower) court," the monarch says—

> " Down, down, I come; like glistering Phaeton,
> Wanting the manage of unruly jades.
> In the base court? Base court, where kings grow base
> To come at traitors' calls, and do them grace.
> In the base court? Come down? Down, court! Down, king!
> For night-owls shriek, where mounting larks should sing."

During the civil wars, Flint Castle was held for the king by Roger Mostyn, who surrendered it, in 1643, to the Roundheads, commanded by Sir W. Brereton and Sir E. Middleton. Originally, the building was of a parallelogramic form, with circular towers at each angle. One detached from the walls appears to have been an additional work. It consists of two concentric circular walls, six feet in thickness, with an area between, twenty feet in diameter, into which a gallery opens through four entrances —all marks of very great antiquity: this is called the double tower. The court extends over an acre, and the windows on the west side contain pointed arches. The barbacan consists of a square tower, and formerly communicated with the castle by a drawbridge.

As far back as 1283, Flint was made a free borough, consisting of a mayor, two bailiffs, and other officers. In the reign of Henry VIII., in conjunction with other adjacent places, it first returned a member to parliament, the right of election being vested in those who " payed scot and lot." A few years before Turner made the accompanying sketch, the new jail was erected by an architect also named Turner. Over the gateway is the following curious inscription:—

" In the twenty-fifth year of his Majesty George III., in the sheriffalty of Thomas Hanmer, Bart., this prison was erected, instead of the ancient loathsome place of confinement; in pity to the misery of even the most guilty, to alleviate the sufferings of lesser offenders, or of the innocent themselves, whom the chances of human life may bring within these walls. Done at the expense of the county, aided by the subscriptions of several of the gentry, who, in the midst of most distressful days, voluntarily took upon themselves part of the burden, in compassion to such of their countrymen on whom fortune had been less bounteous of her favours."

Adjoining Flint are the remains of a forest, though now only a small wood, where Henry II. fought two battles, and was each time defeated, losing also many of his nobles. The castle must have been much older than the period assigned to it by either Camden or Leland, if we take Shakspere as an authority, for in the time of Richard II. he calls it "ancient," and Bolingbroke bids Percy

" Go to the rude ribs of that ancient castle."

He also speaks of its " tottered battlements."

The estuary of the Dee, as given in the engraving, divides Flintshire from Cheshire, and we have in it a fine specimen of the marvellous management of light, in which Turner stands unequalled; and, perhaps, there is no engraving, up to this period, that bears such marks of the master-hand, and which, at a glance, any one familiar with his drawings, would, without hesitation, pronounce "a Turner." Instead of representing Flint by a lot of little spots the size of pins' heads, he has thrown a dazzling light over the distance, under which we "feel" there is a town, for the whole air seems alive, and amid that shipping and sunshine there is the stir of life.

WESTMINSTER BRIDGE.

WESTMINSTER has been a city of Palaces, from the days of Saxon Edward, up to the present time, though all that remains of the ancient palace, where the Saxon King reigned before the silence of our shores was startled by the braying of Norman trumpets, and where fiery-tongued Elizabeth ruled, is to be found in portions of Westminster Hall, and the vaults of St. Stephen's Chapel; for a great portion of the buildings which, for so many centuries, and through so many changes, formed the ancient Palace of Westminster, were with few exceptions destroyed by fire in 1512. The palace was afterwards built at Whitehall, and from one of the windows of the banqueting-house, Charles I. was led to execution, about 100 years before Westminster bridge—as painted by Turner—was opened. But many interesting remains connected with the ancient palace existed at the time the view was taken, and which were swept away in the great fire that consumed the old Houses of Parliament in 1834. Amongst these were the Painted Chamber, hung with ancient tapestry, in which the court was held that decided upon Charles I. being brought to trial in Westminster Hall; and in which his death-warrant was at last signed by Cromwell and the rest of the king-killers. The Star Chamber, in which Prynne was tried, also then remained, together with St. Stephen's Chapel and cloisters; the latter had been standing 500 years. Excepting the Abbey, the Hall, and the few remains above enumerated, there is but little remaining of what may be considered really ancient and truly venerable about the neighbourhood of the bridge. The number of buildings swept away by the fire of 1834, and to make room for the present New Houses of Parliament, the site of which is given, will be best ascertained by a reference to the engraving. With the exception of a few of the houses in New Palace Yard, the church of St. Margaret, Westminster Hall, and the Abbey, the tall towers of which heave up behind, every other vestige our great artist has represented in his " Westminster Bridge," is destroyed. But thankful we are that the most ancient and the most interesting remain; and now that the New Houses of Parliament are completed, we can only regret that the same master-hand is not here to place them in one of his own unsurpassed effects, and to leave the princely pile flooded in that dreamy glory in which he loved to revel. Westminster bridge was built by Charles Lubelye, who was a native of Switzerland; and since old London bridge was taken down, it is the oldest bridge that spans the Thames in the neighbourhood of the Metropolis. It was begun in 1739, and opened in 1750, and consists of 14 arches, the largest of which has a span of 76 feet. It is now in a dilapidated state, and fears are entertained of its falling; although no longer ago than 1846, it was closed for carriages, and released from the weight of many hundred tons, and the whole of the high and heavy parapet, with the arched recesses, represented in the print, were taken away; yet, in spite of the relief obtained by the removal of such a ponderous mass of masonry, and the lowering of the carriage road, it was pronounced incurable; and no marvel, since it had originally no better foundation than a number of timber rafts, placed in such a manner as no architect in the present day would trust a pier upon, even in the centre of a rapid brook. The consequence was, that these wooden cassions were soon undermined by the current, and the piers began to give way, especially after the removal of old London bridge, which increased the rapidity of the tide; and the bridge has gone on cracking and sinking ever since. Before the heavy mass of masonry was removed, the bridge contained twice the number of cubic feet of stone consumed in the erection of St. Paul's Cathedral, according to the statement of the builder. A French writer gravely asserts that the lofty parapet was erected to prevent the English people from committing suicide. The alcoves, or recesses, have given shelter to many a houseless wanderer; and it was no unusual sight, in passing over the bridge early on a summer morning, to see each covered archway occupied by a tenant. In one of the centre recesses on the side opposite to that given in the view, the bridge-keeper had a snug box, that shut in, and in which he oftener slept than kept watch. Westminster bridge will shortly be removed, and a new bridge erected on a plan already approved of, and designed by the architect of the New Houses of Parliament; and which is to be in harmony with that princely pile of buildings. When this is done, Turner's view, beside its great artistic merit, will be preserved as a record of the past; and, perhaps, in some future edition of Wordsworth's poems, be engraved a vignette, above the sonnet composed by the author of the "Excursion," early one morning in the September of 1803.

ON WESTMINSTER BRIDGE.

"Earth has not anything to show more fair;
Dull would he be of soul who could pass by
A sight so touching in its majesty;
This city now doth like a garment wear
The beauty of the morning; silent, bare,
Ships, towers, domes, theatres, and temples lie
Open unto the fields and to the sky,
All bright and glittering in the smokeless air.
Never did sun more beautifully steep
In his first splendour valley, rock, or hill;
Ne'er saw I, never felt a calm so deep!
The river glideth at his own sweet will:
Dear God! the very houses seem asleep;
And all that mighty heart is lying still."

Before Westminster bridge was erected, the great highway across the Thames—excepting over London bridge—was between the horse-ferry at Milbank, and Lambeth pier, adjoining Lambeth Palace, and near to which several very old houses still remain. This was the only horse-ferry across the Thames, near London, and the tolls or fares belonged to the Archbishop of Canterbury, and formed a valuable addition to the revenue of the see.

BAMBROUGH CASTLE.

THE village of Bambrough, which gives name to one of the six wards into which the county of Northumberland is divided, was, in former ages, a place of some importance, as we find that it contributed its quota of ships to our early fleets, and sent two representatives to a parliament summoned by Edward I. All traces of its former consequence have, however, disappeared, with the exception of the old castle, which still

"From its tall rock looks grimly down."

In regard to natural strength, there is not a situation in all Northumberland equal to that of Bambrough, or one in any wise so well adapted to the ancient rules of fortification. It is built on a rock which rises abruptly from the sea, to the height of about a hundred and fifty feet. The principal entrance to the castle is on the south-east, and is approached by a steep ascent, at the top of which there was formerly a ditch, crossed by a drawbridge. The gateway is defended by circular towers, beyond which is a flight of steps leading to the inner ballium. To the left of these steps, proceeding northward, is the chapel, beyond which are two towers, erected to guard the pass to the keep, and for the defence of the inner court. In the castle there is a well, a hundred and fifty feet deep, from which it has been ascertained that the overlying rock of basalt is seventy-five feet thick, and that it rests on a fine-grained red and white sandstone. The exterior walls enclose an area of about eight acres, nearly in the centre of which stands the keep, a square and massive pile, on the basement of which, says Chatto, certain sharp-sighted antiquaries have fancied that they could perceive traces of the architectural style of the Romans. It is scarcely necessary to observe, he continues, that such persons might find similar traces of Roman architecture in almost every old castle in the kingdom. The general character of the building seems to indicate that it was erected about the outset of the twelfth century; though it is not improbable that one of the towers on the exterior walls to the west, was built at an earlier period. Bambrough, or Bebbanburgh, as it was termed by the Saxons, was a royal residence, and a place of great strength, under the Saxon kings; and, according to Matthew of Westminster, and other ancient chroniclers, was first built by Ida, who ascended the Bernician throne in 559, and named by him Bebbanburgh, in honour of his queen, Bebba.

That the important position of Bambrough would escape the notice of the Romans is very unlikely. Roman coins have been found here, and the presence of Roman materials in the keep would seem to show, that the remains of a former fortress have been used up in the Norman erections.

Bambrough, being a place of considerable importance, is frequently mentioned in the history of the Saxon period, as the scene of conflict between contending kings. It was also more than once taken and pillaged by the Danes. In the reign of William Rufus, Bambrough Castle appears to have been in the possession of Robert de Mowbray, earl of Northumberland, who defeated and killed Malcolm, king of Scotland, before Alnwick, in 1093. Rufus, after this, becoming jealous of the earl's power in Northumberland, required him to desist from further fortifying certain castles which he had begun to repair. As the earl did not immediately attend to this injunction, Rufus sent his brother, Henry, with an army to the North to compel obedience. Mowbray, to avoid the impending storm, retired to Bambrough Castle, which was in vain assailed by the Royal army. Finding the place impregnable, to distress the garrison they cut off all succours of men and provisions, erected a fortress in the neighbourhood, according to the art of war practised in those days, which was named *Malvoisin*, or the bad neighbour, in which he placed a strong garrison, and drew off the main body of his army southward. The earl, by means of a secret correspondence held with some of the garrison of Newcastle, had entertained hopes of making himself master of that place; with this intent, under cover of the night, he set out from Bambrough, accompanied by thirty horsemen; but being observed by the garrison of Malvoisin, was pursued. When he arrived at Newcastle he found the gates shut against him, and the garrison apprised of his intention. He now was under the necessity of flying to the monastery of Tynemouth, where he was besieged six days, and wounded. At length, he and his followers having retired to the sanctuary, in defiance of the holy prescription were dragged forth and delivered up prisoners. Thence he was conducted towards Bambrough, which was still held out by his wife, and Morel his kinsman and lieutenant, in defiance of every assault, and every device then practised in sieges. Wearied with this unsuccessful procedure, Henry led forth his prisoner before the walls, and threatened instantly to put out his eyes, and deliver him to the torture, if the garrison did not surrender. Morel, overcome by the threatening calamity which impended over his lord, capitulated, and Mowbray was despatched to die in the dungeon of Windsor.

From the days of Rufus, to the time of the civil wars between the houses of York and Lancaster (it has been well observed), Bambrough Castle, as if it were too important a fortress to belong to a subject, appears to have continued in the possession of the kings of England, by whom a constable or governor was appointed. In the frequent contests between the partizans of Henry VI. and Edward IV., the castle sustained great damage, and, as it does not seem to have been thoroughly repaired either by Henry VII. or his successor, it ceased, from this time, to be of importance as a place of strength. In the reign of Elizabeth, Sir John Forster, warden of the Marches, was governor of Bambrough; and one of his descendants, in the reign of James I., received a grant of the old building. It continued in the possession of this family till the commencement of the reign of George I., when it was forfeited by Thomas Forster, Esq., M.P. for Northumberland, who was one of the leaders of the rebel army in 1715. Forster was taken prisoner, condemned to death, and committed to Newgate. His sister, Dorothy, rode to London on a double horse, behind an Adderstone blacksmith, in the quality of a servant, and, procuring an impression of the prison key, liberated her brother, and, like Madam Lavalette, remained in his place. Forster got clear off to the Continent, where a reward of £1000 was offered for his apprehension. He died abroad in 1738, and his body was privately buried in Bambrough crypt, being brought in a one-horsed hearse, with a solitary attendant.

The manor and castle of Bambrough were afterwards purchased of the Crown by Nathaniel, Lord Crewe, bishop of Durham, who was married to Forster's aunt. Crewe's life (says Surtees, the historian of Durham,) was one continued scene of political tergiversation and courtly meanness. Attached to the Stuarts, he yet, in spite of indifference and insult, paid the most servile homage to the princes of Nassau and Hanover. But his private virtues and active benevolence have veiled his public errors. His wife was reputed a beauty, and not without reason, if we may trust her portrait at Bambrough, which represents her with delicate features, blue eyes, light hair, a complexion beautifully fair, and a soft good-natured countenance. She was buried in 1715, at Stene, in Leicestershire. The bishop often spent hours in contemplation at the foot of her funeral monument; but he took occasion to express to Dr. Grey, his disgust at the sight of a ghastly skull which the sculptor had placed there; and Dr. Grey, ever ready to spare his beneficent patron a moment of uneasiness, immediately sent to the artist, and asked him whether he could not convert the skull into some less offensive object. "Yes," said he, after a short consideration, "I can change it into *a bunch of grapes;*" and it was forthwith done. The prelate on his decease, in 1720, left the manor of Bambrough, with other valuable estates, to trustees, to be applied to charitable uses; and in compliance with the intention of the testator, a noble charity is established at Bambrough, for the succour of shipwrecked seamen, the education of children, and the relief of indigent persons. Since the castle came into the possession of Lord Crewe's trustees, the keep has been repaired, and fitted up as a place of residence, where one of them generally takes up his abode for two or three months in the summer. The exterior walls and towers, which were in a more dilapidated state than the keep, have also been repaired, with due regard to the ancient style of the building; and an immense quantity of sand, which had accumulated in the castle-yard, has also been cleared away. In a strong wind from the eastward, fine particles of sand are drifted up from the beach to the castle and the village, and find an entrance into almost every room.

At the castle are kept blocks and tackles, warps, cables, mooring chains, anchors, kedges, pumps, and other articles for the use of stranded vessels; and there are also storehouses for the reception of such goods and stores as may be saved from a wreck. Apartments are kept ready for the accommodation of shipwrecked seamen; and in stormy weather two men patrol the coast for eight miles, day and night, in order to look out for vessels in distress. During a thick fog, a bell is rung at intervals from the castle, and a gun fired every quarter of an hour, as a warning to seamen, and as a guide to fishermen in making for the land.

There are extensive granaries within the castle-yard, where corn is stored, which, after being ground into flour at a mill which stands on the cliff, to the north of the castle, is sold at a reduced rate to poor families, who are also supplied with groceries at the cost price. A surgeon is paid to attend to the sick poor, and there is a dispensary in the castle, where they may obtain, free of expense, such medicine as is ordered. Schools are established for the gratuitous education of poor children; and there are twenty girls, above the number of those who attend as day-scholars, that receive board, clothing, and lodging at the castle, until they are old enough to go to service. There is also a library at the castle, from which any person residing within ten miles of Bambrough, may obtain the loan of books on payment of half-a-crown, which entitles him to the privilege for life.

To the eastward of Bambrough lie the Farne Islands, the largest of which, called the House Island, is little more than two miles distant from the castle. The nearest of the group, called the Staples, is about a mile and a half eastward of the House Island. The Great Farne, or House Island, was St. Cuthbert's favourite place of retirement, who, on resigning the bishopric of Lindisfarn in 678, again took possession of the cell which he had formerly built there, and in which he died two months after his return. The island was, in consequence of the saint's reputation, regarded as a place of great sanctity; and a cell of Benedictine monks, dependent on the abbey at Durham, was afterwards established there, and which continued to the time of the dissolution of the monasteries by Henry the Eighth. The island affords pasturage to a few sheep and cattle, and there are two light-houses, as well as a farmhouse, upon it. The lighthouses were originally erected by Sir Francis Liddell, in conjunction with the Trinity-house of Newcastle, a few years before the Restoration. "At the north end of the isle," to borrow the description of Pennant, who visited the Farne Islands in 1769, "is a deep chasm, from the top to the bottom of the rock, communicating to the sea, through which, in tempestuous weather, the water is forced with vast violence and noise, and forms a fine *jet d'eau* of sixty-six feet high. It is called by the inhabitants of the opposite coast, the *Churn*." The Farne Islands was the scene of the heroic exploit of the lighthouse-keeper, James Darling, and his daughter, Grace Darling, in saving so many persons from the wreck of the *Forfarshire* steamer. An excursion to the Farne Islands, and thence round the Staples, touching at the Crumstone, the Broomsman, and the Pinnacles, to see the nests of the eider-duck, (says Chatto in his 'Rambles,') forms a very pleasant trip in fine weather. By this course, from Budle to Holy Island, or from

Budle to Budle again, the distance is about eighteen or twenty miles; and with a breeze from the south-west, which will both fetch and carry, the trip may be performed in about six hours, allowing ample time to see everything likely to engage the stranger's attention among the islands.

HAMPTON COURT.

HAMPTON COURT, with its extensive park, ornamental water, avenues of ancient trees, herd of deer, and standing in its green seclusion, is one of the few ancient abodes of our old English aristocracy, that has stood through all the storms and changes of time, and ever remained habitable. Situated within the beautiful county of Herefordshire, it contains within its spacious enclosure—an area of eight miles—almost every specimen of the exquisite scenery of that far-famed shire. The broad sheet of water, nearly a mile in length, reflects every variety of tree that grows in the overhanging woods, out of which the deer come trooping to drink, and stand wondering at their own shadows as they gaze in the silver mirror. A river also murmurs through the wide domain, and gives a voice to the landscape, as it frets and flows over its rocky bed, or along the slopes of greensward, which are here and there bordered with wild flowers. In the woods, the brooding voice of the ringdove is heard; and there all the birds sing, that make up the great band of summer, like "little angels in the trees," while the rooks are ever "cawing" amid the old "ancestral elms." Nor are these the only sounds that break through the surrounding silence; for sometimes after heavy rain, the swollen waters, churned into white foam, come tumbling headlong, with thunderous voice, over a mass of rock, and the restless cascade "shakes its loosened silver in the sun," as it rolls down the jagged height, until lost amid the angry torrent at its base. But in sweet summer-time—

> It seems like Eden's angel-peopled vale,
> So bright the skies, so soft the river's flow;
> Such music floats upon the scented gale;
> The very air seems sleepily to blow,
> And choicest flowers enamel every dale.

Hampton Court, which was the seat of George Capel Coningsby, Earl of Essex, until disposed of to Richard Arkwright, Esq., in 1809, was built under the auspices of Henry IV., by his favourite, Sir Rowland Lenthall, who was Yeoman of the Robes to his Royal Master. "He being a gallant fellow," says quaint old Leland, "either a daughter, or very near kinswoman of the king's fell in love with him, and in continuance was wedded unto him; whereupon after he fell into estimation, and had given to him one thousand pounds by the year, for the maintenance of him and his wife, and their heirs; among which lands he held Ludlow, for one part. He was victorious at the battle of Agincourt, and took many prisoners there, by which prey he began the new building of Hampton Court, and brought from a hill a spring of water, and made a little pool within the top of his house." It is asserted that the lady Sir Rowland married was a co-heiress of Richard Fitz-Alan's, Earl of Arundel; but how the estate descended is not clearly made out, though Camden says, "it was for some time possessed by the Coningsbys, a famous family in these parts," and that they purchased it of the Cornwalls, Barons of Burford. Frances, the daughter of Thomas Earl Coningsby, married Sir Charles Hanbury Williams, Knight of the Bath; their daughter Charlotte married William Holles Capel, fourth Earl of Essex, whose son George, the fifth earl of this family, sold it to the Arkwrights.

The mansion stands on a magnificent lawn of nearly a hundred acres, which comes sloping down to the water's edge, like a carpet of green velvet, and which, when the sun shines on its watery border, looks as if edged with silver. It is a princely structure, half castellated and half monastic, and, like many similar buildings of the middle ages, calls up the battlemented fortress and grey abbey, as if it had rung back the sound of the warden's trumpet, and echoed to the chanting of matin and vesper. The buildings surround a quadrangular court, over the north entrance of which frowns a majestic square tower, deeply embattled, and with space enough on the summit for two or three score archers to ply their cross-bows, and shoot their bolts from behind the embrasures, as they have no doubt done many a time since it was first reared. There are also two smaller towers at the opposite extremities, the eastern one of which joins the chapel. Portions of this splendid old building are sadly defaced by the barbarous alterations that were first began in the reign of William of Orange, and carried on through many years; and though a great deal has since been done to alter the portions that were defaced and destroyed, it can never be wholly restored to what it once was. Still, while ever it stands, it will wear the majesty of antiquity; that can never be destroyed, until its massy walls are levelled to the earth.

Some years ago it contained a portion of the ancient furniture which had stood within its walls for two or three centuries, some portions of it probably longer. In one of the rooms stood the state bed, with its tall canopy and rich hangings of damask crimson, just as it stood when William the Third slept on it, when he was the guest of the noble Coningsby, who distinguished himself by his valour at the battle of the Boyne, and stanched the blood with his own handkerchief when the warrior king was wounded in that engagement. This relic is still preserved in an ebony casket, on the lid of which are miniatures of the Monarch and Lord Coningsby, copied from their large portraits by the Lady Essex. There are several valuable paintings in Hampton Court, and amongst them pictures by Jansen, Holbein, Vandyke, Lely, Kneller, Reynolds, and others. Amongst these is a very ancient portrait, which has been engraved by Vertue, and which Walpole has pronounced an "undoubted original" of Henry the Fourth. A medallion, suspended by a chain, hangs from the neck, and on it are the arms of the Fitz-

Alans, earls of Arundel. This picture bears the following inscription:—" Henry the Fourth, king of England, who laid the first stone of this house, and left this picture in it, when he gave it to Lenthall, who sold it to Cornwall of Burford, who sold it to the ancestors of the Lord Coningsby, in the reign of Henry the Sixth." Seldom has the history of a portrait been handed down through four or five centuries so free from doubt; and there is every reason to believe it has never been removed from Hampton Court, since King Henry the Fourth first presented it to his yeoman of the robes.

The chapel, with its quaintly carved timber roof, appears to have undergone but little change, excepting what the corroding finger of time has made. It is ornamented in the pointed style peculiar to the period of its erection, and contains several very whimsical figures similar to what may be found in many of our early churches, and the origin or meaning of which has long puzzled both our architects and antiquarians. Several of the windows are filled with painted glass, and which, like those in Henry the Seventh's Chapel at Westminster, are honeycombed through age and the action of the atmosphere. Among the devices represented are the arms of Lenthall. As for the gardens and shrubberies, they abound—

> In many a quaintly shapen bed,
> And many a mazy path that leads
> To alcove, grotto, bower, and hall,
> Through winding paths of evergreen;
> Holly and laurel, dark and tall,
> Where many a crystal fountain's falling,
> And many a hidden bird is calling,
> To waving trees, and flowing streams:
> It seems a living land of dreams.

CARLISLE.

NATURALLY associated in one's mind with wild and stirring tales of border warfare, is the name of Carlisle—" Merry Carlisle," as the poets and romancists term it, but, in sooth, sad Carlisle, as the more sober historian, and especially the philanthropist, would be inclined to call that ancient place which has witnessed so many bloody encounters, and changed masters so often, in the bygone days of lawless violence and strong-handed oppression. As of old, " the sun shines bright on Carlisle's walls," but, thank God! not as of old does it shine upon helm and haubert, and the broad claymore—now gleaming aloft in unsullied brightness, now dimmed with the purple stain of a fellow-creature's blood. Not as of old, when that sun has tinged with its setting beams the broad bosom of the Solway Firth, do the watchers upon its garrison walls look forth apprehensively, expecting to see the lurid glare of the bale-fire flashing from hill to hill amid the gathering darkness, and to hear "the slogan's deadly yell," and the shrill pibroch of Donald Dhu, or some other kilted chieftain, sending upon the night-gale its knell for the fierce onset. Disturbed no more by raid and foray, by national animosities or civil wars, Carlisle may sit peacefully by the confluence of her three rivers, and, like an aged warrior, show her scars, and tell her strange and terrible stories of violence and vicissitudes. Here may she, in her own rugged dialect, the patois of swart miners and wild shepherds of the moorland, tell how once the woad-stained Britons paddled their coracles upon her gentle stream; how the fair-haired Saxon came and dwelt upon her hills, which were afterwards fortified by the mailed

cohorts of Agricola. How Antoninus, in his Itinerary, called her name *Luguvallum*,* which the Saxons corrupted into *Luel*, with the British prefix *Caer*, a city, thus making it *Caerluel*,† as her own children pronounce it to this day. And she will tell, too, or we may tell for her, how, about the end of the ninth century, the Danes ravaged her borders, and destroyed all that was beautiful and stately about her; and how she lay prostrate amid her desolation until the hand of a Norman, William Rufus, raised her up once more, built her strong castle, and girt her about with thick walls and stately towers. Once before she had been laid waste by northern invaders, and rebuilt by Egfrid, king of Northumberland; and, many times after, it was her lot to suffer great reverses and disasters, of which the record is preserved in history. Occupying a strong position, close upon the borders of Scotland, down to the time of the union between the two countries she was constantly subjected to attacks from the North; was often taken and retaken, and, of course, suffered much damage in the various sieges which she underwent. She has at times, too, been the abode of royalty, the scene of princely festivity, and of grave and solemn gatherings for national legislation. Here Edward I. occasionally abode, and here, in 1306-7, held a parliament. Here the unfortunate Mary Stuart stopped, in her flight after the battle of Langside, previous to her imprisonment and death in England. In the last civil war with which our country was afflicted, the inhabitants of this place declared for King Charles, and were subjected to a close and protracted siege, which brought them to the verge of starvation. Charles Stuart, commonly called the Pretender, made this place, for a short space, his head-quarters, and brought upon it a severe chastisement from the Duke of Cumberland, who, when he had taken it, put many of the principal citizens to death.

---

* Some difference occurs in the spelling of these names by various authorities; we have followed the "Penny Cyclopedia."

† Some authorities derive this name from Luil, a British king, who, say they, founded the city before the invasion of the Romans. According to them it is *Cuer-luil*—Luil's-town.

But let us leave these historical reminiscences, and turn our attention to Turner's view of the old border city. The artist's position seems to have been on the right bank of the river Eden, which flows past the city in a north-westerly direction, taking its rise in Westmoreland, and running into the head of the Solway Firth. The bridge, which forms the great foreground object of the view, is now replaced by a handsomer structure of white freestone, with five elliptical arches; it was built in 1812, at an expense of £70,000. Just beyond the bridge we see the fine old castle, in which the last half century has made but little alteration. It stands on an eminence overlooking the river, which, in its winding course, flows between it and the city. This castle is of an irregular form, with a gatehouse, and three towers or turrets, and is still maintained as a garrison fortress. Once it was considered the western key of the Scottish border, as Berwick Castle was the eastern; and what a host of memoirs and associations linger around its walls, to render it interesting to the poet, and the historian who follows the chain of events which lead him back, link by link, to the days of the red-headed, strong-handed Norman monarch; and, further still, to those of the Northumbrian king, Egfrid; ay, and further yet, to those of the all-conquering Roman, whose lines of circumvallation, it is probable, invested the very hill on which the present castle stands; and this, it may be, was the exact spot which Antoninus calls *Luguballium*, or *Luguvallum*, signifying the fortress by the wall, on account, as some authorities say, of its contiguity to the wall of Severus.

Turning again to the picture, we see, crowning the opposite hill, the ancient cathedral, built of red freestone, and displaying specimens of various styles of architecture—some, it is said, as early as the Saxon. Turner's pencil has depicted it pretty much as it now stands, no material alteration having taken place to effect a change in the general outline. This is one of the plainest of the English cathedrals; the original cloister, chapter-house, and a great part of the nave, are entirely gone, together with the west front, usually the most highly ornamented part of these ecclesiastical buildings. The tower is very low, and has no pretensions whatever to architectural beauty. At the north-east angle of it is a turret, like a pepper-box, with a vane on the top. It has a choir, however, exceedingly rich in sculptured tracery and other ornamental work. The window at the eastern end of this is considered by some to be the very finest in England; so that, like many other things with a plain exterior, Carlisle cathedral has something worthy of admiration and regard within; and, like the castle, it, too, has many interesting historical associations, on which, however, we must not dwell. In it are interred the remains of Dr. Paley, who was archdeacon here, and wrote several of his chief works while residing in the city.

In Turner's view, only one of the rivers which invest Carlisle is seen; this, as we said before, is the Eden, famous for salmon. The other two are the Caldew, or the Calder, and the Pettrel, or Petreil, both mere streams ordinarily; but in high floods, in the winter season, they frequently overflow their banks and the adjacent low lands. On such occasions, the city appears like an island arising from the midst of a vast lake, whose waters go foaming and whirling along on every side, as though they would ingulf the whole of the buildings which they enclose.

Let not our readers imagine that old Carlisle has been so engrossed by dreams and recollections of the past, that she has made no efforts to keep pace with the progressive movements of the age. Every year she has become more and more of a manufacturing city; she has thrown down her three gates as useless incumbrances, has levelled her ancient walls, and keeps stretching further and further out into the fair meadows amid which she is seated. She has built her up tall chimneys, which send forth volumes of smoke and steam into the clear sky, and huge factories with many windows. Her new streets are wide, clean, and comfortable; and walking in these, out of sight of the two ancient relics of her bygone glory and grandeur, we may fancy ourselves in a quite modern manufacturing town. Much of this commercial activity has manifested itself within the last half century, and could Turner now revisit the spot, he would see many changes, on which, as an artist, he would not look with pleasure. It only remains to add, that the principal manufactures of Carlisle are woollen and cotton goods and ginghams, together with two extensive biscuit works. The ancient lady has also turned her attention to the making of such trifles as whips, hats, and fish-hooks—better commodities, certainly, than feuds and forays. They are small things, but they help to build up, and to render stable, the great structure called "National Prosperity." All honour, then, to Carlisle! May her coasting trade increase, and her inland commerce flourish exceedingly; and the next time she sits for her portrait, may it be to as great an artist as Turner!

GREAT MARLOW.

Great Marlow, with its river, its little islands, and wooded scenery, is one of those dreamy old towns, in which a peace-loving and retiring man would delight to spend his days—

"The world forgetting, by the world forgot."

Not in sour misanthropy—for no man can be a lover of nature and a misanthropist—but in that sweet seclusion, which good old Izaak Walton loved, and wrote so charmingly about in his never-wearying 'Angler.' You look at its comfortable inns and peaceful fishing stations—at the meadows which lie around—and think of him, and the rooms which smelt of lavender, of his poetical dish—fish fried in cowslips—his draught of red cow's milk, and Maud the milkmaid's song, and, above all, of the flowers, which were too beautiful to look upon, "excepting on Sundays or holidays;" and while you dream of these things, you love the old man, and the old world in which he lived, and you look upon Great Marlow as a little Eden, and feel as if you could never live amid "the fever and the fret" of busy London again. You stand upon its banks, and hearken to

"The distant bells with silver chime,
Come floating o'er the peaceful shore."

And while you listen, fancy that

"Though you have heard them many a time,
They never rang so sweet before."

It looks like a place purposely made to whisper a tale of love into a fair lady's ear—a spot to lose your heart in, and feel thankful for the loss. In which you would walk and talk with a bashful maiden leaning on your arm, and, thinking of mellifluous Suckling, look through the modest twilight into the depth of her eyes, and exclaim—

> " I prithee give me back my heart,
> Since I can not have thine;
> For since from yours you will not part,
> Oh! why should I from mine?
> Yet now I think on't, let it lie,
> To have it back were vain;
> For thou'st a thief in either eye,
> Would steal it back again."

Or, if you are not in love, but only in the meditative mood, and fond of brooding over the past, there it is mapped out before you, from the very dawning of history. You have only to recall its name, and picture the watering Mere that once covered the spot on which it now stands, when, according to the ancient Welsh Triads, England was only known as the Island of Sea Cliffs; and saving Prydian, or Brydian—after whom it was called—there was no man alive upon it when he and his followers came over the hazy ocean; "nothing but bears, wolves, and the oxen with the high prominence." Or upward, along the current of Time, that flows onward to the present day, and on which floats the memory of old events, the mind may picture Saxon Algar—like the immortal Cedric of Rotherwood, in 'Ivanhoe'—located in his ancient grange, when the commissioners came from the Norman Conqueror, with their horn-tablets in their hands, to make the dreaded entries for Domesday Book, and to demand a return of the fish he yearly caught in the river, the hogs he fed in the forest, what his estate was valued at in the days of Edward the Confessor, and how many hides of land he held. And we can picture the Saxon thane in his low-browed doorway, the battle-axe behind him, which he had taken from the smoky rafter, and the angry look, as he hesitated for a moment whether to make a return, or, like his forefathers, strike a blow at the invaders of his peaceful home. It may be that some blue-eyed Edith, with her golden hair floating about her fair shoulders, stood behind him ready to grasp his brown muscular arm, and prevent him from shedding blood on his own threshold. Perchance a pet doe, with her little fawn, stood by looking in wonder on the armed invaders, and waiting to frisk and play with golden-haired and blue-eyed Edith.

But the country around, in former times, must have been well wooded, as it is recorded in Domesday Book to have supplied mast* for a thousand swine—a large number compared with the returns made of other places by the commissioners of William the Bastard, as he frequently signed himself. Excepting changing proprietors, it seems to have had but little share in the stirring events that shook England at a remote period. This earl hawked, and that baron hunted in the surrounding forest, until the one fell in battle, and the other died under the ancient roof-tree; then came his successor, and he, perhaps, was beheaded; and so the cycle of years went round, and many of their names are now but unmeaning sounds. They loved the tramp of the war-horse and the battle-cry a thousand times better than the domestic hearth. They had no household ties, no home affections, but sat yawning over the wood-fire in the hall, and dreaming of the chase or the combat; longing to hear the death-mott,† or the war-note, better than the tender voice of woman, or the babbling of childish tongues. The manor was in turn held by various barons, whose names figure in the pages of history; but their ambitious schemes and dangerous conspiracies had not much effect on Marlow beyond a change of owners. Their heads were graced with a coronet, or rolled from the scaffold, but the old town stood unchanged. The swineherd blew his horn, and drove his charge among the beeches, where the bucks bellowed, and Marlow stood

---

* Acorns, beechnuts, chestnuts, or whatever the forest afforded.
† Notes blown on the horn at the death of the stag.

reflected in the waters of the undated Mere, as if dreaming of the times of Saxon Algar.

Marlow, at the Conquest, was taken from Algar the Saxon, by William the Norman, and given to his queen, Matilda, from whom it came to the Clares, De Spencers, Beauchamps, and Neville the king-maker, and so down to the Pagets and Claytons of Marlow Cottage. It has returned two members to Parliament from a very early period; and, since the passing of the Reform Bill, includes within its franchise Little Marlow, Medmenham, and Bisham. Its principal trade is in corn, malt, and timber, the manufacturing of paper, rope, black silk lace, and other descriptions of lace which Buckinghamshire is famous for producing, also the Temple copper-works, together with a busy little market every Saturday, which is well attended. Up to 1812, it occasionally wore something of a martial look, as gallant soldiers, "famed for deeds of arms," were ever riding to and fro to visit the youths who were then educated at the Military College, and which, since the above date, has been removed to Sandhurst. In 1835, the present beautiful suspension bridge was built—it has a span of 225 feet, and is a great ornament to the river; yet, with the exception of the bridge, the features of the place have undergone but little change since Girtin made the accompanying beautiful drawing.

Great Marlow is described in the 'Beauties of Engand and Wales,' as consisting of two principal streets, and three smaller ones; the High Street spacious, with a gradual descent, and containing several good houses. The Market-house is comparatively a new building. The church, dedicated to All Saints, is large and ancient, "consisting of a body and two aisles, with a transept dividing it from the chancel;" the wooden spire was built in 1627; the oaken altar is handsomely carved. The "monumental inscriptions," says the author of the article in the above work, "are not deserving of particular notice," which is rather surprising, considering the antiquity of the church.

Of the old bridge but little appears to be known, beyond that the tolls taken were to be expended in repairs, and that a portion of it was destroyed in the civil wars, in 1642, by General Brown.

" Some faint traces," says the same authority, " of a corporation are discoverable in the records concerning the town, but it does not appear that any charter for its government was ever obtained. The last mention of the mayor and burgesses occurs about the conclusion of the fourteenth century;" and, no doubt, prior to that period, the mace and mayor, and the portly burgesses, went in procession, on All Saints day, to the old church, then returned to feast on the brown haunch which had once bounded through the neighbouring forest.

The almshouses were founded in 1608 for poor widows, six of whom still divide amongst them forty-two pounds per annum. There are also free schools for boys and girls, the former of whom have forty shillings when they are apprenticed, and the latter of whom were taught to knit, spin, and make lace, until Nottingham, with its bobbin-nets and improved machinery, reduced lace-making by hand to " a sorry trade," and the trustees " allege that the estates are inadequate to allow of its now being taught."

WOOLWICH.

Between the Woolwich of to-day and the Woolwich of sixty years since, the difference is so great, that one is puzzled to discover the point of view from which Girtin drew his picture. We have traversed the ground in all directions, and even taken counsel of that infallible authority, "the oldest inhabitant;" but after all our trouble, are obliged to confess that the question is one on which we are unable to come to any decision. But what matters? the picture is, no doubt, a faithful transcript of one lovely aspect of nature, as it presented itself to our artist's delighted vision; and the blame is not his, if it is now altered and defaced by the handiworks of man. These old pictures, how we should treasure them! rapidly as the face of our "tight little island" is becoming changed, built upon, and bored through, and cut up in all sorts of ways; we shall very soon be glad to refer to them as the only remembrancers of the sweet rural aspect of things in the times gone by—of the woods and green fields, the leafy groves and purling streams, and all the beauties and delights of country scenery. Fawns and dryades have long since left the woods, and full soon the birds must leave them too, for they are fast becoming, like St. John's Wood, all streets, and squares, and stacks of chimneys; the fields are turning into brickfields, the gardens into market gardens, where the only flowers are cauliflowers; the green hedgerows, alas! are fast disappearing, and all the old picturesque divisions of the landscape are being swept away. They are sticking up invisible fences, that one breaks one's shins against; and laying down iron rails, that one dares not cross, lest one

should be trampled to atoms by the iron horse, that goes through the land breathing out fire and smoke like a dragon. No sylvan nooks and corners, where one may sink to sleep, lulled by

"The shivery leaf-sounds of the solitude."

No bosky dells, home of the freckled foxglove; no mossy "bank, whereon the wild thyme blows;" only banks of deposit, with which poets, and such like poor people, have nothing to do. No commons for cows, and geese, and donkeys; but very "short commons" for all common sort of folk. No spots for poesy and imagination to rest upon, and plume their wings for far-stretching flights into dream-land. But we are forgetting Girtin and Woolwich, while listening to this Jeremiad of the "oldest inhabitant," for it was he, gentle reader, and not ourselves, who was speaking. To us all these changes are signs of progress and prosperity; and dearly as we love a bit of rural scenery, yet do we love our fellow-creatures more; and knowing that the over-increasing millions cannot live upon song and sunshine, we rejoice to see all these means and appliances for their sustenance and comfort brought into operation, although they do disfigure the face of nature, and defile her green garb with smoke and the stain of burnt bricks. But let us, as we said before, treasure these old pictures; they are to us, and they will be still more to those who come after us, like the faces of friends dead and gone, speaking of the past, and carrying the thoughts back from things as they are, to things as they were. Look now upon the one before us, with this glorious old tree giving shade and shelter to the wayfarer. We stood awhile beneath just such a one, and, without any stretch of Eastern hyperbole, wished that its "shadow might never be less." Look at this *beau ideal* of a country road, with its Arcadian cart, and quaintly-dressed rustics, and sand-banks, and bushes tumbling about in all directions, and encroaching where they like, without the slightest fear of billhook or spade. Look at that undulating expanse, beyond the straggling hedgerow; no straight lines there, all curves—true lines of beauty! Think of the blackberries on all those hedges, and the hazel-nuts in the copses, and ask yourself if this is not truly English—the England of sixty years since! Cannot you fancy you hear the chime of bells from the church tower up there, mingling with the songs of the skylarks above, and the soft *coo-coo* of the doves in the woods behind, from which this foreground tree stands out like a sentinel, probably the advanced guard of some thick wood. But what about Woolwich? Of Woolwich, gentle reader, as it is now, we see little, and might almost doubt if that in the picture is Woolwich Church, which is a plain brick erection, with stone facings, bearing date about 1726, and dedicated to St. Mary—a comfortable well-fitted structure inside, but neither imposing nor picturesque externally, and having stuck on to it a vestry, with a tall chimney very like a wash-house. There are, besides, chapels out of number for all denominations of Christians, and two other district churches in Woolwich; but as these have been built since the view was taken, the church in the picture cannot be either of them. Standing on the spot whence the relative positions of the tower with regard to the rest of the building, would lead us to suppose Girtin might have taken his view, we see—what, of course, the artist could not—the intervening space in great part covered with buildings; but we see not several prominent objects which appear in the picture, and which we are assured by the "old inhabitant" aforesaid, never did exist in Woolwich, as far as his memory carries him back. The question then arises, may it not be Charlton church that Girtin has taken for Woolwich? The two are but a mile or so apart, and the places themselves are so closely connected, that an artist, not well acquainted with the locality, might easily fall into such an error. Both churches have square towers, and the body of each, somewhat foreshortened as in the picture, would look very similar. There is nothing like the old range of buildings to the right now existing in either Woolwich or Charlton, nor can any such be remembered. They may be part of the Dockyard buildings, which came up very close to the sacred edifice at one time. Beyond we see the river Thames, and this would seem to strengthen such a supposition. There is no object in the present aspect of Woolwich, from the direction whence Girtin must have looked, at all corresponding with the large house on the hill to the right of the picture; but if we go to Charlton, there is Charlton House, the seat of Sir Thomas Maryon Wilson, Bart., a fine old Elizabethan mansion, occupying an elevated site, and about the same relative position with regard to the church. After all, however, we must leave the question as we took it up. Our readers had better visit this interesting locality, and decide for themselves. Were we to attempt to describe all the changes which have taken place here since the date of Girtin's picture, we should find it necessary to give nearly the whole contents of the modern 'Guide to Woolwich and its Environs,' which may be had, in a very cheap and compact form, of any bookseller in the place.

Hulviz, or the dwelling on the creek, as Woolwich is called in Doomsday Book, has indeed outgrown its once limited dimensions; a few fishermen's huts, in a wide waste of marsh and woodland, was the nucleus around which its present population of about thirty thousand souls has gradually gathered. But we need not look so far back into the dim past, for proofs of its rapid rise into a town of first-rate importance. We see by this picture that, in little more than half a century, it has so thickened and extended itself, that it can scarcely be recognized as the place whose then familiar features Girtin transferred to his canvas. People of the present generation look at the picture, and shake their heads: "This can't be Woolwich," they say; "where are all the streets, the houses, the churches, the chapels, the barracks, and one knows not what? This can't be Woolwich!" Oh! but it is, we reply, Woolwich as it was sixty years since, when the Dockyard, of which mention is made as early as the time of Henry VII., was not above half its present size; and the arsenal, now covering about 250 acres, was a *warren*, with just a single iron foundry, gun-wharf, and powder-magazine, occupying but a small portion of it; when the Military Academy was a poor mean

o

building, very different from the present spacious and handsome structure; when the Artillery Barracks were not, nor the Marine Barracks, nor the Ordnance Hospital, nor the Sappers and Miners Barracks, nor the Repository with its store of warlike curiosities, nor ——. But our catalogue of things that were not then, and are now, might be extended *ad infinitum;* so we had better stop and close our paper with an observation or two upon a few generalities of the neighbourhood.

Girtin had no railroad, with its Deptford, Lewisham, Blackheath, Charlton, Dockyard and Arsenal stations, to whisk him down in a jiffy, and deposit him wherever he pleased, all fresh and vigorous for his work; not that a walk on a bright breezy day, over Blackheath, or through Greenwich Park, or across Woolwich Common, is a thing to be despised. Many are the delicious bits of land and river scenery, which now, as they did sixty years ago, present themselves to fascinate the eye of an artist, and to arrest his steps. And what locality is there so thickly strown with historic memoirs and associations as this? Blackheath and Shooter's Hill; Greenwich, with its Park and Palace; the old Palace at Eltham; and half a hundred other spots, which we have but to name, and straight there rise before us Bluff Hall and Queen Bess, Jack Cade and Wat Tyler, and a whole host of the chief *dramatis personæ* in the drama of English history. We remember, that not far off lies the little village of Swanscombe, or Swane's Camp, which the Danes, under their victorious leader Swane, made the centre of their plundering operations; and where, at a later period, the great Norman Conqueror, when he had subdued the rest of the kingdom, was met by the stalwart men of Kent, who presented such a bold front that he deemed it prudent to accede to their demands, for the maintenance of their ancient laws and privileges of gavel-kind, or give-all-kin, and the like. Some historians treat this account as a mere silly legend; but we have it on the authority of Lambarde and others, that the yeomonry, or common people of this county, had ever a certain pre-eminence in right of their manhood; " and it is agreed by all men," saith the old perambulator, "that there were never any bondmen or villaines (as the law calleth them) in Kent." In memory of their manful bearing towards the Norman king, the term Men of Kent has been applied to those dwelling above the river Medway, while those below are called Kentish men. Perhaps we may not inappropriately conclude this paper with a few stanzas from

A SONG FOR KENT.

Pleasant are the hills of Surrey,
   Pleasant are her gliding streams;
Sussex hath historic memories,
   Glorious as sunset gleams;
But to thee, my native county,
   Fondly, gladly do I turn,
And with breathing thoughts would crown thee,
   Uttered in the words that burn.

Proudly dost thou stand, my county,
   Beating back the foaming brine,
Rise thy chalky cliffs like ramparts,
   Strength and beauty both are thine;
Stately oaks are in thy woodlands,
   Bright flowers spring their roots among,
And thy maids as these are lovely,
   And thy men as those are strong.

Oh! thy soil is very fruitful,
   Thick thy valleys stand with corn,
Orchards rich, and cultured gardens,
   All thy length and breadth adorn;
Herds are in thy grassy meadows,
   On thy hills the white flocks feed;
Thou dost give of food abundance,
   To supply man's every need.

Thou hast old ancestral mansions,
   Girt with trees of mighty bole,
Thou hast parks where deer are trooping,
   Streams where glide the finny shoal;
Thou hast many a stately ruin,
   Rich with relics of the past,
Many an ivied tower and steeple,
   Where the grey owl sitteth fast.

Thou hast harbours safe, and roadsteads,
  Wherein fleets may safely ride,
And a river broad which floweth
  Inland far with briny tide;
And cathedral fanes majestic,
  Monuments of human skill,
And dismantled piles monastic,
  Where the beating heart grows still.

Thou hast monuments Druidic,
  Huge grey piles that mock at time,
Records of the Dane and Saxon,
  Theme of many a Runic rhyme;
Norman William's keeps are frowning
  Grimly on thy sons of toil,
And the tread of Roman legions,
  Is imprinted on thy soil.

Thou hast worn the yoke, yet conquered
  Even those who conquered thee,
With thy sturdy, stern endurance,
  And the will that *would* be free:
Roman, Saxon, Dane, and Norman,
  Singly with the past are blent,
And their better parts compounded,
  We behold in " men of Kent."

'Twas of Christ and His salvation
  First to thee the tidings came,
On thy hills the cross was lifted,
  To the land a beacon flame—
Warning, guiding unto safety,
  Teaching sinners where to fly,
Better this than deeds of prowess,
  Kent, thy name to glorify!

County of the old INVICTA,
  " Civilest place in all the isle,"
Home of learning and of genius,
  " Land of Cantii " called erewhile:
Bards and sages out of number,
  Have thy praises said and sung,
Till in earth's remotest corners,
  Thy great name hath loudly rung.

WINDSOR.

What space the forests and parks may have occupied in former times, which the royal towers of Windsor overlooked, and which were included in the length and breadth of its princely domains, it is impossible at this remote period to ascertain; though it is recorded that the circumference of Windsor forest once exceeded an hundred and twenty miles. It extended into Buckinghamshire, included Chobham and Chertsey, in Surrey, and ran along the side of the Wey, up to Guildford. Even so near our own time as the reign of James I.—without including the liberties of Buckinghamshire—it had a circuit of seventy-seven miles, and was divided into fifteen walks, each of which was under the care of several keepers, whose duty it was to guard the vert and venison.

Early in the reign of George III. and a little before the appended view of Windsor was taken, the Great Park, which was then surveyed, contained 3800 acres, two hundred of which were covered with water, some hundreds overrun with fern and rushes, and abounding in dangerous bogs and impassable swamps, over which three thousand head of neglected and half-starved deer then ranged. The alterations that have been made since that period are marvellous; for Windsor Park, at the present time, is one of the most beautiful sylvan scenes in England.

The principal alterations in the castle, since Girtin's drawing was made, are the George IV. or Wyatville tower, so sometimes named after the architect, and the state dining-room, altered by George III., and which completely changed the features of the old north front. Sir Jeffrey Wyatville's alterations alone, would fill the present volume were they fully described; they are seen in the ground terrace, nearly a thousand feet in length; in the Brunswick and Cornwall towers; the rich oriel window of the state drawing-room; the buildings of Henry VII. and Elizabeth; the Norman tower, with the range of walls that run up to the Winchester tower; and it will also be seen that in Girtin's time the northern slopes were not planted. But the greatest achievement was raising the round tower, or keep, sixty feet, and then erecting a watch tower on this immense elevation, the summit of which comprehends a prospect of twelve counties; while it rises a proud landmark above the scene, commanding a view of numberless miles of the most beautiful rural landscape scenery in England. We have not space to enumerate the further additions and alterations made by Wyatville; they may be seen in the Prince of Wales's tower, the Chester, Clarence, and Victoria towers, all of which he raised and enriched by stately windows. See also the winter garden—its orangery, fountain, steps, terrace; then turn to the south—to the Victoria tower, with its battlements and oriel windows, at the eastern corner; the glorious gate bearing the name of George IV., and opening into the long walk, which was laid out in the time of Charles II.; and then you will confess that Sir Jeffrey worked wonders. Most of these alterations are visible in 'Evans' View of Windsor,' published in 1837.

Glancing at the ancient history of Windsor Castle, and passing by Arthur, his Round Table, Merlin, &c., we find that the place took its name from its winding shore, round which the waters still flow. William the Conqueror obtained it, in exchange for other places, from the Abbot of Westminster, as it was surrounded with wood, and abounded in game; though what he built at Windsor was probably nothing more than a hunting lodge. Here his son Rufus—who was shot in the New Forest by Tyrrel—also followed the chase. Henry I. erected some kind of royal residence on the present site, though all that remains is supposed to be the basement of the round tower. Henry II. added a vineyard to the castle-gardens, and made a few alterations. King John resided here when his bold barons compelled him to sign Magna Charta, in the neighbouring meadow of Runnymede. Henry III. spent much money, and made many improvements, and to him we are indebted for the Curfew, the Garter, and the Salisbury towers, the walls of some of which are thirteen feet in thickness. Henry had some trouble to hold Windsor against his stormy barons, and many sieges, and many fights took place at the foot of those green slopes, of which we have no record. In the reign of Edward I., Windsor began to grow into importance, and was made a free borough. Edward III. was born in Windsor Castle, and was called Edward of Windsor. He established the Order of the Garter, which had its origin in a slight accident at a dance, when the Countess of Salisbury's garter, which was of blue velvet, slipped off, and was picked up by her royal partner. He held many a joust and feast at Windsor Castle on St. George's day. John, King of France, who was defeated at the battle of Poictiers, by Edward the Black Prince, was a captive in Windsor Castle. The celebrated William of Wykeham was at this period superintendent of the works of the castle. He built the Winchester tower, to which a few additions were made in the time of George IV. Here the queen of Edward III. died. James I. of Scotland, while a prince, was prisoner at Windsor—his captivity in the round tower, his love for Jane of Beaufort, and his poetry, are things to dream of while wandering in sight of Windsor in a summer sunset. Henry V. kept his court here, and here also Henry VI. was born. But it is to Edward IV. that we are indebted for St. George's Chapel, the tomb of so many of our English kings, though it was not completed during his reign, for the exquisitely groined ceiling was not commenced until far in the reign of Henry VII. Here lie buried Edward IV. and his queen; Henry VI., Henry VIII. and his queen Jane Seymour, the only one of his many wives; Charles I., and many others. Here Wolsey intended to have been buried, and went so far as to commence his own monument, which now covers the remains of the gallant Nelson in St. Paul's Cathedral.

Richard III. held the feast of St. George at Windsor; Henry VII. added to the building; so also did Henry VIII. Here the boy-King Edward VI., who founded Christ's Hospital, resided for a short time, and here his successors Mary and Elizabeth held their court. James I. often hunted in the Great Park. Charles I. resided here, and made a few alterations; then came Cromwell, and sat down in this ancient seat of England's Mighty Kings! Those who followed are, so to speak, a part of the history of our own age. The brazen beauties of Charles II., who lounged on the slopes and lawns, next succeeded; then came William of Orange, with whom Windsor was no favourite haunt; Queen Anne, who planted the Queen's Walk, and laid out a garden on the north side of the Castle; and next good George III. who spent so much in the restoration of St. George's Chapel; and with him and his successors we may close our sketch of Windsor Castle, which brings us down to our Gracious Queen. Long may she enjoy the green shades of her Royal Ancestors!

WAKEFIELD.

Turner—with his fine appreciation of the picturesque—has here given such a view of Wakefield as no other artist has attempted, during the last sixty years, although the number of views of this celebrated place are "plentiful as blackberries." Beside an extensive view of the town, our great painter has seized upon the most beautiful and the most remarkable objects in the locality—such as the ancient bridge, with its far-famed chapel; the old soke mill adjoining it; the churches of All Saints and St. John; with the river Calder filling the foreground, and giving a soft silvery finish to the scene. The whole is also overhung with one of his own inimitable skies, since so world-wide famous, and made purposely to light up every object he wished to render prominent, and to throw into shade what he considered neither picturesque nor poetical—a hint not to be lost, in the limited space allowed us, to glance at these, the all-but-forgotten specimens of the earliest works of this great English master.

Wakefield is a place of great antiquity, and was well known in the time of the Saxons, from one of whom it no doubt took its name, as its earliest proprietor was called Wach or Wak, and the land belonging to him called Wak's field—a very natural and very proper origin, and nothing more likely than that it was so called after its most ancient and original proprietor.

The grant of the privilege of the soke is very ancient. The Old Soke Mill stands at the head of the ancient bridge, and near the beautiful chapel. Roger of Hovenden relates the following legend—though it is no proof that the building is so old as the period of the story he narrates—and the substance of which is that, " In the year 1201, a Norman abbot came over to England, and endeavoured to persuade the people of Yorkshire, that the Sabbath ought to be held from three o'clock on Saturday to sunrise on Monday; and that his authority was a record found on the altar of St. Simon, at Golgotha. But the miller of Wakefield —paying no regard to the Norman abbot—continued to grind his corn at the old mill in the prohibited hours, when," says the historian, " his corn was turned into blood, and his mill-wheel stood immoveable amid the current of the river Calder." The soke has recently been purchased by the town, and in 1854 will cease to exist.

The Chapel of Our Lady, on the bridge, was founded by the inhabitants of Wakefield about 1357, in the reign of Edward III., with a royal endowment of £8. 10s. 3d. annually to William Kaye and William Bull, and their successors for ever, to perform divine service therein. The endowment was further increased after the hard-fought battle of Wakefield, in 1460, to £14. 15s. 3½d.,—no doubt to pay for masses for the souls of those who fell in that memorable battle.

About seven years ago, the chapel was restored at a cost of £3,000, and it is now again open for divine service, after having been used, during the last three centuries, as an exchange, a warehouse, an old clothes' and flax-dresser's shop, a news-room, cheesecake house, dwelling-house, and corn-factor's office. Little did our English kings dream, when they endowed it, of the "vile purposes" it would be brought to. The tower is still standing, on which a light was burnt at night, for the guidance of travellers, both on land and water; and many a prayer would be offered up to Our Lady, by the ancient wayfarers who went from town to Thorpe, in those perilous times, when they set out on their journey or returned, as they looked toward that guiding light, which would throw a trail of rippling gold on the face of the Calder, from the chapel on the bridge. Our engraving represents the east end of this ancient edifice, which is built upon a little island in the river, and in whose waters it stands reflected, as if dreaming of the past, and the many changes that have taken place since it was first mirrored on the calm surface of the Calder. The west front, which faces and is entered from the bridge, is rich in architectural ornaments and scriptural story, of which some notion may be formed from the tracery in the east window, as shown in the present picture. But whom and what the figures in the west front were intended to represent, it is difficult to ascertain.

A description of the chapel, written soon after the accompanying Plate was engraved, may be found in the 'Gentleman's Magazine' for 1806, or seven years after the author visited it. The article is entitled "Pursuits of Architectural Innovation;" and, among other matters, states that the east window at that time (1799) contained much tracery, that the parapet was perforated, and that the windows on the north and south sides of the building were equally rich. He says that "the basso-relievos on the west front" were then "much mutilated," but that he could make out sufficient to discover that the "Nativity, Resurrection, and Ascension" were represented. Other authorities, however, have interpreted the figures differently; but we prefer preserving this description, as it was written about the period when the drawing was made by Turner.

The next prominent object is the tower and spire of All Saints' Church—the tower of which alone is ancient—and, there is but little doubt, forms a part of the original Norman edifice, which remained till the beginning of the reign of Edward the Third, whilst John, Earl of Warren, was tenant of Wakefield for life. The next erection was the building consecrated by William de Melton, Archbishop of York, in 1329, or some quarter of a century before the chapel on the bridge was built. As for the body of the church, both the north and south sides have been rebuilt. The other church shown in the engraving was erected in the thirty-first of George III., and was quite new when the accompanying sketch was made.

SHEFFIELD.

SHEFFIELD is one of those English towns that has become famous by its own industry, and we believe that there are but few of its spirited and independent inhabitants that would care to pluck the finest plume from the wings of antiquity, to add to the celebrity which they and their fathers have given to it. It is stamped with the nobility of labour and enterprise, and its proudest heraldic device is the thews and sinews of hard-working and earnest men, who, like the Corn-law Rhymer, while labouring at the mine, the wheel, and the forge—

"Shaped their own divinity."

So far back as the time of Chaucer, who makes one of his "Canterbury Pilgrims" carry a Sheffield whittle (or knife) in his hose, it was celebrated for its present manufactories. Perhaps there is scarcely a town in England that has made greater progress, since the present sketch was taken by Turner, than Sheffield. Could Robert de Buisle, who held the manor at the Conquest, see it now, he could never be brought to believe that on that very spot he had chased the hart and the hind, and flown his hawk at the herons which then sheltered amid the rushes and sedge beside the Don. Nor need we go back to this remote period to marvel at the wonders which time has worked, but we will compare the Sheffield of the present day with what it was when the accompanying drawing was made by Turner, whose view is taken from Derbyshire Lane, a road that runs under the village of Horton. The valley shown in the engraving is now built upon, the glimpse obtained of the river Porter long since

shut out by houses; and, with the exception of the churches, the whole scene has undergone a mighty change. The moor, rising in the background, was then covered with golden gorse and purple heather, and abounded in grouse; but as the buildings drew nearer to their ancient haunts, they took wing and flew away in search for other solitudes: the hills on which they once nestled are now covered with the villas of the wealthy manufacturers. But, perhaps, the most striking feature of the engraving, is the entire absence of those tall chimneys, which form such prominent landmarks in most of our large manufacturing towns in the present day, since man has called in the power of steam to his aid. To say nothing of the churches and other lofty buildings which have since been erected, the absence of the towering smoke-conductors gives to the engraving that quiet primitive look which it wore in the days of our forefathers. The masses of foliage in the foreground are all but swept away, and the silence of those "green eternal hills" are now broken up by the abodes of man. The hearth smokes, and children prattle on the very spots where, sixty years ago, the wild grouse sheltered its brood beneath its wing. Still the Sheffielders, as if in memory of the old green retreats that hung around the homes of their fathers, keep two or three subscription packs of harriers; and though they have to go further a-field than their fathers, this prevents them not from leaving the "noise and smoke" now and then far behind, and joining in the hunt, with as much glee as ever the same pursuit was followed by their ancestors. No marvel that the good citizens of Sheffield are a race of hunters, while their town is still overlooked by Foxley Wood, which tradition and the old ballads fix upon as the birth-place of that famous killer of the king's deer, Robin Hood, and where his Well is still pointed out. His very name calls up sweet images—

"In summer-time when leaves are green and long."

To the 'Beauties of England and Wales,' we are indebted for the following remarks on Sheffield:—

"There are few situations better adapted to the manufacturing system here established than that of Sheffield. Coal mines abound in the neighbourhood; and the rivers Don and Sheaf, which run close to the town, afford great conveniences to its trade, a great number of works being erected on their banks for the purpose of forging, slitting, and otherwise preparing the iron and steel for the manufactures. The Don being navigable to Tinsley, within three miles of Sheffield, is a great advantage to the commerce of the town, by facilitating its communication with every part of the kingdom.

"The name of Sheffield, or Sheaffield, is evidently derived from the smaller river that runs on its eastern side, and appears to be of Saxon or Danish etymology. But the origin of the town is wholly unknown, and it possesses but little historical celebrity, its importance being comparatively of modern date. Here was, however, in former times, a strong castle, situated at the north-east corner of the town, at the confluence of the two rivers. It was of a triangular form; on the north side it was guarded by the river Don, and on the eastern side by the Sheaf; towards the town it was fortified with a strong breastwork before the gates, which were pallisaded with a trench eighteen feet wide, and twelve feet deep, full of water, and a wall fifteen feet thick.

"This Castle was built in the reign of Henry III., and, with the manor of Sheffield, descended from the family of Lovetofts to the Nevils, Lords Furnival. From them it passed to the Talbots, Earls of Shrewsbury. George, the sixth Earl of Shrewsbury, was appointed by Queen Elizabeth the keeper of that unfortunate princess, Mary, Queen of Scots, who was placed under the care of this nobleman in the year 1568, and resided at the manor-house in the park till 1584. During the civil wars, in the reign of Charles I., Sheffield Castle was garrisoned for the king; and the town had, consequently, some share in the calamities of those unhappy times. On the 1st of August, 1644, the Earl of Manchester sent Major-General Crawford, and Colonel Pickering, with a detachment of 1,200 infantry, and a regiment of cavalry, to attack the Castle. Having summoned the governor, Major Thomas Beaumont, to surrender, and received an insulting answer, the Parliamentarians entered the town, and in the night and the following day erected two batteries within sixty yards of the outworks of the fortress. But the artillery making little impression, and the garrison seeming determined on a vigorous defence, application was made to Lord Fairfax, the Parliament's general, who sent an iron demi-cannon, and a large piece, called the queen's pocket pistol, which being mounted, so heavy a fire was poured on the Castle from the batteries, that, on the 10th of August, the garrison beat a parley, and obtained an honourable capitulation. The Castle was afterwards demolished by order of Parliament; but scarcely any vestiges of it now remain, except that the names of Castle-hill, Castle-ditch, Castle-green, Castle-orchards, &c., are still retained by several places in the vicinity.

" The lordship of Sheffield descended from Henry, Earl of Norwich, Earl Marshal of England, and great-grandson of Gilbert, Earl of Shrewsbury, to the illustrious family of the Howards, Dukes of Norfolk. The greatest part of the town was till lately comprised in the ample estates of that family, and the different portions were usually let on long leases to the inhabitants; but the present Duke has sold the greatest part to individuals, though his Grace is still lord of the manor.

" The history of its manufactures, though comprising comparatively only a short period, exhibits such a display of ingenuity, and such a series of improvements, as render it important, and, in a commercial point of view, highly interesting. From the town seal, and various other circumstances, there is reason to believe that, from the year 1297, this town has had a staple for the iron manufactory, especially for falchion heads, arrow piles, and a sort of knives called whittles. Dr. Gibson, who published his edition of Camden in 1695, says, that Sheffield has been for three hundred years the staple for knives.

" The cutlery trade, in the town and neighbourhood, was prosecuted in the various articles of sheath-knives, scissors, sickles, and scythes; and, about the commencement of the seventeenth century, an ordinary sort of tobacco-boxes began to be made. In 1625, an act was passed for the incorporation of the master manufacturers, by the name of the Company of Cutlers of Hallamshire. In 1638, the people of Sheffield began to make clasp or spring-knives with handles of iron, which they soon afterwards covered with horn, tortoise-shell, and other ornamental materials."

Up to 1750, the Sheffield trade was confined to England chiefly, and the goods carried from town to town on the backs of pack-horses. After that year, the trade was extended to the Continent, and the Don made navigable to within three miles of the town; and then—(how we smile in this age of railroads and steamboats)—a stage-waggon was started for the conveyance of goods and passengers to London; and—greatest stride of all, and which shows a progress for which mighty Manchester may spare a leaf from its free-trade laurels—" several factors, now establishing a correspondence with various parts of the Continent, *engaged foreigners as clerks in their counting-houses.*"

In 1760, Sheffield started its first stage-coach; in 1765, opened its first coffee-room; and, about this period, erected its theatre and assembly rooms. Then came its bank, new market-place, and general infirmary, all stepping-stones in its onward progress, over which it passed to become what it is, one of the most celebrated manufacturing towns in the world, and employing in the making of cutlery above three thousand hands at the present time, without enumerating any of its other branches of business. Numbers of the working-cutlers are men of small capital. Its gas-works, water-works, museum, literary institution, mechanics' institute, news-room, botanical gardens, benevolent institution, bridges, churches, and schools, rank amongst the noblest in England, and show how intellect and charity, wherever they meet, travel in harmony together, hand in hand, in that progress, whose great end and aim is to benefit mankind.

THE MARINE BARRACKS AT STONEHOUSE,
PLYMOUTH.

WE think we may safely assert that few Cockneys exactly understand the meaning of the word "marine"——

Don't stare, good Madam! in such amazement at our impudent assertion, when you know that, being deluded by a Times' advertisement of "a genteel *marine* residence, elegantly furnished, to let," last summer, you took possession of a plaster-and-lath cottage at Ramsgate, where the roof was far from water-proof, and the windows from air-tight; where the doors had an obstinate prepossession against closing, and the paper to remaining on the drawing-room walls; and where, indeed, "things in general were so far from being "passable," that all your infantile Johnnies and Jemimas "caught colds," (running up the doctor's bills, as dear Charles said, "to an extent truly awful;") and when your cousin, John Peabody of the Customs, from whom you had "great expectations," sojourned with you for a week, to such trials and inconveniences was that respectable old bachelor put, that before the expiration of that time he rushed back to "town," and made a will, bequeathing all his "real and personal estate, whatsoever," to the "Flannel-stocking and Shirt-giving Society." Well do you remember how, when you asked those Muffletons (who give *such* "at-homes" when at home, but only go into lodgings at Ramsgate) to dine with you, the culinary apparatus was so defective that cook came to you, with tears in her eyes, immediately before the arrival of the

Q

company, to say, "that she could not by no manner of means serve up for an hour; and as for soup, no sich thing was possible, for the plaster had come down the chimley and spoilt it," leaving you in doubt as to what the pronoun might refer. Well, too, do you remember how, when that horrid Horace Muffleton, who prides himself on being an "Oxford man," and denominates "the gowned students on the banks of reedy Cam," by the flattering appellation of "snobs," (we believe your Augustus, dear Madam, is just entered at Cambridge) endeavoured—stimulated by juices of the fruitful vine—to show his celebrated balance trick, those fragile pieces of manufacture, set together with glue, and by the care and ingenuity of "French artistes," (in consideration of which Mrs. Fleeceem let you have them, "as a favour, at two guineas a-piece,") yclept chairs, broke down beneath him—involving Master Horace, tables, and decanters, in general ruin; while Mrs. Muffleton took occasion to inform you that lodgings were more fashionable, and indeed more expensive, than marine residences.

We think, after perpetrating two such sentences as the foregoing, we surely might be allowed to draw breath; but we must not leave you, sweet Miss Clara, with whom the mention of "marine" is associated with a hazy recollection of bathing-machines, new novels, and flirting on the moonlit sands, to pout that pretty lip so pettishly. We speak of the word as applied to that amphibious class of individuals, familiarly called "Joeys;" but in Admiralty despatches, and "all genteel societies," "marines." What! those men whom you saw when at the great naval review, loitering about the streets of Portsmouth in blue frock-coats; those men with waspish waists, and a-would-be-sort-of-a-gentleman-air? Yes! precisely so, those were marine officers, whom you may remember that "love of a Fitzgun" of the Guards distinguished by the title of "muffs." Nevertheless, as Sir Charles Napier would have said, "the marines have seen some service;" they are no drawing-room soldiers; no moustachoed dandies sickening at a cruise off the Nore, and endeavouring to appear unconscious of the danger, on a perilous two hour-voyage to Calais; and surely those whom Nelson could endiadem with praise, are worthy of something better than the sneers of a Regent Street idler, or even than the slighting appreciation of a ball-room belle.

To enter into a long history of the circumstances which led to the formation of a "marine corps" would, to use the stereotyped phrase, be neither interesting nor expedient; suffice it to say, that if the substantial building, which is represented in the accompanying engraving, be not a sufficient proof of their necessity, the friendship which subsists between them and Jack, the laurels they have won, are "proofs fresh and abundant," of their valour and worth.

The Marine Barracks at Stonehouse were built about eighty years ago, when the increasing wants and numbers of the Plymouth division induced the then Lords of the Admiralty to give up the barracks at Long-room. A site had been chosen at Five-fields, at the northern extremity of Plymouth, but Mr. Bewes, the owner of the land, demanded too exorbitant a price from the Government; when the Earl of Mount Edgecombe, with true foresight and sagacity, offered them the site on which the barracks are now erected on very advantageous terms. By so doing, he created the town of Stonehouse, and thus increased the value of his surrounding land in a proportionate degree; which will be still more valuable when the Great Western Docks, which are at present excavating, are completed. Here, at no far-distant day, "flags of all nations" shall float in the breeze, and extending commerce and prosperity prove the truth of the old aphorism, that he who by prudence and calculation makes two blades of grass grow where but one grew before, is a benefactor to his species.

The barracks are built on a level piece of ground; on the one side of which the excavations are going on for the docks, and on the other lies the township of East Stonehouse. They are of an oblong form, consisting of three ranges of buildings, enclosing a broad and spacious parade-ground. That which stretches from north to south on the dock side, is given up entirely to non-commissioned officers and privates for mess-rooms and sleeping apartments; while the opposite range contains a guard-room, store-rooms, &c. At the north end is a range of officers' dwelling-houses; and at the south (in order, we presume, that the officers may enjoy a clear and uninterrupted view) is — a dead wall! Since Girtin gazed upon it many changes have taken place, both in the original structure and in the surrounding neighbourhood. The quay and landing-place at its rear has been taken away, and many of the adjacent outbuildings have been destroyed. The large peninsular piece of land, which in his sketch lies at its southern extremity, is now occupied by the Victualling-yard for her Majesty's navy; and, emblematic of the world's progress, at the foot of the slope on which he sat with his pencils stands a Mechanics' Institute. Where he beheld a barren bay, dry at low-water, hundreds of "navvies" (a race unknown in his day) are at work, preparing a receptacle for future commerce; where he wandered through green fields, there are now streets, and houses, and shops, adorned with all the conveniences and beauties which men in these days are capable of conceiving. Nature alone remains unchanged. There is the Hamoaze, lying as placidly as ever beneath the sun's bright smile; and there, in the back-ground, are the woods of Mount Edgecombe, still as beautiful, whether Spring decks them with all her blossoms; whether clothed in the rich panoply of burning Summer, or the sad yet gorgeous array of silent Autumn; or whether Winter

"Robes with pure snow, and crowns
Of starry ice, the grey grass and bare boughs."

The Hamoaze is an estuary formed by the junction of the river Tamar with the sea, and is, as it were, a nursery for our ships of war; here they repose in times of peace, in a kind of dignified half-pay respectability. For four miles they stretch away — we beg our nautical friends' pardon — lay away up the estuary; and among them are many whose names are famous in the annals of our wars. Here is a battered veteran of Trafalgar, lying quietly beside a prize taken on the same "glorious day;" here is the hero of Algiers; and here, floating on her own shadow — her ports all closed, her pennant hanging listless in the summer air — is a new and beautiful frigate, a monument of the intellect and skill of the "young generation."

Crotchetty old gents, who still have a great affection for dry arguments and plush small-clothes, may lecture to us on the futility of war and the blessings of peace; but here is a nobler argument against the one, and at the same time a better guarantee for the preservation of the other, than the most brilliant eloquence can supply.

Mount Edgecombe has been called " the Paradise of England," and to many a hard-worn artizan in life's great workshop, who can step aside for awhile from the trials and struggles of the active world to pause amid its sylvan scenes, and feel the breath of heaven " blow full upon his cheek," it is more than this; for by its beauty his " heart of hearts" is touched, and the holier and serener feelings are awakened, which were else in danger of being utterly lost " in the mire of life." Nature does indeed stand between God and man as mediator, purifying and exalting our earthly affections. When will legislators learn that, better than the strictest codes, better than moral homilies, better than sermonising, and educating, and writing essays " On the Prevention of Crime"—better than all these things for instructing their poorer brethren, and leading them up to a knowledge of the Beautiful and True, is an intercourse with all the lovely and holy forms of nature?

Mount Edgecombe, indeed, is a paradise. Well might the French Admiral covet it for his own; but that, thanks to Jack and the Marines, it will never be. Though laid out and adorned with all the taste of art, it is yet allowed to retain the freedom and symmetry of nature. There are no miserable clap-traps, no mountebank shows, to deface its beauty; and if in our wanderings we do stumble upon a temple dedicated to Milton, or startle a nymph at her fountain, we can plunge into the gloom of primeval woods, or stand on jagged precipices, with the sea thundering solemnly for ever at our feet. Many a time, as the eyelid of the morn went quivering up, and the deep blue laughed forth, have we stood upon its slopes, and watched the white-sailed ships, rippling the golden sunlight round their bows. float out into the mist. Many a long summer's day have we lain—

> "Under a roof
> Of cloistering boughs fretted with the blue sky;
> Beneath which an eternal eventide
> Muses the trancèd years away.
> Through these green arches odours faint,
> Mingled with sweet bird-echoes, and hushed sighs
> Of the long spear-grass, ripple all day long.
> Like a swift cataract of falling light,
> The stream shoots down the verdant precipice
> Into the black deep pool, where, like pale stars
> In the deep heavens, broad water-lilies rest;
> And then goes murmuring for evermore
> Through the green twilight to a silent sea."

Many an eve have we lingered in its dells until the mild pale stars,

> "Those asterisks, filling up
> The solemn blanks of God's great mystery,"

came out; and oftentimes, as we have oared our pinnace homeward through the night, have we been ready to say,—

> "Blessings be on the painter and the poet!
>   *   *   *   *   *
> They are God's messengers on earth.
> The unutterable mysteries, which lie
> On Nature's passive face, like weird dreams
> Upon the marble features of a Sphynx,
> They give a voice to, and make eloquent
>   *   *   *   *   *
> The cast-out portions of humanity.
>   *   *   *   *   *
> They bring old scenes before us, and awake
> Hopes, dreams, and tears forgotten."

Blessings be on them both! may Poetry and Painting yet prosper to the exclusion of vice and sin! may the Muses, taking the genius of the coming age by the hand, lead it upward from ignorance and sin to the dawn of Truth's eternal day—onward from misery and death, from worn-out creeds and shattered systems—onward for ever to the perfect life!

RICHMOND.

Richmond, the gem of the North of England, is in every respect deserving of the name. Apart from the charming scenery which has ever been its chief attraction in the eyes of the visitor, it is rich in all the glorious associations of an age of feudal magnificence and Norman grandeur; " the capital of a land, whose riches of romance are scarcely exceeded by any other district in England; the chosen seat of its own Earls, the Scropes, Marmions, and Fitzhughs; and those setters-up and pullers-down of kings, the wealthiest, noblest, and most prudent race of the North, the lordly Nevilles;" boasting of a castle coeval with the Conquest, which opposes an almost unbroken front to the winds which have beaten against it for centuries, and frowns upon the spectator, as it was wont to do when its walls re-echoed the war-cry and the clang of arms; a structure, whose desolate halls are eloquent with stories of the past, and carry us back, in thought, to the time when Britain was in her infancy as a nation.

The beauty of the place is proverbial, and it has worthily employed the pencils of our artists. Situated on the sloping banks of the river, it has an irregularity of outline extremely picturesque; the castle forms the prominent object in the landscape, and will amply repay our close attention. " In every point of view it is a magnificent object, and in ancient times, on its almost perpendicular rock, it must have been considered as next to impregnable; the imposing dimensions of the keep, the freshness of its masonry, the pertinacious dislike to vegetation on its exterior, strike the eye as it gazes on the towering stronghold, and are evidences of an almost indestructible durability. But the hand of Time has shown itself on all around: the ivy clings to the mouldering walls, and clothes them with a beauty which the keep despises."

The year 1071 is said to be the date of the erection of the castle. To confirm his conquest, William gave to the more zealous of his followers the various patrimonies which fell into his hands: thus 164 manors, composing the later Richmondshire, were awarded to Alan Rufus (son of Eudo, duke of Brittany), along with the title of Earl; and he, not satisfied with the existing castle of Gilling, which in point of situation possessed few natural advantages, pitched upon the present site for an erection fitted to hand down his name to posterity.

The outer walls of the castle form the earlier building; the keep has evidently been a later addition. It is attributed to Conan, the fifth earl, who lived a century later, and is built with more regard to durability; the stone has all the sharpness of outline which it possessed when fresh from the mason's chisel. It is stated, that in the inquiry instituted by Government for the purpose of ascertaining the localities where the best stone could be obtained for building the new Houses of Parliament, the keep of Richmond Castle was pronounced to be the best material, but the quarry was worked out. The enormous strength of the place has, perhaps, deterred besiegers, for Richmond plays but little part in recorded warfare; defended on three sides by an abrupt slope overhanging the river, and with its weakest point protected by this magnificent tower, it afforded few hopes of success to a warlike assault.

A terrace has been constructed round the walls, forming a delightful walk midway between the castle and the river. The varied beauties here presented to the eye, in a small compass, are unequalled by any in England — the towering battlements above, the precipitous descent at our feet, the opposite banks clothed with foliage, and throwing a dark shade over the stream, which is now calm and placid, now dashing over the opposing barriers of rock, and at length precipitated over the Force at the turn of the river, is lashed into foam, and rushes onward to the quieter pools below the town.

The castle is now the property of the Duke of Richmond, who derives his title from it.

The Friary Tower, the only relic of a house of the Franciscan Friars which has survived the dissolution, is another graceful subject for the pencil. It has been a central tower, and rises from four elegant arches: a turret staircase at the north-west corner gives a graceful outline to the building when viewed from that side: two windows of the south aisle remain. It is said to have been built by Ralph Fitz-Randal, Lord of Middleham, in 1258, but part of the credit attaches to the Scropes. The house was dissolved in 1538.

The Parish Church, dedicated to St. Mary, is situated near the entrance to the town by the railway bridge; it is built upon the hill-side, and the peculiar character of the place causes the walls to be unusually high, and the east windows to appear awkwardly elevated: repeated pointing with a blue lime, peculiar to the place, gives to the exterior a cold grey aspect. There are many traces of Norman architecture in the interior, particularly in the chancel, and at the west end of the nave. There is a large east window, with some remains of stained glass; but the entire building has a most undevotional aspect, being choked up with galleries and high pews, which modern enlightenment and good taste would do well to remove. The chancel contains some fine carved stall-work, which was brought from the neighbouring abbey of St. Agatha at the dissolution.. The tower is good, and has a fine window at the west and a peal of six bells. It is said to have been built by Ralph Neville, first Earl of Westmorland, and his saltire occurs under the west battlement.

Trinity Church, in the Market-place, has been aptly compared to a fossil set in limestone; it is in reality " a masterpiece of desecration:" the chancel and south aisle have entirely disappeared; the arches of the latter are filled up with windows; the western tower is separated from the nave by a dwelling-house, and another house is built against it. The north aisle is walled-off, and is used as the depository for the wills of the archdeaconry, the basement being occupied with shops.

The whole of the east and south sides are built up with dwelling-houses. There is no authentic account of its origin, and it presents few traces of its original architecture. Leland mentions a "chapel in Richemonte toune with straunge figures on the waulles of it." The present entrance is modern; it was repaired and fitted for public worship in 1744, at the expense of the corporation, who have the appointment of the minister.

The Grammar School, founded by Queen Elizabeth in 1566, from the spoils of some of the smaller charities, is one of those many acts of beneficence which have endeared her memory to Englishmen. The original structure, a plain, unpretending building, is situated at the east corner of the churchyard; a modern building, at the opposite side of the road, is the present school-house. It was erected in 1850, by subscription amongst the pupils of the late master, Canon Tate, as a testimony of respect to his memory. Many a clever man and a wrangler has emerged from this school; and such was its fame during the earlier part of the present century, that Richmond men were dreaded at Cambridge. The pupils of the late Mr. Tate gained more honours at Cambridge than those of any other master.

It were wrong to quit this subject without making mention of Herbert Knowles, the youthful poet who promised so fair, but was cut off at the early age of nineteen, whilst under the tutelage of the late Mr. Tate. It may not be deemed out of place to insert here the lines which were written in Richmond churchyard, as they may not be known to all our readers:—

LINES WRITTEN IN THE CHURCHYARD OF RICHMOND, YORKSHIRE.
October 7, 1816.

"It is good for us to be here: if thou wilt, let us here make three tabernacles; one for Thee, and one for Moses, and one for Elias."—*Matt.* xvii. 4.

Methinks it is good to be here:
If thou wilt, let us build—but for whom?
Nor Elias nor Moses appear;
But the shadows of eve, that encompass the gloom,
The abode of the dead, and the place of the tomb.

Shall we build to Ambition? Ah, no!
Affrighted he shrinketh away;
 For, see! they would pin him below,
In a small narrow cave, and begirt with cold clay,
To the meanest of reptiles a peer and a prey.

To Beauty? Ah, no! she forgets
The charms which she wielded before:
 Nor knows the foul worm, that he frets
The skin which but yesterday fools could adore,
For the smoothness it held or the tint which it wore.

Shall we build to the purple of Pride—
The trappings which dizen the proud?
 Alas! they are all laid aside,
And here's neither dress nor adornment allow'd,
But the long winding-sheet and the fringe of the shroud.

To Riches? Alas! 'tis in vain—
Who hid, in their turns have been hid;
 The treasures are squandered again;
And here in the grave are all metals forbid,
But the tinsel that shone on the dark coffin-lid.

To the Pleasures which Mirth can afford—
The revel, the laugh, and the jeer?
 Ah! here is a plentiful board!
But the guests are all mute as their pitiful cheer,
And none but the worm is a reveller here.

Shall we build to Affection and Love?
Ah, no! they have withered and died,
 Or fled with the spirit above:
Friends, brothers, and sisters, are laid side by side,
Yet none have saluted, and none have replied.

Unto Sorrow? The dead cannot grieve—
Not a sob, not a sigh meets mine ear,
 Which Compassion itself could relieve!
Ah! sweetly they slumber, nor hope, love, nor fear:
Peace, Peace, is the watchword, the only one here.

Unto Death! to whom monarchs must bow?
Ah, no! for his empire is known—
 And here there are trophies enow!
Beneath the cold dead, and around the dark stone,
Are the signs of a sceptre that none may disown.

> The first tabernacle to Hope we will build,
> And look for the sleepers around us to rise ;
> The second to Faith, which ensures it fulfill'd ;
> And the third to the Lamb of the great sacrifice,
> Who bequeath'd us them both when He rose to the skies.

To the west of the town is a modern tower, erected to commemorate the battle of Culloden, and forming an ornament to the grounds lately attached to the mansion of the Yorkes, which is now razed.

St. Agatha's Abbey is a sweet spot, situated on the north bank of the river, about a mile below the town. It was founded by Roald, constable of Richmond Castle, in 1152, but eventually passed into the hands of the Scropes, along with Roald's other possessions.

About a mile from the town is a remarkable earthwork, known by the name of Scots Dyke, which is traceable, at intervals, across the country : at this point it is well defined, and has the aspect of a formidable barrier. It is supposed to have been a boundary or defence erected by the ancient Britons, as circumstances justify the conclusion that it was constructed anterior to the Wall of Severus.

The neighbourhood of Richmond abounds in places of interest, which cannot be enumerated here. Rokeby, the scene of Scott's poem ; Hornby Castle, the princely residence of the Duke of Leeds ; Aske, the seat of the Earl of Zetland ; Bolton Castle, where Mary Queen of Scots was immured, are amongst the number. It will ever retain its character for beauty, and will afford abundant employment for the pencil.

APPLEBY.

APPLEBY is a town of great antiquity, and in ancient times, when Northumberland was a Saxon kingdom, divided into six shires, and extending far beyond its present limits, Applebyshire formed one of the six counties, and gave its name to what at present is called Westmoreland, or the land of the western meres, or lakes. The neighbourhood, no doubt, in early times abounded in apple-trees, and from these it was called Apple-town. It is supposed that the fourteenth station on the Roman wall was here, and that it was the ancient *Galacum*. That it was a place of some importance at an early period is evident, from Edward the Confessor giving its name to one of the shires into which he divided Northumberland. William, king of Scotland, took the castle, and destroyed the town in 1173; and Henry the Second imposed a fine of five hundred marks on Gospatric, and smaller sums upon other families in the country, for allowing the castle to be surprised. After it was restored he received forty marks for granting the town a charter, which freed it from the payment of " tollage, stallage, pontage, and lastage throughout England, except in the city of London." Pontage was a toll collected for the repairing of bridges; lastage, for the freightage of vessels. King John renewed this charter. In 1388 the Scots again set fire to it, and into such a state of decay had it fallen in 1555, that instead of paying a fee-farm rent of twenty marks a-year, as it had done in the reign of Edward the Second, though it had been gradually recovering from the last conflagration, yet above one hundred and seventy years had elapsed, and " nine parts of it still remained in ruins;" so, instead of twenty marks, it only paid " two marks " a-year, so much had it suffered through the ravages of war, and so slow was the growth of its recovery. Foundations of its ancient buildings have been bared by the plough for two or three miles around the present town; proving how much further it extended than it does in our own day. The place is built very irregularly on the slope of a hill, on the summit of which stands the castle, and at its base the old church of St. Lawrence, by which the river Eden flows through the ancient two-arched bridge, so beautifully pictured by Girtin in the present engraving; and a man may now wander a long summer's day, before he can find such a ponderous and primitive cart as that drawn by the horse which is drinking. Excepting the scythes, one can almost imagine that the ancient Britons had such lumbering wheels, as we here see, affixed to their war-chariots.

Appleby had sent two members to Parliament from the time of Edward the First to the passing of the Reform Bill, when it was disfranchised; though it is still governed by a mayor, twelve aldermen, and sixteen burgesses. At the foot of the bridge stood an old chapel, afterwards used for many years as a gaol, until the new gaol was built.

The chapel was built about 1480, and probably the bridge is of about the same date: it was guarded by a gateway, which was pulled down above half a century ago. The cloisters which stood at the entrance of the churchyard, and were used for many years as the market-house, were taken down in 1811, and the present elegant Gothic building erected, from a design by Smirke. At each end of the town stands a stone obelisk, one of which is inscribed with the words, —

"Retain your loyalty,
Preserve your rights."

Anne Clifford, the celebrated Countess of Pembroke, who, with Margaret the Countess of Cumberland, collected the materials for the three large manuscript folio volumes which are still preserved at Appleby (or were, a few years ago), fortified the castle in 1641 for King Charles, and gave the government of it to Sir Philip Musgrave, who held it until after the battle of Marston Moor. In the autumn of 1648 it surrendered to Cromwell's forces, under Lieutenant-general Ashton, when five knights, twenty-five colonels, nine lieutenant-colonels, six majors, forty-six captains, seventeen lieutenants, ten cornets, three ensigns, twelve hundred horse, with five pieces of cannon — in short, the whole wreck of the Royal army which had a little before blockaded Cockermouth, gave themselves up prisoners, with all their baggage : but the Countess seems to have been left unmolested.

There is but little doubt that Appleby Castle was a famous stronghold prior to the Conquest, and that Edward the Confessor would not have made the place a county town unless it had been well fortified. The Countess of Pembroke calls the keep Cæsar's Tower, and says it was built by the Romans. Before the year 1422, John Lord Clifford built the gatehouse of the castle, and his successor repaired the eastern portions; such as the hall, the chapel, and the great chamber, "which were then fallen into great decay." And they were again terribly shattered in 1648; for the little band who had retreated into Appleby from Cockermouth did not surrender without a struggle. Indeed it was, up to the Restoration, a little fiery loyal town. Though Cromwell gave them a new charter they kept their old one, and would not give it up, "and at the Restoration the mayor (who was too wise a man to do it before) took Cromwell's charter, and in the face of the court cut it into pieces with his own hands, and then looking about, he espied some tailors, and cast it to them, saying, " it should never be a measure unto them." Bravo, little mayor of Appleby! he knew that grim Oliver, and many of his stern old Ironsides, were then in their graves, and so the little dog played with the once dreaded paws of the dead lion. And where was the brave old Countess of Pembroke all this time? She was right loyal, " hip and thigh," and would not surrender until the old castle of her ancestors came rattling about her ears, and the dead and dying lay around her in all directions.

The Restoration was celebrated with as many bonfires as there were houses in Appleby, and "after service done at the church the Countess of Pembroke, with the mayor, aldermen, and gentry of the county, with the sound of trumpets, and an imperial crown carried before them, ascended two stately scaffolds at each end of the town, hung with cloth and arras of gold, where they proclaimed, prayed for, and drank the health of the king on their knees. The aged Countess seemed young again to grace the solemnity." Pity that the "Merry Monarch" was unworthy of such staunch loyalty. The brave old Countess expired at Brougham Hall, at the age of 85 ; and a few years after her death James the Second demanded all the old charters of Appleby: they were delivered up, "*and have never since been heard of.*" This is quite in keeping with his throwing the Great Seal of England into the Thames on the night he fled from Whitehall, crossed the river, and landed at Lambeth Stairs. The charters of Appleby would not have been delivered up so readily if the old Countess of Pembroke had been alive. But she then slept in the family vault of the Cliffords, in the ancient church of St. Lawrence, where there is a marble monument erected to her memory, and over it the pedigree and armorial bearings of her ancestors, ranging as far back as the reign of King John. And that old church dates from the time of Henry the Second; and never, perhaps, from the day of its erection, had so much money been expended on repairs as by the good old Countess of Pembroke, who, twenty years before her death, repaired it at a cost of seven hundred pounds: when, to quote her own words, "I caused a vault to be made in the north-east corner of the church for myself to be buried in." She half rebuilt the church of St. Lawrence. The good Countess also founded an hospital for twelve poor widows and a mother, concerning which she says, "And the 23rd day of the said April, 1652, two days after, I was at the laying the first foundation-stone of my hospital or alms-house, here in Appleby town, for which I purchased lands: namely, the manor of Brougham, the 4th day of February following; and the lands called St. Nicholas, near Appleby, the 29th day of December: which alms-house was quite finished, and the mother and twelve sisters placed in it in January 1653." In 1574 Queen Elizabeth founded a free grammar-school, and granted it many privileges. One hundred years after the governors, for the sum of 380*l*. gave the nomination of its master to the provost and scholars of Queen's College, Oxford.

In the "Beauties of England and Wales," 1814, from which a great portion of the preceding account is taken, it is stated that "the principal edifice of the present structure is of a square form, and was built in 1686, by Thomas earl of Thanet, out of the ruins of the old castle. In it are portraits of the different members of the Thanet and Bedford families, of Queen Elizabeth, and some of the kings of the house of Stuart, but none of them by eminent artists. At the upper end of the large hall is a copy of the great family picture, the original of which is at Shipton Castle, and is described by Pennant in his account of that place; it is tripartate in the form of a screen. In the middle stand, at full length, George earl of Cumberland and his amiable Countess, with their two sons, Francis and George, who died in infancy. Above the two principal figures are the heads of the Earl's two sisters, Anne countess of Warwick, and Elizabeth countess of Bath; and the Countess's two sisters, Frances, married to Philip lord Wharton, and Margaret countess of Derby. The two side-leaves show the full-length portraits of their daughter Anne; in the one, at the age of fifteen, standing in her study, dressed in white, embroidered with flowers, her head adorned with great pearls; one hand is on a music-book; her lute lies by her." Among the books represented in the study are Sir Philip Sidney's "Arcadia," the fashionable and favourite romance of that age; "Godfrey of Boulogne," Camden, and others. "Above are the heads of Mr. Daniel, her tutor, and Mrs. Anne Taylor, her governess. In the other leaf she is represented at the age of seventy-five, as a widow, dressed in a black gown and black veil, and white sleeves, and round her waist is a chain of great pearls; her hair long and brown; her wedding-ring on the thumb of her right hand, which is placed on the Bible and Charron's 'Book of Wisdom.' The rest of the books are of piety, excepting one of distillations and excellent medicines." The several inscriptions, which occupy the other parts of the picture, were composed by Anne Clifford, with the assistance of Judge Hales, who methodised for her the necessary papers and evidences.

In the drawing-room are four half-length likenesses of the Countess of Pembroke, taken in the states of childhood, youth, middle, and old age. They are oval, and united in one picture. In her diary, in 1619, she says her picture was drawn by Lanking. Pennant mentions a picture similar to this at Shipton Castle, and says that Mr. Walpole showed him a medal with the head of the Countess, exactly resembling the last in this picture; on the reverse is Religion, represented by a female figure, crowned, and standing; in one hand the Bible, the left arm embraces a cross.

There is also preserved the magnificent suit of armour worn by George Clifford in the tilt-yard, as champion to his royal mistress; it is richly gilt, and ornamented with fleurs-de-lys: his horse-armour, of equal splendour, lies by it.

It will be seen from the above brief description that Appleby, in the old time, was a stirring town, when—

> "Banners hung on high,
> And battles passed below."

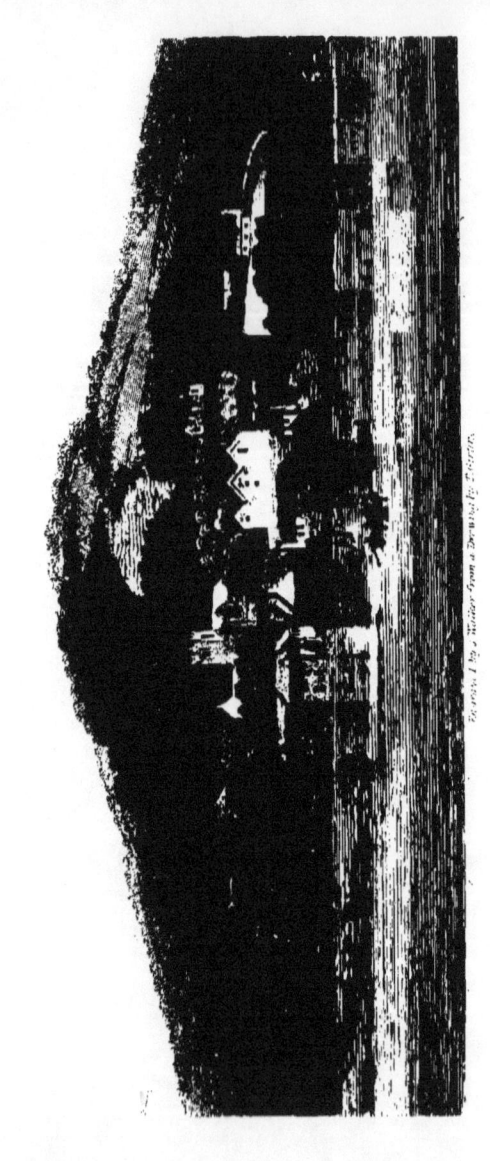

KINGSWEARE.

FEW scenes in Devonshire can exceed in beauty the basin formed by the surrounding hills at the mouth of the Dart. The shores rise in two steep ranges of heights from the water; at the foot of one is situated the little town of King's Weare. The banks of the Dart, as seen in the voyage thither from Totnes, are of enchanting loveliness, displaying a delightful interchange of green meadows, and woodlands speckled with grey rocks, and country seats, and parks, and cheerful villages; but among their many fair scenes, perhaps none is more worthy of notice than the stately woods of Sharpham, which overhang a fine bend of the winding river in the form of an amphitheatre, where the sturdy splendours of the oak, and the unwithering, though sombre green of the fir, contend with the richly luxuriant leafage of the chestnut, and the lighter graces of the beech:—woods beautiful alike in Summer, when

> " All the tree-tops lie asleep,
> Like green waves on the sea,
> As still as in the ocean deep
> The ocean woods may be;"

or in the season when

> " Autumn, laying here and there
> A fiery finger on the leaves,"

causes then to appear

> " One vast mass
> Of mingled shade;"

and when the fading foliage is indeed

" Clothed
In rainbow and in fire;"

or,

" At the season when the Earth upsprings
From slumber, as a spherèd angel's child,
Shadowing its eyes with green and golden wings."

Kingsweare is a small town, containing about 250 inhabitants; it has an old church, but no other building of note, though some handsome villas are scattered about in its neighbourhood. The town stands on a steep slope, and commands a fine view of the harbour, with the town of Dartmouth lying on the opposite shore, and the abrupt and lofty hills behind it,—also of the castle of Dartmouth, and of the remains of the one called after itself, towards the sea. This latter ruin is very venerable, and commands an extensive view of the Channel.

From the heights at the back of Kingsweare the eye wanders over a wide extent of prospect, comprising the beautiful abounding river, both above and below the town, flowing between green hills in its oceanward course,—Dartmouth, with an old fort built by Cromwell, on the water's edge, and the fine old church of St. Saviour's,—Mount Boone, the seat of Sir Henry Seale, situated in pleasantly-wooded grounds,—and at the mouth of the river, Dartmouth Castle, which is a prominent feature in all the best views from Kingsweare and its neighbourhood. The old castle was built at the close of the fifteenth century, when Edward the Fourth entered into a covenant with the corporation of Dartmouth, whereby they agreed to build "a stronge, and mighty, and defensyve newe towyr, and bulwark of lime and stone," for the protection of the place, to "garnish it with guns," &c., and to find a chain to be laid across the mouth of the harbour: in consideration of this they were to receive an annual grant from the crown of 30*l.* The remains of this old building are yet visible immediately above the present one, though in the last stage of ivied decay. There are two modern forts, which face the south and command the entrance of the river; these in the late war were mounted with twelve long 18-pounders; and a small fort adjoins the castle on its northern side, with three long 6-pounders. The castle itself consists of two towers, one square and the other round, for the purpose of drawing the chain tight across the harbour. In the rear of the castle is the church of St. Petrox, with its wind-swept burial-ground; and on the hill above it are the ruins of an old fort, called by Sir Thomas Fairfax "the Gallant's Bower." From the crown of this hill is to be obtained, perhaps, the widest and finest view in the vicinity, and happy is he, who, with a heart to appreciate its beauties, and a spirit to add to the loveliness and the loneliness of the hour,

"The light that never was on sea or shore,
The consecration, and the poet's dream,"

looks out upon the wide sea, and the fine river, and the shadowy hills around, beneath a harvest-moon. Perhaps the imagination would find few uncelebrated places that more abound with the spirit of "localised romance" than this, with the memories of the Cavaliers still clinging, like its ivy, about it, and its venerable ruin above the castle, and the deep fissures in the rocks below; which busy fancy finds it not difficult to people with many

"A silver fay
That at night's hushed noon
Dances thought away,
'Neath the argent moon,
Upon the yellow sands, to ocean's solemn tune."

It would be unpardonable to conclude a description of Kingsweare and its neighbourhood without noticing the church of St. Saviour's, in Dartmouth. It is a fine and spacious structure of the fourteenth century, having been dedicated a chapel by Bishop Brantingham in 1372. It is built cathedral-wise, and possesses great internal attractions; having a handsome altar-piece, representing "Christ raising the Widow's Son," by Brockedon, and presented by him to the corporation; also a rich and ancient wooden screen, said to have been brought from Spain; and a rood-loft, finely carved. The pulpit is highly interesting; it is of stone, and has many enrichments carved in wood upon it, evidently added at a date subsequent to its erection. The communion-table is surrounded with seats having arabesque ornaments and arms; the table is supported by grotesque figures, and the four evangelists with their symbols. In front of the communion-table is a curious old monument of brass on stone, to the memory of John Hawley and his two wives. He was a prosperous merchant and representative of Dartmouth in the reign of Henry IV., and his large shipping property gave rise to the rhyming adage, still frequent in the mouths of the ancients of Dartmouth,—

> " Blow the wind high, or blow it low,
> It bloweth well to Hawley's hoe."

The mouth of the Dart on which Kingsweare stands, seems, in its singular beauty, a fit termination to the fine scenery that the tourist meets with everywhere along the banks of this loveliest of the streams of Devon,—the loveliest where all are lovely! Proud, indeed, may the native of this peerless county of Devonia—the garden of England—be, of the place of his birth. Land of green meadows, feeding deep-uddered kine! Land of rich apple orchards! Land of free-flowing and abounding streams! Land of breezy uplands, wealthy with golden grain! Land where cloud and sunshine succeed each to each as beautifiers! Land of the wild, impassive Tor, and the wide moor, grand in its savage loneliness! Surely to the pilgrim hither from the town, life must seem renewed :

> " For before every man the world of beauty,
> Like a great artist, standeth day and night,
> With patient hand retouching in his heart
> God's defaced image."

CHRISTCHURCH ABBEY,

HAMPSHIRE.

THE view represented in the annexed engraving is taken from a meadow immediately below the precincts of the Church, known by the term "Paradise," and is separated from the churchyard by a beautiful stream, which, diverging from the river Stour, about a mile distant, skirts in its course the picturesque ruins of the Castle and Governor's house, and flowing by the west end of the Priory Church and the remains of the Conventual buildings southwards, turns a water-mill, which anciently belonged to the convent, and unites itself again with the main river a little below it.

There is no spot from which the church is more picturesquely seen than the one chosen by Girtin, for though it fails to present an extended view, by which all may be at once seen, it throws into distance the least attractive parts of the building, and gives prominence to the singular design of the east end, exhibiting to advantage the Ladye Chapel, surmounted by its curious Scriptorium known as "St. Michael's Loft," and the more early and interesting portions of the structure comprised in the east angle of the north transept. The low point also, from which the view is taken, excludes the whole tower, excepting its embattled top, and best presents the massive north porch, which with its Parvise completes the group.

In plan and arrangement this structure shows all the magnificence of a cathedral, and may be considered an epitome of architecture, having specimens of every style, from the Norman Conquest to the decay of art in the seventeenth century.

There is very little evidence to show by whom the different parts of the church were built, but from the heraldic badges and cyphers upon the bosses of the stone vaulting, and a list of the Priors (which has been fortunately preserved), we can with tolerable accuracy assign the leading features to some of the Ecclesiastics, with whose names we are thus made acquainted.

A few words will convey an historical sketch of the ecclesiastical establishment connected with this building. The origin and early history of the priory of Christchurch are unknown; it was supposed to have been founded soon after the Order of St. Augustine in this country. In King Edward the Confessor's time, there were a dean and twenty-four canons belonging to the Church of the Holy Trinity. After the Conquest, the office of dean was held by Ranulph Flambard, subsequently made Bishop of Durham, and he commenced the erection of a new and larger church, and advanced as far as the partial completion of the nave and transept, when, probably, his elevation to the see of Durham suspended the works. There is a great similarity between the architecture of the nave of Durham and Christchurch, with its singular reticulated work in each transept, as well as like combinations in the nave, arcade, and triforium; so that, even had records been wanting to prove that Flambard designed these parts, the fact of his early connexion with the priory of Christchurch, and the internal evidence mentioned, would at once have pointed to him as the architect of this portion of the fabric. Manner and treatment are observable in different schools of painting, as well as in the works of individual artists, and many pictures are identified with eminent names solely on account of peculiarities which the artists were known to adopt. The works of mediæval architects may with equal probability be ascertained, where names are wanting, by comparing one building with another, and minutely examining details. The diocese of Winchester furnishes an additional illustration of this kind in the churches of St. Cross, near Winchester, and St. Mary Crondall, near Farnham. The former church was founded by Bishop Blois, brother of King Stephen, in the year 1136, and the portion of the building erected by him affords a fine example of the Transitional style, which was speedily succeeded by the first Pointed style. Now, an examination of the ornaments, &c. of this celebrated building, and a comparison of them with the details of Crondall Church (also a noble structure), will show not only a close resemblance, but that the workmen adopted probably the same drawings or "face-moulds" which were used at St. Cross. There is also the same principle of composition apparent in the general design. Considering, therefore, the proximity of Crondall to Farnham Castle, the episcopal residence, it may fairly be assumed that this pleasing church owes its excellence to the mastermind of Bishop Blois.

To return, however, to the more immediate subject, the prominent place which the ambitious prelate, Flambard, filled (being made Justiciary of England and Procurator-general by William Rufus), and his influence with that monarch, no doubt induced the latter to become a benefactor to the church, as mention is made of many grants and privileges to the Church of Christchurch, Twynham, by him; it would appear also, that Flambard changed the constitution of the establishment by placing "canons regular," instead of "secular canons;" and during his presidency as dean, as well as after his elevation to Durham, his conduct was marked by tyranny and avarice; but the violent and sudden death of William Rufus put an end to Flambard's influence, and on the accession of Henry I., in consequence of the many accusations against Flambard, he was committed to the Tower, deprived of his estates, offices, and benefices,—amongst the latter, that of the Holy Trinity at Twynham, which was conferred by the king upon a clerk named Gilbert de Dousgenels, who, with the consent of his brethren, travelled to Rome to obtain privileges and immunities for the new church, but died on his journey home. The king then conferred the patronage of the church and the government of the whole province to Richard de Redvers, earl of Devon, who appointed Peter de Oglandres, granting him all the rights and privileges possessed by preceding deans. On his death a new dean was appointed, named Radulph, who seems to have carried on the architectural improvements begun by Flambard; and it is

T

recorded that, before his death, several of the conventual buildings were covered in, and part of the church itself. He was followed in his office by Hillary, a clerk or chaplain to the Bishop of Winchester. It was during the presidency of Dean Hillary that the religious establishment was made a priory of canons regular of the order of St. Augustine, the secular canons being superseded. This alteration was effected under Baldwin de Redvers, earl of Devon, son of Richard, to whom the patronage of the convent had been granted by Henry I.

From subsequent grants and charters of various royal and noble benefactors, the priory obtained a large accession of property and fresh privileges : thus the new establishment was benefited by Kings Richard I., John, Edward I., Edward II., Edward III., Richard II., Henry IV., and Henry V.

There is a continued list of the priors from 1150 to 1477, during which period there appear to have been twenty-six, the last being named John Draper, who surrendered the priory to King Henry the Eighth's commissioners on the 28th of November, 1539.

Within a year after the surrender, the king granted the immediate site of the priory and precincts to Stephen Kirton and his wife for ever: since that period the estate has passed through the hands of various possessors. On the 23d of October, 1540, the fabric of the Priory Church, with all its appurtenances whatsoever, was granted by the king to the wardens and inhabitants for ever. James I. confirmed this grant, and from that time the Priory Church has been appropriated for parochial worship.

Of the numerous persons who presided successively over this once important priory, with the exception of Flambard, whose history is fully known, nothing is really recorded of the others to show that they were distinguished by any learning or other high quality : it may be asserted, however, that Priors Eyre and Draper were well qualified in architectural skill, and, doubtless, contributed liberally from their means towards the portions of the edifice carried on during their presidency.

Although extensive priory buildings once stood to the south of the church, scarcely anything but rude masses of stonework covered with ivy now remain; there is a late pointed couplet window, however, which ornaments a small stone cottage to the west of the the church, having the initials J. D. on its label, and identifies this portion with the last prior; the little building may, perhaps, have been an entrance-lodge to the priory.

Few persons, on seeing the Priory Church from a distance, would expect to find so noble an edifice within; the absence of a central tower (as originally intended by Flambard), and the construction of a tall perpendicular tower at the west end, give the building externally the appearance of a huge parish church; although in plan it has all the appointments of a cathedral, comprehending in arrangement a nave and aisles, a transept with chapels projecting eastwards, a choir and aisles, a lady-chapel western tower, and a capacious north porch: there are also traces of the cloisters on the south side. With the exception of St. Alban's, it is the largest parish church in the kingdom.

As before observed, beyond the nave, it is not known by whom any other part of the church is built; but it is probable that the Montacutes, earls of Salisbury, whose arms are prominent on the bosses of the chancel vaulting, and who were great benefactors to the priory, may have contributed largely to the erection of the choir; and the initials W. E. may reasonably be those of William Eyre, as the date of the architecture would agree with the period during which he was prior. The nave is separated from the chancel by a solid stone rood screen, which has been carefully restored within the last few years, and is a good example of Edward the Third's time.*

The choir has a beautiful vaulted ceiling, with emblazoned bosses

---

* It had been grievously mutilated by the erection of galleries, and its upper tier of niches cut away to make room for the organ; fortunately, the entire compartments were spared at each end, so that it is now a faithful renovation, wanting only its polychromatic decoration, of which some traces remained : but neither its authority nor the means at command were sufficient to restore this part of its ornamentation.

and pendants; and its east end terminates in a very elaborately sculptured altar-screen, representing the genealogy of Jesse.* This screen is unrivalled, and is a fine specimen of Edward the Third's time. It has probably belonged to some other church, being surmounted by a cornice of much later character than the screen itself, added in order to accommodate its dimensions to the choir. There is a most enriched chantry chapel within the sanctuary, on the north side, adjoining the screen, which was erected to receive the remains of Margaret countess of Salisbury, granddaughter of Richard Nevil, earl of Warwick and Salisbury, distinguished by the name of King-maker.

The design of this monumental chapel exhibits, in a remarkable manner, the mixture of perpendicular and Italian detail, which subsequently developed itself in a complete but debased style during James the Second's reign. This chapel was evidently executed by Italian artists; the various string courses and friezes are completely of cinque-cento character; and no better example can be found in this country to illustrate the combination of Gothic and Italian features than this little building. The remains of the unhappy Countess were interred in St. Peter's Chapel, within the Tower of London; but the recent discovery of two spaces for coffins beneath the floor would seem to indicate that they were intended to receive the remains of the Countess, and perhaps her son, the Cardinal Pole.

The western portion of the choir is fitted up with oak stalls, thirty-six in number; two of them, assigned to the prior and sub-prior, have distinct canopies: these stalls are of late date, and show traces of mixed character. The sub-sellæ have a profusion of carvings, with representations of a grotesque character.

This brief notice of the choir cannot be closed without reference

* The recumbent figure of David, and the principal group of figures in the large central niche, are of natural size; they are finely conceived, and the drapery is exceedingly bold and effective. There is a good illustration of this sculpture in Carter's work on "Ancient Painting." This screen had also been originally coloured and gilded; and wherever the numerous coats of whitewash show a defect, slight appearances might be seen. To show the diligence with which the former authorities whitewashed this church, it may be sufficient to state that the scrapings were sold as manure for the sum of five guineas!

to the richly-carved modern altar-table given by the late A. Welby Pugin, Esq., whose skill in mediæval art was unrivalled in his day, and to whom this age owes the revival of sound principles of Gothic architecture. It need scarcely be observed, that the altar-table was presented by him before he changed his faith; his admiration of this church was well known, and was evidenced by the offering alluded to, and the significant fact of his selecting it to receive the remains of his first wife.

The north and south aisles, together with Ladye Chapel, are probably of contemporaneous date; the latter is singularly graceful in design. There are numerous inscribed Purbeck slabs in various parts of the flooring, recording the several priors who have been interred, and three chantry chapels well worthy of notice, particularly one built by the last prior, John Draper, exhibiting the same mixture of character referred to in the Countess of Salisbury's Chapel.

It is beyond the object of this short notice to enter into a minute description of the different parts of this most interesting building, as they may be found elsewhere; but it may be remarked, that few ancient structures have less of their original design left than this church : perfect as it is in plan, there is no corresponding beauty in its external design. Judging by the impression of the conventual seal, the earlier church at Toinham, or Twynham, as it was then called, which was demolished by Flambard, possessed a well-developed elevation, and the Norman portions of the present larger church are sufficient to show, that had Flambard carried out his design, the exterior character of the church would at once have indicated its collegiate intention. Tradition states, that the fall of the centre tower destroyed the nave vaulting; whether this was the case or not, the existence of the stone springers upon which the modern plaster vaulting is formed, shows, at all events, that a stone canopy to the nave was intended.

The super-imposed walls on the four great piers of the central transept afford further proof that a Norman lantern was intended at the junction of the nave, chancel, and transepts. The elongation of the nave roof in later times entirely obliterates this interesting feature in the exterior. The Norman apsidal chapel on the east side of the south transept, together with a wall arcading on the north transept and south aisles, all confirm the notion that a noble Norman church was contemplated by Flambard some recent openings at the west end of the south aisle of the nave have also disclosed traces of an early western tower, evidently of Norman date. Little doubt can therefore be entertained, that Flambard intended the west end of the church to terminate with two towers, in the usual Norman manner, of which so fine an example existed in his native town of Bayeux. The general plan of all large churches embraced two western towers, and it is somewhat remarkable that the great cathedral of the diocese, in which the Norman work is so extensive, should be without them; but late excavations, made during the meeting of the Archæological Society in 1845, brought to light the complete foundations of two Norman towers, which originally flanked the western front of the cathedral. There is no reason, however, to suppose that these towers were standing in Wykeham's day, and the probabilities are against such a supposition, as he would, doubtless, have moulded their massive forms into the prevailing architecture of his time, in the same marvellous manner in which he transformed the ponderous piers and arches of the nave into their present majestic proportions.

Had the Norman design of Christchurch been fully carried out, the building would not have been inferior to any of the same date in England; for Flambard's work at Durham affords undoubted evidence that he was possessed of great ability as an architect, and though on a smaller scale, what he did at Christchurch is fully worthy of him.

Christchurch, like other monastic foundations, is not without its legends, but they are scarcely worthy of record: the tale of the "Miraculous Beam," which in the morning was found too short for its purpose, and subsequently found too long, has ceased to be told in connexion with the church; and the removal of the materials from another site near the town (through supernatural agency) to the spot where the church now stands, may amuse the credulous, but is hardly worthy of notice.

These few remarks will have shown the interesting character of the church as an architectural monument; it must also be noticed as a feature in a general view, for it is in close proximity to the ruinous keep of the castle, and the remains of the "Governor's House," a curious Norman building, with a most characteristic Norman chimney-shaft. The whole group of buildings, when seen from an ancient bridge which crosses the Avon at the entrance to the principal street in the town, presents a picturesque combination which can scarcely be surpassed, and no visitor can leave Christ-church without a vivid recollection of so interesting a view.

TARNAWAY OR DARNAWAY CASTLE,

MORAYSHIRE.

We here present to our readers a scarce view of a very celebrated castle, of which, unfortunately, the greater part has now been demolished. It will be seen to belong to that peculiarly stately and picturesque class of buildings of which so many interesting remains have of late been *illustrated* by Mr. Billings, especially in Aberdeen and Kincardineshires, and which (half the ordinary *feudal* castle and half the *French* château) may justly be called the national *Scottish* style of architecture. In these baronial remains, while ornament was not neglected, there was no *weakening* of the defences by an unnecessary array of windows and doors; and hence the solid, gloomy walls, always stand out well grouped with the rugged hills and tall "ancestral trees" by which they are surrounded.

Of those castles of the olden time, of which Scotland still is proud, that of the redoubted Randolph, earl of Moray, is associated with very interesting scenery and historical events. Himself the nephew of the good King Robert Bruce, and the companion of Wallace, he was one of the foremost of that little but intrepid band of warriors who battled successfully against fearful odds for the independence of Scotland, both in Church and State. Randolph was a man of great personal strength as well as courage, and at the battle of Bannockburn the van or centre of the Scottish host was committed to his leading. His perseverance and prowess contributed not a little to the splendid victory then gained over "proud Edward's power;" and no wonder that he was afterwards rewarded by his sovereign with very extensive grants of land in

the northern counties, chiefly portions of the estates of the old Cumings of Badenoch, whose power fell with that of the Baliol faction, to which they were attached. Here the rough Earl ruled with a power and rude magnificence little short of regal, and which on the death of Robert Bruce, in fact, became such; for, during the minority of David II., Randolph was appointed Regent of Scotland. On the confines of the ancient Caledonian forest, which here stretched uninterruptedly from the sources of the river Earn or Findhorn, far up among the Monaliah mountains (the hills of the mist) to the *laigh*, or flat cultivated lands of Moray bordering the sea, the Earl erected a sylvan palace, or hunting-lodge, which was called Tarnaway or Darnaway. It consisted chiefly of a single castle hall, an apartment 90 feet long by 35 feet broad, inferior to none in Scotland, and which resembles much the Parliament House of Edinburgh. This magnificent hall is still entire. The walls rise to the height of 30 feet, and a carved roof of solid black oak, divided by large knobs and compartments, forms the arched ceiling. A suitable fire-place that would roast a stalled ox, an enormous oaken table, and some carved chairs, still garnish this hall, on the floor of which, it is said, a thousand armed men could easily muster, and stand without touching one another. It was not, however, the Earl's chief country residence, as, in the charter of erection of the earldom, the castle of Elgin, "manerium de Elgyn," is appointed "pro capitali mansione comitatus Moraviæ." It appears also, from a charter of Robert III. to Thomas le Graunt, son of John le Grant, dated in 1390 (Regist. Morav. No. 22, p. 473), that there was an older royal castle of Tarnaway, which was previously in the keeping of the Cumings, and afterwards of the Grants; and in fact the Cuming family, earls of March, seem to have been introduced at an earlier period from Forfarshire, as the great instruments for exterminating, or at least suppressing, the insurrections of the clan Chattan, who were thus, in all probability, the principal aboriginal Celtic inhabitants of Moray.

By subsequent additions to the old hunting-lodge, and the floor of which, strewed with heather and rushes, sufficed at night, no doubt, for the sleeping-place of many hundred warriors and huntsmen, the castle became the large and spacious building indicated in our drawing, and the principal residence of the Earls of Moray. Unfortunately, about the beginning of the present century, the whole was knocked down, and a modern restoration substituted for the old castellated mansion. The roof of the hall, supported for a time on wooden props, was alone left in its pristine state; and its imposing massiveness and grandeur cause the visitor deeply to regret that the newer apartments were not erected in the same style.

Darnaway Castle is still further interesting from being situated in the finest woodland scenery, just where the cultivated district gives place to the rougher inequalities of the upland pastures. It is in the close vicinity of the river Findhorn, one of the most magnificent of our Scottish rivers, and which exhibits a greater variety of rock, of woody glade, and grassy brae, than any of them. Alongside one of the most beautiful reaches of the river's bank, overhung with beetling cliffs, and old oaks and pine-trees, at no distance from the castle, is a celebrated heronry, where the habits of the stately heron could, until of late, be studied to the greatest advantage, and without disturbing the birds. The increase of the common and hooded crow, which has recently been permitted in the neighbourhood, has greatly reduced the number of nests; for these predacious gentry steal all the herons' eggs they can pounce upon, and so annoy the old birds as to cause many of them to desert the spot altogether.

Immediately beneath, or to the north of Darnaway, lay the wild "hard moor" of Brodie, where, according to tradition and the immortal dramatist, Macbeth met the "Weird Sisters," and which to a recent period was, indeed, a "blasted heath!"

But next to its hall, Tarnaway was wont to draw the visitor to see it on account of the magnificent oak and pine-forest, in which till very recently it was almost buried. The finest trees have now yielded to the axe, but they were the largest in the North Highlands, and the zone of the oak forest, with a plentiful undergrowth of hazel, beech, ash, and holly, crossed the precincts of the park in a broad belt, backed towards the inner and higher grounds by the more gloomy and impenetrable masses of the native pine. This forest harboured the largest stags, both of the roe and red deer, to be seen in the country; and in the language of a huntsman, who wrote not above a dozen years ago, " few knew what Tarnaway was in days not long gone by, almost untrodden, except by the deer, the roe, the foxes, and the pine martins ; its green dells filled with lilies of the valley, its banks covered with wild hyacinths, primroses, and pyrolas, and its deep thickets clothed with every species of woodland luxuriance, in blossoms, grass, moss, and timber of every kind, growing with the magnificence and solitude of an aboriginal wilderness — a world of unknown beauty and silent loneliness, broken only by the seugh of the pines, the hum of the water, the hoarse bell of the buck, the long wild cry of the fox, the shriek of the heron, or the strange mysterious tap of the northern wood-pecker."*

* See " Lays of the Deer Forest," by John Sobieski and Charles Edward Stuart, vol. ii., and Anderson's " Guide to the Highlands."

TOTNES.

HAPPY is the wanderer, whether poet or painter, or only dreamer of sweet dreams, who, free from the graver cares and occupations of life, goes forth, as of old, a knight in search of heroic adventures, to look for new and undiscovered beauties in Nature and Art. Hope is his morning and evening star, ever in the ascendant. He has no thought of what the morrow shall bring forth, but ever willingly leaves it in sweet uncertainty. The roadside inn is his home; and his friends and companions those whom accident brings in his way, and the everlasting features of Nature. He looks abroad upon the world smiling beneath the sunshine, or darkened by the shadowy wings of the storm, "in gladness and deep joy." Night and solitude are holy to him, and the moon and stars more than to the busy habitant of towns; for he feels them to be, as he wanders on his path, "eternal lamps in the bright city of God." He loves all the sweet influences of the seasons: things inanimate are, in his eyes, possessed of life; and the old ruin, and grey relic of antiquity, "pleading haughtily for glories gone," speak to him in voices which the ears of men filled with the sound and stir of every-day life hear not, and never will.

Far have we wandered on such pilgrimages, and few places have we met of more interest than Totnes. It is the most ancient borough in the county of Devon, and the oldest town in the kingdom; for it was there, as legends say, that Brute landed

with his followers from Troy. It consists principally of one street, about three-quarters of a mile in length, terminated on the east by a new stone bridge: a handsome and massive, though rather heavy structure, spanning the beautiful river Dart by three arches.

In the time of the Romans, according to Westcote, it was considered the most southern part of the kingdom; and the Fosseway, which passed through Devonshire into Somerset, and thence led to other parts of the country, began here; and, though fifteen hundred years old, is still visible. It was formerly surrounded by walls, having four gates, and defended by a castle: the building of which is ascribed to Judhael, or Joel de Totnes, to whom the manor was given by the Conqueror. Its circular keep is still remaining, as are also some portions of the town walls and the south gate. The church seen in our view is ninety feet in height. Totnes has returned members to parliament since the reign of Edward I., and was presided over by a mayor as early as the time of King John. It has a weekly market, and an endowed grammar-school, and possesses a population of about 4000.*

The site of this venerable borough-town is peculiarly fine. It extends along the brow of a steep hill, which commands a rich view of the Dart and the blue heights in the distance, and from which its main street leads down an abrupt declivity to the margin of the river. Many of the old houses still remain, with the piazzas in front and the upper stories overhanging the under. The church is an interesting fabric, having a finely-wrought tower with fretwork pinnacles: its interior is graced with a very elegant stone screen, enriched with tabernacle-work, and also boasts a fine pulpit on a pedestal, sculptured with gothic tracery and shields. It was rebuilt in 1432, as was discovered by some old records, brought to light by the destruction of the southernmost pinnacle in a storm of

---

* The town gave a striking example of its loyalty to the house of Brunswick, by an address to King George I., on occasion of the Vienna treaty between the Emperor and the King of Spain; when the good people of Totnes assured his majesty of their readiness, not only to grant him four shillings in the pound land-tax, but, if his service should require it, to give him the other sixteen likewise.

lightning some years ago, whereby an old chest, in which they were contained, became exposed.

The scenery of the neighbourhood is very lovely, and a good panorama of it may be beheld from the keep of the old castle, which stands on a large artificial mound of considerable altitude. The last time we visited it was on one of those fine days in October —"the sunset of the year"—which seem as if they were belated children of the summer born after their time; and which the poet describes in those fine words,

> "That beautiful autumnal weather,
> When gloom and glory meet together."

The foliage was thoroughly tinted,

> "The trees
> Wore their golden liveries,
> Servitors of autumn;"

and the hour was in every way propitious for the worship of Nature. To the south-east we obtained a delightful view of the Dart, which, in that direction, has the appearance of an oblong lake cradled among the hills. The right bank is pleasantly wooded, and the left slopes backward with "a mild acclivity" of meadowy hill, while the view is bounded by more distant heights, far-off, and indistinct. To the north, the Dart, then blue with the heaven its clear waters seemed to have wooed to their bosom, was traceable flowing toward Totnes; while in the horizon we saw the dim-discovered Dartmoor Hills and Haytor. On the north-east was the hilly ground, over which the annual steeple-chase takes place; while in the direction of Plymouth the eye followed the windings of a rich valley, bounded far-off by the Brent Hills. Though the views of the Dart from this spot are, perhaps, hardly equal to those of the Teign, from the lovely churchyard of the village of Highweek, yet a panorama so very beautiful and various can never fail of drawing thither the admirers of Nature.

Of the beauties of the neighbourhood we cannot speak adequately: for what words could do justice to the green walls and venerable ruins of Berry Pomeroy, so festooned with ivy, that of them it may be truly said, in the words of a great living author,—

> "Time smit with honour,
> Of what he slew, cast his own mantle on him,
> That none might mock the dead;"

and the decay of which tells us, in language more than ordinarily eloquent, the story of the sad and slow triumphs of time; or, what words could do justice to the banks of the Dart, either skirting it in its journey towards the sea, with their glorious variety of wooded, or meadowy, or rocky hill and dale, between which the river (called, not without reason, the English Rhine) rolls along in grand harmony with the scenery; or skirting it while flowing down from the solitary pool of Cranmere, through the wild lonelinesses of the moors, and the richly-wooded valley of Holnchase, and the green meadows and rich apple-orchards of cultivated Devonia; or to the view from Sharpham, looking toward Totnes—unsurpassed even in this delightful district; or to that from Totnes Down Hill, whence the eye glances over a lovely and wide tract of country; or, lastly, to the beautiful scene which the accompanying engraving illustrates, with the fine old castle on the hill, and the church tower rising over the rich and full foliage of the trees. Well may we apostrophise Devonshire, after looking on such scenes, in Carrington's words,—

> "Rich
> Art thou in all that Nature's hand can give,—
> Land of the matchless view!"

ABERNETHY ROUND TOWER.

This ancient and mysterious landmark, respecting which nothing is really known, stands in the beautiful little town of Abernethy, and is one of the oldest monuments in Scotland. When it was built, or by whom, or for what purpose, is not, and probably never will, be known. It rears up a relic of the past, and seems to stand dreaming on the border of an old world, every vestige of which, saving itself and its companion tower at Brechin, have centuries ago passed away. Those who built it, and those who occupied it, have left no record behind; and when we grope about the dim twilight of Time to discover who and what they were, we stumble amid the deep darkness that lies behind those old undated centuries, lose our way, and, after the wearisome research, return no wiser than we were.

What we can see of the remote past through the deepening shadows of Time is as of a great and unknown sea, on which some solitary ship is afloat, whose course we cannot trace through the clouds which every way gather around her, nor tell what unknown land lies beyond the horizon to which she seems bound. A long night of deep and unbroken mystery has for ever settled down upon the early history of our island; and the first dawning which throws the shadow of man upon the scene reveals a rude hunter, clad in the

skins of beasts of the chase, and we know no more:—and so, in as few words, might the early annals of many another country be written. Here and there a colossal barrow heaves up above the dead; we open them, look within, and find a few bones or a few rude weapons, either used in war or the chase, and these are all. Or, turning to such remains as our artist has here pictured, we see that the hand of man is there, and that is almost all we know; whether posterity would understand the enduring monument he reared seems not to have concerned the builder, and we cannot tell whether it was the temple in which he worshipped, or the pile which he erected above the dead. He lived not for us.

We stand at the base of the tower, and as we look up seem to hear that solemn Voice which spake to Job in the years of old, and exclaimed, "Hitherto shalt thou come, but no further!"

At a very early period a portion of Scotland was inhabited by the same people as Ireland; and as so many similar monuments are found in the sister kingdom, it is not improbable that the Round Tower of Abernethy was built by these unknown colonists. The original language of Scotland was Irish, as Welsh was the oldest language of England: the Gothic was not spoken in our island until the Saxons landed. These are facts, admitted by all who have carefully studied our ancient chronicles. Scarcely anything is known of the Pictish language; we may, perhaps, glean a scattered word here and there in the name of some old headland, mountain, river, or valley, but that is almost all; and while we are pondering over it, the Celt and the Gaul step up and claim it for their own, and we seem left in the old primeval silence, looking upon that ancient Round Tower to unravel the mystery—but it stands "grey in its hoar antiquity," and makes no sign.

From the "History of Brechin," by Mr. David Black, published in 1839, we quote the following amusing and interesting description of the Abernethy Tower, candidly confessing, on our own part, that we know no more of its origin than we have above stated, and that if we ever visit it we should never wish for a more agreeable guide than the Thomas Simpson, beadle of Abernethy, who figures in the following excellent extract :—

"Thomas Simpson, the Beadle of Abernethy, informed us readily that it was built by the Picts, thirteen hundred years ago, and that a gentleman had read the whole account of it out of a book to his daughter. Thomas was otherwise very communicative and obliging, and under his superintendence we made a survey of the tower. We found that the height was about eighty feet; the door-way, which is on the north side, and attained by three steps (evidently of modern architecture), is about seven feet high and three wide; the diameter of the tower inside, level with the door-sill, seven feet ten inches; the thickness of the wall at the doorway is three and a half feet, but as the rabbet of the door projects two inches, the true thickness of the wall here is three feet four inches. The doorway is of very wide (?) architecture, composed externally of six stones, one serving for the door-sill, four for the side rabbets, and one put into a curb or arch for the lintel. The top of the tower is attained by means of four ladders, resting upon wooden floors, supported by rings or corbels, exactly similar to those of the Brechin tower. By the help of the four ladders, the aspiring antiquarian may reach the floor where the bell is hung; but those who wish to attain the leads of the tower must apply to Thomas Simpson to keep the bell stationary, and then they will gain the highest floor, which is about three feet from the extreme top. The floor is covered with lead. Measured at this height the internal diameter of the tower is six feet eight inches and a half, and the walls two feet seven inches thick; but as the top is covered with stones, which project with a moulding of about seven inches beyond the wall, the real thickness of the top is two feet, and, consequently, the external diameter nearly ten feet nine inches. This projecting moulding was added about the middle of the last century, previous to which the tower must have had a very unfinished appearance. Thomas Simpson says, the Picts built it all in a night, and were about to put on the roof in the morning, when an old woman, looking from her window, frightened them away, and hence the building was left unfinished. At the top, and immediately below the highest internal ring or corbel, which supports the leads of the building, there are four windows, but these do not look to the cardinal points. Each window measures inside about six feet in height, and two feet in width; they are all arched, and externally there is a higher circle, about a foot above that which gives light; and small carved pilasters—of which a few yet remain—have supported or ornamented the external arch. In this respect they differ from the tower of Brechin. Upon the south side of the tower, without the dyke of the churchyard, and opposite the Cross House, in which the councillors make their elections and hold their magisterial feasts, affixed to the wall of the tower, are those ancient instruments of punishment, the jugs (or jougs), an iron collar of three pieces, attached together by two joints, and which, opening in front to receive the culprit's neck, was then secured by a padlock."

"The question has often been discussed, for what use or purpose the curious towers of Abernethy and Brechin were erected. Some allege that they were not only intended for the confinement of those under ecclesiastical punishment, but also for summoning the people to public worship, by the sound of horn or trumpet, before the introduction of bells; others contend that they were watch-towers, from the summit of which a sharp look-out was kept. A third and more recent opinion respecting the tower of Abernethy is, that it was erected as a burying-place for the kings of the Picts. In short, no one knows anything about the matter." Such was the conclusion arrived at by the late John Parker Lawson, M.A., the talented editor of the "Gazetteer of Scotland."

Abernethy is beautifully situated about two miles from the Tay, that mighty river, which (rising where Loch Tay sleeps under the shadows of its overhanging mountains, above which Ben Lawers towers, like a watching sentinel) pours more water into the ocean than any other river in Great Britain. Many of its primitive houses are covered with thatch, while the Ballo burn murmurs along the glen by which it stands, and in spring-time reflects the white and crimson blossoms of the fruit-trees, for which it is so famous. In ancient times it is said to have been the capital of the Pictish kingdom, and that it was at an early period a town of note—its far-famed Round Tower, as quaint John Bunyan says, still stands,

" The same to testify."

The history of Abernethy comes not within the compass of our pages, as the present sketch is only devoted to the Round Tower, so beautifully drawn by Girtin; and those who look into the engraving will see that his hand "never lost its cunning," or forgot the lessons he learned while copying the "mutilated masonry" among the ruins of the Old Savoy Palace.

www.ingramcontent.com/pod-product-compliance
Lightning Source LLC
Chambersburg PA
CBHW032352230426
43672CB00007B/676